THE
WRITING ROOM

THE
WRITING ROOM

A Resource Book
for Teachers of English

HARVEY S. WIENER
City University of New York
LaGuardia Community College

With an Annotated Bibliography
on Basic Writing by

TED SHECKELS
Beaver College

New York   Oxford
OXFORD UNIVERSITY PRESS
1981

Parts of Chapter 1 and of Chapter 2 appear in "Basic Writing: First Days' Thoughts on Process and Detail" in *Eight Approaches to Teaching Composition,* ed. Timothy Donovan and Ben McClelland, Urbana, Ill.: National Council of Teachers of English, 1980.

Some of the material in this book has appeared previously in *Creating Compositions,* 2nd. ed., and in the Instructor's Manual for *Creating Compositions,* copyright © 1977, 1973 by Harvey S. Wiener. Reprinted by permission of McGraw-Hill Book Co.

Library of Congress Cataloging in Publication Data

Weiner, Harvey S
The writing room.

Bibliography: p.
Includes index.
1. English language—Rhetoric—Study and teaching.
2. English language—Grammar—1950– —Study and
teaching. I. Sheckels, Ted. II. Title.
PE1404.W5   808'.042'071173   80-18020
ISBN 0-19-502826-0 (pbk.)

Printed in the United States of America

IN MEMORY OF
MINA P. SHAUGHNESSY

friend, advisor, teacher

Preface

I have many debts to acknowledge in the creation of this book.

For much of its scope I owe thanks to the diverse public schools and colleges of New York City, laboratories in which I have taught more than a dozen years the boys and girls, the women and men of dreams and ambitions.

To Pennsylvania State University I express appreciation. If not for the complex problems of student writers on campuses scattered throughout Pennsylvania and if not for the need to standardize instructional goals in the name of the University, I doubt that I would have drawn together the principles that guide my own teaching and the programs I have helped develop. Members of the PSU Freshman English Committee provided guidance as they read, edited, and discussed, piece by piece, the draft of *The Writing Room* that I prepared as a resource book for the English Department in 1977. The Committee's suggestions about form and content helped me smooth out the rough spots for the first complete edition used by teachers of English 4 (basic writing skills) on the Commonwealth campuses and at University Park. Those suggestions also guided the major changes I had to make for this book in its current form to serve even more divergent audiences than one finds among teachers and graduate assistants in a large, diversified state university system.

Others have read this manuscript, whole or in parts. I want to acknowledge with thanks good advice from Nancy Sommers at the University of Oklahoma, Andrea A. Lunsford at the University of British Columbia, Robert Lyons at Queens College of the City University of New York, and Nora Eisenberg at LaGuardia Community College of CUNY, colleagues in the basic writing effort who helped me strengthen the text. I want also to thank Edward M. White, at California

State College, San Bernardino, William D. Lutz, at Camden College of Rutgers University, and Evans Alloway, at the Educational Testing Service: they helped me gather and interpret the data I needed for an introduction to testing. Marian Arkin at CUNY LaGuardia suggested valuable information for the section on Writing Centers. By agreeing to prepare a comprehensive bibliography in basic writing, Theodore F. Sheckels of Beaver College brings an essential element to my project, and I am grateful to him for undertaking the task and for accomplishing it so professionally.*

I owe thanks to John Wright, editor at Oxford University Press. His unflagging support and warm yet sturdy advice kept this project alive amid urgent relocations of mind and body, and sudden new projects rearing up to deflect attention from this book.

To the community of teachers of writing at the City University of New York, to the members of the CUNY Association of Writing Supervisors (CAWS) past and present, to my new friends and associates at the Council of Writing Program Administrators (WPA), and to other colleagues around the country I am indebted for their advice and encouragement.

To the unforgettable Don Marion Wolfe whose spirit guides me still as a teacher and a writer I continue to owe much of what I am. And to Mina P. Shaughnessy whose memory and work inspire me I dedicate this book as evidence that her work lives on and grows.

Finally, to my wife Barbara, to my children Melissa, Joseph, and Saul I write of my love and my thanks for allowing a writer to live with them.

Massapequa, N.Y.   H.S.W.
January 1980

*Dr. Sheckels would like to thank the Department of English of The Pennsylvania State University, which funded his initial work on the annotated bibliography; Professor Robert Worth Frank, Jr., its former head; and its efficient clerical staff. In revising the bibliography, Dr. Sheckels was aided by the advice of Professor Harvey S. Wiener and Professor Richard Larson. He wishes to acknowledge their assistance.

Contents

Introduction

This is a book of ideas for beginning teachers who must teach beginners of a special sort—those who are just starting to learn the writer's craft in any serious and comprehensive way. It is a book about traditional composing tasks taught to "remedial" or "developmental" students, happily called *basic writers* (BW) now at many enlightened colleges and high schools, which have accepted Mina Shaughnessy's thoughtful tag. Such students are working to *qualify* for instruction in the usual sequence of English courses. Thus, we are talking about students viewed as unlikely to meet with much success as they face the demands of "regular" course instruction. Despite the alarming increase of such students and the courses created to teach them, other than some new volumes focusing on theory and, in them, occasional chapters on how to teach specific skills—Shaughnessy's extraordinary book *Errors and Expectations* leaps to mind first—not much appears as a guide through day-to-day classroom activities for the teacher of beginning writers.

The Writing Room is such a guide, a collection of activities for setting and achieving goals, for motivating reluctant beginners, and for practicing, stretching, and mastering basic writing skills. But it is more than an idea bank. The context for all its suggestions and proposed techniques is the traditional classroom setting: one teacher, anywhere from 15 to 35 (and, sadly, often more) beginning writers, and a four-walled room where they meet from three to five times a week. Hence, this is just as importantly a book about planning courses and about accommodating instruction to classroom realities. Though it encourages and recognizes experimentation with learning configurations, *The Writing*

3

Room attempts one kind of answer to the sobering question: "How much may beginning writers reasonably achieve in typical classroom instruction within a term's work?"

Unfortunately, the icy truth for anyone who regularly faces undeveloped writers is, of course, that like beginners of any kind, they need everything all at once—all the skills in language, form, and structure that each writing task demands.

Among the very first papers I read from college basic writers was this one:

Women's Liberation

Wmen's liberation is good in one way, but not in another way. Wemen should be paid the same amount of money as a men, in some field, for example. If wemen have the knowlegde to become nurse, doctor or any other field, wemen should be paid the sam amount of salary. If she doesn't have the knowlegde for that particular field, then she should not be paid the same salary. I think that wemen should have the same rights as a man. Because if a lady doctor is examining a patient, if she doesn't have the knowlegde, the patient eighter will become very ill or die. There are some job's in which wemen cann't work at, for example, sanatation department, plumer's ETC.

A paper like this, calling for help in every direction at once, suggests an absurdity to sequence, certainly. Yet experienced teachers know that they must begin somewhere and end somewhere else, both points defined in some way. Undoubtedly, by what activities fill the early days of instruction and by what follows and in what order, teachers announce (perhaps too inadvertently) their view of what is essential about composing. Admittedly, it's not hard to avoid introducing skills progressively in the crush of student needs. But the basic course is desperation for anyone bent on meeting all those needs as they arise. The most painful classroom lesson I have watched teachers teach has a class viewing as if at a circus a weak student essay like "Women's Liberation" for all its offerings at once: its indiscretions in style, language, form, detail, usage, grammar, and spelling. The teacher is a ring master shifting attention from comma faults to squinting constructions to imagery to misspellings to tone to transitions and back again, one alongside the other; and in sheer multiplicity the student is lost, struggling to keep an eye on events in the next ring and never fully appreciating any.

Although it is easy to understand how humaneness might suggest for the unskilled presenting everything they need as they need it instead of as bits served up one or two at a time, nothing will prevent success for the beginner more than instructional overkill. Incremental learning and mastery of clearly defined concepts (apart from their often unfortunate trappings like *behavioral objectives, learning contracts,* and other Madison Avenue formulas) still bring students closer to achievement than any other approaches I know. And if I seem to be laboring the need for curricular structure, it is fruitful toil, I am convinced. All too frequently the basic writing course is a diluted English 101 that the teacher greets each morning with the same grim question, "What am I going to do today?"

Now it's true that the "regular" English course and the course for beginners that often precedes it both aim at building skills in writing. However, the first course in the sequence is not simply a version of the second in slow motion or with complicated units omitted or with handouts on subject-verb agreement to ballast instruction. Teachers of basic writing must explore language and composing tasks on a much more fundamental level of awareness than, say, English 101 demands. Of course, instruction requires thoughtful, restrained pacing and attention to correctness; yet the concepts that define the first course and the materials that teach those concepts distinguish a strong basic writing curriculum from any course that succeeds it. Taking five days in class instead of three with Orwell's "Politics and the English Language" simply will not do.

What will, then? *The Writing Room* attempts to flesh out *in one way* the answer to that question and to others that face the instructor. The chapters present ways of approaching rhetorical strategies and language skills that most inexperienced writers need to practice. There is an introduction to testing and its concepts for the beginning teacher; there are suggestions about what to teach after the basic writing course; there is an overview of services that can support classroom instruction in writing at any institution. An appendix offers two possible daily plans that identify specific areas of instruction for each day.

Although I have for the most part avoided theoretical issues here (in my wish to attend to the classroom they would steal space from this book and would move me quite apart from my purpose), experienced teachers will hear in my suggestions resonances of Wolfe, Christensen, Shaughnessy, Hirsch, Britton, Corbett, Winterowd, D'Angelo, Moffett, Bruffee, and Lindemann among others. As a guide to the valuable literature of the composing process, through the careful work of Professor Ted Schekels of Beaver College, I present a comprehensive annotated bibliography for basic writing teachers so that they can read freely to build upon my suggestions and to construct their own course plans. But the essential *mise en scène* here is not footnotes, but desks and chalkboards in the classroom, my classroom, and several adjusted images of it created by trusting colleagues and students.

That classroom is a classroom of writers, where writing is the day's business. In regard to the two major areas of instruction associated with composition teaching, "rhetoric," and "usage" or "grammar," I will insist throughout this book that the first define the course. I'm sorry even in these days when writing has made major strides as a legitimate area of study and research to have to explain the need for a program rooted more in composing than in grammatical systems and in correctness. After examining countless syllabi for beginning writers over the country, I have found that "remedial" students suffer daily doses of run-ons and apostrophes as the program of cure for sick writers. With rare exceptions almost every syllabus I studied worked from a heart of grammar and mechanics, each day's toil a new effort at labels and definitions and a new attempt to apply them through underlining and circling and connecting subjects and verbs and commas and adverbial clauses. In only some cases was frequent writing demanded of the student.

Starting off as many courses do with intensive grammar instruction and drill, which are sustained throughout the term, is wrong for many reasons but especially because it is a miscue. Although I am the first to admit the excitement in and importance of exploring the structure and the history of the language, in a basic skills course no such instruction will make good writers, I am sure. Though I am refreshed somewhat by the winds of change, I point only to Erika Lindemann among many other talented theoreticians who must argue this in 1980:

> we cannot improve our students' writing abilities if we focus exclusively on the code, on grammar or on the surface features of the written product. Students who cannot find anything to say, even though they write not the first misspelled word, can be as ineffective as communicators as students who have brilliant ideas but ignore the reader's need to have them presented in reasonably punctuated sentences.

Basic writing courses are still dark forests of nouns and verbs and nominitive absolutes, of parsing sentences and of fragments and run ons in other people's prose. If all *The Writing Room* does is to cut a path through those assumptions by insisting upon *writing,* I shall have achieved an important goal. The underlying premise of a basic writing course must be that students required to take it are inexperienced writers who need practice. My assumption is not that there is anything wrong with the student or that he or she requires corrective instruction; I assume that these men and women are apprentices—it is again, Mina Shaughnessy's word and a perfect one at that—who need experience as writers, experience instructors have to encourage and stimulate. In that frame the more writing students do, the better the chances for success. Hence, I recommend with Shaughnessy 1000–1500 words per week for each student in the class. This is not to insist upon ten formal writing assignments, each of a thousand words. That would surely suffocate an inexperienced writer. But through a variety of activities—some sentence combining and embedding, some original sentence construction based upon patterns, some very short sentence groups on provocative topics, some longer paragraphs—an instructor can approach the suggested word goal with relative painlessness for student and teacher alike.

The formal writing I suggest focuses upon the paragraph and upon experiments with three basic types—description, narration, and illustration—only because these are easily accessible to inexperienced writers and because they are vehicles of practice (as a result of that accessibility) for basic language skills and for skills in organization, in form, in the use of detail, and in correctness. I appreciate, though do not fully agree with, the point James Britton makes intelligently in *The Development of Writing Abilities (11–18)*, that the four traditional categories of writing (narration, description, exposition and argument) "will not serve as a conceptual framework for the study of writing." Certainly it is right that these categories must not be rigidly defined; that they must be taught as streams running into and beside and around each other; that an overly fussy attention to them as forms blurs the process of writing for the product. But admitting as artificial the boundaries drawn to define these rhetorical categories, one recognizes that their value as five finger exercises is hard to challenge. (Britton and his colleagues do not consider this point satisfactorily.) Even if a student will never again write a description of such highly sensory appeal as

the first suggested theme in *The Writing Room,* what he*
learns and practices there about focus, form, and language
has importance in the growth of his craft. Of course there's
no guarantee of transferability, that skills honed in one task
will cut through other difficult challenges. But by expanding
upon skills taught, learned, and practiced, the beginner
builds on early attempts, a good teacher recalling these
achievements and insisting upon their continued application
and expansion.

By focusing the course upon the value of meaningful expression and upon an intention to get students to see that
they have meaningful things to say in writing, teachers
create a setting that lends itself favorably to correctness.
Unless the students believe that they need to function as
writers because they have important information to com-
municate, all the instruction I could offer in grammar and
punctuation falls on deaf ears. But I do not ignore the conventions of Edited American English; quite the contrary, I
view those conventions as inseparable from good writing. To
put Lindemann's point in a slightly different way, a student
with brilliant ideas written in unintelligible prose is a bad
writer—as is a student with poorly formed ideas written in
perfect grammatical English. In classroom instruction you
sometimes need to separate those skills required for developing and communicating ideas from those skills that allow
writers to follow conventions of correctness, teaching one,
then the other, as the calendar allows. This is pedagogical
expediency. But it is not to suggest that content and form

---

*For a book so largely based in the conventions of written English I choose the
conventional masculine pronoun, recognizing the uneasiness it arouses in
some readers, but unhappy nonetheless with what proposed alternatives do to
a writer's style. But let me quote Mina Shaughnessy here:

> "After having tried various ways of circumventing the use of the masculine
> pronoun in situations where women teachers and students might easily out-
> number men, I have settled for the convention, but I regret that the lan-
> guage resists my meaning in this important respect. When the reader sees
> *he,* I can only hope *she* will also be there."

are separately weighted. If we tell students not to worry about correcting errors until *after* they sustain an idea in clear prose, that is not to say that being correct is unimportant. Rather, it is to keep the cart where it belongs—behind the horse. Most important, it is to establish in a piece of original writing of power and clarity a context for the desire to be correct, to observe convention, to write free from troublesome error. That as I see it is the light that flickers full of hope at the end of the long passageway through which anyone seeking skill in writing must move.

1

Making and Carrying Out Assignments

WHAT TO DO ON THE FIRST DAYS*

Since major efforts and advances among beginning writers proceed to a large degree in collaborative settings, instructors need to establish the kind of atmosphere that from the first day encourages interaction among strangers. Students will have to work together, sharing their writing, listening and responding to each other; and without a plan that right from the outset weaves personal identity into the fabric of the course, group efforts may unravel and shred. From day one you want to avoid anonymity.

First things first. When you meet your students on the first day, begin immediately to deal with issues about the course that will concern the class. You announce the name of the course, you distribute and read aloud the syllabus and goals for the term, you name the number of assignments and how you'll respond to them, you call attention to the required dictionary and to the textbook. You'd be wise to take some time showing how to use the text—especially if it's a handbook— by looking together at the correction chart, the table of contents, the index, the subheadings in a sample chapter. There's the value of good attendance to explain (missing class in a skills course pushes the beginner down the ladder more rungs than anyone can count); there's the reading of the roster and the careful pronunciation of students' names (invite correction so that you say them right); there's the spelling of your name on the board and a few seconds look-

---

*The arrangement of tasks in this and subsequent chapters follows the sequence of skills in the suggested daily plans I propose in Appendix A. Readers will find an overview of that sequence helpful before they proceed.

ing at how to say and to write it. (I'm amazed each year anew when scores of basic writing students turn up in the department office to ask questions about grades but can't remember their teachers' names. For the secretaries it's Twenty Questions: "Is it male or female? Young or old? Moustache? Tall or short?") You announce your office hours, and you explain about conferences (see pp. 204–5).

Then there's data gathering on department questionnaires or on index cards: names, addresses, phone numbers, names of faculty counselors. What's the first language the student spoke? What language(s) does the family use at home? Has the student taken this course before, or has he taken, in fact, *any* course in writing? What year is the student in? (Don't be surprised to find sophomores or juniors.) What's the student's program—what days and what hours does he sit in class, what hours at the school are unassigned? Does an after- or before-school responsibility place demands on the student's time? (a job? child care?)

Some teachers expand the department's questionnaire, using it to get students to disclose briefly attitudes towards and feelings about writing. Nancy Sommers at the University of Oklahoma suggests these, for example:

1. What do you want to learn from this course?
2. What fears do you have about taking this writing course?
3. What specific comments did your last teacher make to you about your writing?
4. What is the most difficult thing for you when you write? What do you worry about when you write?
5. What is the easiest thing for you when you write?
6. What special habits or idiosyncrasies do you have when you write?
7. Describe what is good writing to you.
8. What steps do you go through when you sit down to write a paper?
9. What do the words *rewriting* or *editing* mean to you?

10. How do you decide that a paper is finished and that there is nothing more that can be done with it?

Housekeeping over, as soon as you can manage it, everyone writes for twenty minutes. Explain that these papers will *not* be scored, but that you need an idea of what the writers in this class are like. Don't fuss about a topic—"Write for twenty minutes on how you feel about writing"; "Write a twenty-minute introduction of yourself to me"; "Write about how you feel toward this school." Here are samples produced by students in response to such topics.

Hi There! I am Anthony Edmund Colwell. Who are you? Well, since you will not say anything. I will tell you about myself. I was born in El Paso, Texas. Lived there till my forth graded. during my schooling there I learned spanish, the 4 years of school, In which has proved to be of no help. The problem I have with it is that I try to use the spanish rules of grammar to my english writing. Since I have been away from spanish. I have forgotten. The Lang., but the rules of spanish keeps comeing back when I do my english papers.

My name is Rodney Todd. My life has rewarded me with many unknown adventures that someday I'll tell my wife and children.
I have many personalities that I'll present to you. I'm still undecided about my future. I expect the future to hold different challenges for me to over come and master. I would like to continue my education for the next 7 yrs., I want to develop my mind so that I can produce more than I consume. It is very important that I contribute within my society. There is a burning void inside my heart, I love life and I love food. There is not doubt in my mind I love my life.

Writing the first or second day says more than any careful discussion and lecture can that this is a course in which people write.

But the early brief sample has many purposes. It gives you a quick overview of the general strengths and weaknesses of the class, the assumptions about language form and structure that students bring to your course. It provides you with materials for the first week's work when students are hunting for the bookstore and are trying to locate required texts. It offers a check on placement: a paper stronger than most should send you to examine the score on whatever instrument your school uses to require admission for basic writing. (Many schools have appeals procedures which allow students, on the basis of in-class writing, on the instructor's recommendation, and on the findings of a review committee, to transfer into a more advanced section.) It lets you read and make comments quickly on all the papers, comments that set the tone right away for the enlightened questioning and evaluation you expect students to offer when they read the work of a peer and, ultimately, when they read their own rough drafts. You'll look at these papers humanely, therefore, offering encouragement and support over everything (see pp. 45–55). After all, these are clearly unfinished efforts. Getting them back to their authors by the next session or the one right after it is an important priority.

After early writing, another major task for the first and second sessions is to develop in an overview the concept of writing as a process. Put simply, process means *steps* or *stages*. To the inexperienced the idea of a writer moving from stage to stage to produce a finished manuscript demands patient exploration. Suffering as they frequently do to lay their few words out on a page, beginners sanctify those words, and rarely try to change them. It is the mark of the amateur and not of the accomplished writer, the beginner's thinking goes, to need to change things. Thus, much early work deals with talk and demonstration of how writers behave. Rough draft workshops (see pp. 33–37) built into the course calendar advance and support the notion of the writer's work habits.

Beginners need to consider these various stages of writing:

- Getting an idea to write about (this sometimes means starting from scratch and identifying and narrowing a

topic of the writer's own choice and interest; or, it at other times means limiting a topic within the framework of a class assignment)
- Determining how to support the idea and whether the writer has sufficient resources to develop it (if not, where to turn for detail)
- Getting the thought down and changing it as it refines itself; adding ideas, combining ideas, ripping open sentences at the beginning, in the middle, and at the end in productive exploration
- Preparing the thought for someone else to read

You'll be surprised at the range of misconceptions students hold about writing if you ask them to talk (before you teach anything about it) of various steps writers take to carry out a task. "Based on your past experience with courses in school," you might say, "tell us everything you usually do from the time you get a writing assignment until the time you actually hand it in for someone to read."

Students will talk of their writing habits freely. As discussion ensues, corroborate or question assumptions that arise. Ask for more information. "You mean you start writing as soon as you sit down at the kitchen table? What do other people in the class do?" "You start writing sentences immediately? I start by making a list of everything I can think of." "What do you do if you get writer's block?" "What kind of paper and pencil do you use? Do they matter to you? I *must* use long yellow sheets and pencils." Although work habits that reveal themselves in the discussion may make you weak, honor your students' subjective responses, collecting a major point from one person, then from another, steering the discussion carefully. If you asked a question about process on the questionnaire students answered, read aloud some of the responses, keeping writers anonymous.

About process you can expect a hard loyalty to absolutes, a loyalty that similarly needs questioning. "Where did you learn that every sentence should have ten words, that every paragraph should have five sentences?" "Why *should* you

have to write an outline for every paper?" "Why *should* you
have to wait for inspiration when you write?" Students will
not easily forswear what Karen Horney calls the "tyranny of
the shoulds." Examining the rigid concepts beginners have
about what writers *should* do when they compose, you can
uncover with the class a number of misconceptions that interfere with the writing process.

Ultimately, in this discussion, you'll have touched upon the
various stages in any written effort. You're not establishing
rules here—conditions vary for every task and with every individual—but you're laying out possibilities. (And you'll be
dealing with process throughout the semester so there'll be
lots of opportunities for adjustment and expansion of the
concept.) What you will stress is *options.* There is no *one*
way that writers *should* do anything, but there are lots of different ways that require practice for beginners to expand
their repertoire of choices.

For the most productive instruction in process, you want
to show students what a writer's work looks like at as many
stages as possible. That's why it's important for writing
teachers to see themselves as teaching writers, willing to
share effort and criticism. If you've produced articles or
books, put them on display: they give a habitation to the
practices you believe in, practices you'll ask the class to
follow. Bring your own haphazard jottings and outlines to
class. Duplicate the pages of a rough draft from your own
last written piece and show it to your students. If it's been
published, show copy-edited pages, galley or page proofs,
and final product. Little will impress students more than a
pock-marked sheet of their teacher's own rough drafts
scarred with erasures and cross-outs, with the loops and
arrows all writers use to excavate their territory. With the
class look line by line at the starts and stops on a rough
draft, at your choices and rejected phrases, at your inser-
tions and excisions. Ask students why they think you did
what you did on each line, and if there are changes *they*
might make had they written the piece. Another good idea in
this vein is to find a page of rough draft from an ac-

complished writer. Whether it's a Keats ode, a stanza from Eliot, a page from Dickens, a sheet of Lennon's music, show how tentative, how exploratory are a writer's thoughts when they reach a page for the first time.

I opened this section with a brief reference to classroom atmosphere, and I do not want to exclude a discussion of it in these comments on first days' tasks. It may disappoint you to have to think of chairs and desks and spatial relationships as early order of business but unless you do you'll have avoided enlisting an extraordinary aide in your efforts to personalize the course—the physical environment of the room. Using it, you can impel contact through seating arrangements and through methods of directing questions. Get to class before everyone else on the first day and push desks or tables and chairs around so that students are looking at each other's faces and not at fringes of hair on back collars. Try a U- or a C-shaped layout in single or double rows; try a circle; try clusters of seats in small groups. You'll want to try many of those pictured below until you're comfortable. (I often use different plans for the same class and often switch arrangements during a single session depending upon demands of activities.)

```
                                      XXXXXXXXXXXXXXX
              XXXXXXXXXXX             XXXXXXXXXXXXXXX
              X         X             XX           XX
              X         X             XX           XX
              X         X             XX           XX
              X         X             XX           XX
              X         X             XX           XX
                   1                        2

            XXXXXXXXXXXXXXXXX             XXXXXXXXXX
          X                   X          X X        X
          X                   X        X X           X
          X                   X        X             X
          X                   X        X             X
           X                 X         X             X
            XXXXXXXXXXXXXXXX            X             X
                   3                        4
```

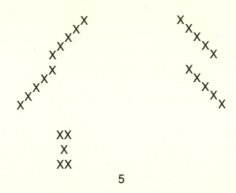

5

You're in for a rough (but not impossible) time if the chairs are bolted to the floor. Having taught too long in rooms with immovable seats, I have learned to shift centers of instruction by teaching from the back and sides and between the rows, and by carefully directing comments and questions from one student to another. If seats are movable, however, get everyone up as close as possible to the front. (I watched once as a graduate assistant taught freshman writing in an enormous room; she stood at the chalkboard while twenty-five students sat in chairs scattered everywhere, none closer to her than ten feet, most lined up against the back wall.) Once you've determined your best plan you'll have to work to keep it the way you want it. Students having prior experience with teachers who ignore movable furniture and who leave desks in single files like army tanks in review are uncomfortable in arrangements that draw eyes together. Latecomers will steal into the room and will gravitate toward empty chairs in the back or to other positions at the fringe of action. But you will have to be vigilant. Where people sit is important, and you've got to convey that. An assistant from the class can help you move desks and chairs at the start of subsequent sessions to suit the arrangement you're after; in a couple of weeks you'll have won this point, the plan you've established finally part of the classroom personality.

A seating arrangement that establishes risks of familiarity

demands extension. Bodies and faces on either side and across the room have names, and the sooner everyone starts using them the sooner the identity of the class takes shape. Try an "ice breaking" activity—go around the room, everyone speaking his name and then trying to remember all the names of the people before him; or, ask each student to speak for a minute about himself or herself from the front of the room—name, background, course of study, impressions of the school. Throughout the term insist that all comments be directed to people by name; no "he said" or "she said" but instead "Carlos said" or "Gloria said." If these steps seem sophomoric or wasteful, they are not. For establishing an air of familiarity and free exchange of ideas no single activity will pay more dividends than name exchanges as soon as possible.

PREWRITING: APPROACHES AND FOLLOW-UPS

For me *prewriting* is a convenient term for all those steps in the writing process before (and sometimes including) the rough draft; and so the word does not *exclude* writing with its prefix but sets off a kind of boundary between thought and idea and any careful, final attempt to mold them. Instructors must teach and must supervise the extensive prewriting process.

Experienced writers advance at least partially by means of some internal conversation (both before they write and while they write) about their intended thought, about what reveals itself in ink, and about how intention modifies and is modified by the written statement. But that is a conversation beginning writers have rarely practiced. Good instruction, therefore, insists on doing out loud in class what a good writer does quietly at home by himself. For the first formal assignments, prewriting offers external models of discussion about writing and its process, models that students must learn to internalize as essential parts of their own writing exercise. It guides the informal collection of ideas, first haphazardly, and then moves to lists or clusters or outlines from which the rough and subsequent drafts grow.

This attention puts a high premium, as you can imagine, upon classroom discussion as an essential element in each formal assignment for the beginner. I cannot stress enough how important this is. Instruction in prewriting techniques often focuses too much and too early upon the writer alone at work. Later on I'll spell out some of those techniques for solitude as parts of the prewriting effort, but right now it is *talking* I want to urge as the first and essential step for the writer learning in the classroom. For early assignments students need to share experiences which might lead to an effective written piece; and students need to listen to what others in the room say as they grapple with the activity, as they look for and evaluate elements of idea and detail.

To take full advantage of the classroom for discussion you need first to make each assignment—as you'll see more fully in Chapter 2—crystaline in its requirements. I discourage until much later on in the writer's development the kind of open-ended assignment that allows free range of topic selection. Though it may seem thoughtful to lay a world of choices at the student's feet, I have found that only carefully defined and structured writing tasks (with lots of opportunity for creative activity within those structures) allow incremental learning that can build upon prior achievement and that can be measured, even if only modestly. The more time you spend, therefore, in thinking about *exactly* what you want students to do, the better the results on a given theme. Write out your assignment. Walk away from it for awhile. Come back and try yourself to write following your own instructions. What problems exist? How can you clarify the sentences which explain what you want?

Once you can state *precisely* what you expect students to do in a given theme, you are ready to encourage class discussion. Let's assume that you're dealing with description (see Chapter 2); that you want students to describe some indoor place; and that you expect details the student offers in support of a topic to be limited by some judgment, opinion, attitude, or point of view. Now, let the class talk the assignment through. One approach I use most often is to put on the chalkboard or overhead projector a list of incomplete sentences that either suggest some opinion about a place or that encourage the student to offer *some* opinion about it. Here are some possibilities:

- The noisiest place I know is . . .
- A summer place I remember most is . . .
- A room that always scared me was . . .
- My brother's (sister's) room is . . .
- Our supermarket is . . .

With a list of at least ten like these I allow some thinking time, and then I go around the room, allowing each student to select any sentence and to complete it aloud. After each response I ask students to explain, extracting detail as I question or—better still—as other students in the class question. "Why do you say your son's room is so messy?" ("Things are all over the place.") "What kinds of things?" ("Oh, a baseball glove and some marbles.") "Just where are they?" ("On the floor near his bed.") "If you were writing about that, what colors and sounds might you add to help someone know the room?" Having introduced the need for sensory diction (see pp. 110–114), I encourage students in the class to help out, suggesting possibilities for concreteness and visual language.

Try to follow a procedure like this one for as many students as you can in a session, each student offering a few sentences of detail. Every member of the class should speak about the assignment in some way. Although students often do not write about the same subject they have discussed with the class, they collect ideas from the people around them; they listen to others coming to grips with the exercise; they learn to expand ideas through questioning. The hope is that students will learn to do all this on their own when they struggle in solitude with a writing task.

Discussions along these lines bring a deductive cast to the piece the writer may ultimately produce. There's first a generalization and then the details to support it. As a student talks about a room, though it's impossible to trace the conscious or unconscious particulars that undoubtedly gave rise to his dominant impression, those particulars certainly exist. However, the student offers the details afterwards to support a general statement to which he has committed himself. With your questioning you can draw out valid particulars, can examine those which fall beyond the generalization, can focus on the generalization itself, which might need modification. When you teach about topic sentences (pp. 63–65), students will be constructing their own generalizations to start paragraphs.

The kind of classroom discussion I've just explained is, of course, only one model. You might simply say, "This week's assignment is the description of a place, one that is particularly lively, one that has some meaning or importance to you. Let's talk about places in your lives that might fit into this category. You might think of a kitchen, a local disco, a fast food restaurant. Let's have some people in the class talk about places of meaning in their lives." Here, too, students talk, and you encourage and raise questions. "Why do you name your kitchen? Show with words what kind of place it is. What colors are the walls? Are there curtains? What does the table look like? What noises would I hear if I were in your kitchen?" Here, impression and evidence, generality and detail proceed together, interacting and refining each other as the student speaks and the rest of the class listens. "What one word would you use to give your overall impression of the place?"

To encourage discussion of a more independent sort, divide the class into groups of three or four. Then give clear directions: "Each person will describe some important, unforgettable place to the rest of the people in the group. One person as secretary will take notes as others talk; the rest of the group will ask questions which will lead to sharp sensory pictures (see p. 110). You might want to ask about location, color, sound, action, people. Don't take more than two or three minutes with each speaker. After each group is finished, the secretary will describe briefly what was said for the rest of the class. And we'll all listen for the clearest description."

These are only suggestions. The point is to bring the class to such a pitch of interest and excitement about the topic through sharing ideas that these ideas will spill over onto a page once writing begins. A second point, of course, is to supervise practice in activities—thinking through the topic, searching for detail, weighing the validity of a generalization—that the inexperienced writer can replicate on his own, alone, before he writes.

Another essential exercise in prewriting for beginners is examining and analyzing student themes written in response to the assignment by others in the past. After explaining a theme and after supervising class discussion, you provide through student models tangible examples of writing that meets the goals for the activity. By reading several papers, you make the point clearly that there is more than one way for writers to do things. And you are offering in this exercise papers of quality which may be recalled or even consulted again as the student struggles with his own creative efforts.

But the activity is no passive one where someone reads and others listen, an occasional comment afterward ("That was good!"), benign but superficial and unconstructive. In the first place, you have to select models purposely. You should be drawing them from files you're keeping as you teach writing classes over the years. If you're just beginning and you have no model themes available, you'd be smart to write them yourself for each paper you require. And if you're shuddering at the hours this will take, I don't think you can spend time more wisely than in preparing good models for your own assignments, models which will be springboards for apprentice writers in the first years you teach the course. Draw your models from students in all your writing courses.

Papers you can identify as those of students or former students at your college have a magnetic hold on beginning writers. In *The Writing Room* I have offered some student samples for writing exercises; the textbook for your course should supply others. Perhaps you can encourage the committee on composition or the department chair to keep an office file of strong student themes. What better way to define goals than to let a piece of writing speak for them?

Next, you've got to be clear about why you're presenting a particular model for the class to examine. Make a list in advance of the features you want the class to note about a theme they are reading or listening to. Devise questions about the models; and ask the questions before examining the theme so you can direct concentration. "Listen to this theme by Helen Chin. Afterwards, be prepared to answer these questions: What main impression is she trying to create? Which sensory details support that impression? Which among the details are most original? Most unnecessary?" By the questions you propose you create a response model that puts forward for consideration immediately what is most important. Don't ask about transitions or about sentence fragments or those questions will announce to students that you value structural elements more than anything. Important as those elements may be, they are on a far lower level in the hierarchy of concerns than issues of meaning and detail. Of course, questions you ask will vary with the task and will reflect the goals of your course syllabus.

For beginning writers, samples from students, as opposed to professionals, have special value. A favorite among teachers, the professional model is often more a threat than a page for emulation; few students think they can write like Orwell or Joyce or Twain or Bacon. These writers are, further, often hard for beginners to understand. Models by students, on the other hand, even by the best students, say something important to the novice: "Here is a piece written by someone a few years ago in a class in writing. The paper may be better than your writing is now, but it's not something you cannot reach if you apply the principles we've been discussing."

After you explain the assignment, after you conduct discussions directed at clarifying it, after you examine samples of student writing, you want to prepare a list of objectives that highlight some *specific* skills demanded by this writing task and by your major concerns as reader and evaluator at this stage. This is not to challenge the holistic nature of the writing process—that writers need everything at once and that readers even if they try cannot overlook certain skills on a page. Rather, it is a way of saying to the student: "Though you're always concerned with all aspects of your writing in every page you do, in this theme you're going to concentrate especially on some key skills, skills you've practiced because this assignment requires their exercise *or* because your own needs in writing demand them. When I look at your paper I shall look *most* at these areas, though I will certainly consider the others."

The list of objectives may take one of several forms. Prepare it as a chart of pointers for success in a particular rhetorical strategy and/or in key areas of language and syntax of recent concern to the class. Go over your suggestions just prior to setting writers on their own. Or—and this in many ways is a more productive exercise—follow a more inductive mode. After discussions, after reading student samples, ask the class to help in the preparation of a checklist for this theme. Such an activity is an efficient way of seeing, from the items that students suggest, how much they have learned about the particular assignment. And this list then becomes *the class'* own set of objectives, recommendations writers make for their own writing, recommendations based upon the selections the class examined together. In this book there are model-goals lists to use in connection with most assignments, but you'll be much more effective if you try to develop an individual list with each group of writers.

To turn this checklist into a self-evaluation device for students to complete before they write their final drafts, state the objectives in question form: "Have I written a topic sentence that states the topic of the paragraph and that gives my opinion toward the topic? Have I used several images of solid sensory diction? Have I checked for run-on errors and have I corrected all such mistakes in my paragraph?" You can ask students simply to write *yes* or *no* alongside, or to check a box, or to grade themselves in each category, A, B, C, and so on. With such questions you are arming the student again with the tools of self-interrogation so vital to the writer's effort as he moves toward completing his work.

All the points I've offered in this section until now are especially important, though perhaps somewhat unorthodox in the context of *prewriting*. If you've followed my suggestions, however, you've laid the groundwork on the first days for those more traditional prewriting activities that engage writers at their workplaces, without teacher, without classmates; and you want to explore now the interesting, if sometimes desperate, options for stimulating, dislodging, tracking, and developing ideas alone at the table amid the anguish of solitary creation. Here you talk first about thinking, about getting up from the chair and wandering about if the idea does not come quickly. All writers first *think* about their subjects before doing anything else, and the thoughts, with their pain and sudden flashes and intermittent pleasures, are a stage in the writing process that requires identification for the beginning writer. Talk about your own despair as a writer in those first moments that you're dealing with a subject. Invite others to share their habits of avoidance and return to task, of the way coffee or soda or cigarettes or other external aids help circle a topic, sometimes opening a path directly to its core.

Stressing the need to read a chapter in a book or an article in a magazine or newspaper will help beginners see another step that can lead to ideas. Faced with a new challenge, experienced writers head instinctively to a library to define a topic and to expand their knowledge. Although students may recognize the library as a place for term paper research, they have not much sense of the role of indexes, card catalogs, and reference books in the developmental stage of a writing task. It is true that you will encourage personal writing almost exclusively, but sooner or later, as they write about a topic beyond their first-hand experience, beginners need to know how a printed record can fertilize an idea.

Continuing instruction in *prewriting,* you want to enumerate and to explain several techniques that help with pencil finally in hand:

• *free association list.* The writer lists all the ideas that come immediately to mind about the topic no matter how farfetched or improbable they seem. The point is to get the ideas down. This page of jottings—some phrases or clauses, others sentences with pieces missing—becomes a mine for excavation, the writer moving through it digging up some nuggets and scrutinizing them, disregarding others.

• *timed writing.* With a watch or clock ticking nearby the writer writes for ten minutes without a stop. The idea is to stop not at all. If a thought dies, keep writing "I have nothing to say. I have nothing to say. I have nothing to say" or some such blank-line filler. The point here is to overcome anxiety, to get the juices flowing simply by spreading out ink in words upon a page.

• *brainstorming.* Armed with a list of questions, writers can stimulate ideas about a topic. An easy brainstorming activity is to write the topic in a word or two on top of a blank page, then to list at two- or three-inch intervals along the side the questions *Who? What? Where? When? Why? How?* Afterwards, start filling in responses. Of course, brainstorming is different for different assignments, each putting forth its own set of questions.

• *subject trees.* Very much like the free association list this technique helps the writer to move from one level of suggestion to another and to follow his thoughts as they develop toward higher levels of specificity. The ultimate product looks like a tree with branches reaching out toward possibilities for more focused writing.

Two different brainstorming efforts

Topic: baseball game

Who?	my brother Pete and I
What?	helped lose the game
Where?	Highland Park in Fairfield, New Jersey
When?	last July
Why?	both poor players, inexperienced, clumsy, nervous
How?	I struck out 3 times, Pete dropped 2 fly balls

Topic: learning to swim

When did I learn to swim? I was eight years old, and I remember being scared. Why? Fell into the creek at Cole's Farm three years before. Who helped me learn? My sister Bertie. How did she get me to do it? Why was I stupid enough to try again, being so scared? She dared me. When was this? June afternoon on the way home from school on the very last day. We were at the creek again. What did the scene look like? What did Bertie say? How did I feel when she held me under my stomach, making me kick my feet and move my arms? How did the water feel? What did I smell, feel, hear at my first swimming lesson?

• *yo-yoing.* After thinking *without* writing, some writers generate and sharpen ideas by constructing consecutive sentences in a first draft, skipping other prewriting activity. When an idea—aroused by a developing thought—intrudes, pencils fly off to the margin, make little notations there attached to lines drawn from it to the paragraph, and then fly back to take up the thought suddenly abandoned for another. Words and ideas in the margin help develop sentences later on.

Prewriting techniques will probably never be fully classified and explained, so varied must they be to suit each writer's needs. You've got to point that out too: what you've enumerated to the class are *only possibilities.* Of course,

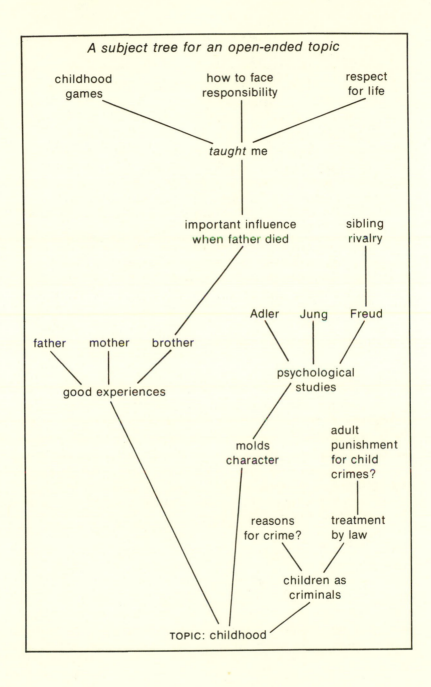

you'll want to give everyone a chance to practice each one. In fact, as you introduce a new theme assignment discuss in depth another of the prewriting techniques. But always present them as options. Encourage the writer to find what works best for him or her in this region of creative development. Again, show your own prewriting artifacts, explaining what you do when you're getting started. And on occasion you'll want to examine what students produce at prewriting so you can help them move on. A major idea, though, is that every writing task demands some kind of prewriting exercise.

A few more points need to be made here. First, be sure some of these prewriting exercises take place during the term under your supervision so you can redirect students' editorial instincts, usually too strong at early stages of creation. Beginning writers rarely know where to edit; if anything they are much too early on engaged in emendations. Timed writing and free association, in their insistence upon rapidly moving on, force concentration away from correctness. (This same stress upon idea formation and away from editing you'll carry over into discussions of rough drafts.)

Next, remind the class of the various stages that succeed prewriting as the written effort moves to completion. You'll deal now with a planning phase where the writer groups written thought-clusters either by recopying or by connecting related ideas with lines and arrows in contrasting ink or by cutting and pasting. Some pieces he'll eliminate if they don't fit his intention; some he'll save for later on, perhaps; others he'll add to develop ideas.

You want to make an important assertion here about outlines. The outline is a tool that *some,* certainly not all, writers use to help them organize their thoughts. An outline can offer help as a road map through dense territory—pages of a writer's notes from sources, quotes and paraphrases, data collected from graphs and charts. Bringing order to the chaos of note cards is in the domain of the outline, certainly. And outlines also seem to work pretty well after the fact;

they can illustrate—after there is a written draft—the form that the writer chose and can point out weaknesses in that form and methods for improving it. To analyze the structure of a paragraph that already exists, you can offer an outline of it as a good aid. But because writers need to discover structure *as they write,* outlines in the early, creative stages of writing are not often helpful. They assume that a precise structure already exists in the writer's mind before he has worked his way through a rough draft. Unfortunately, many students, as a result of prior training, will seem addicted to formal outlining for all their writing efforts, and for questionable reasons. It is important, therefore, to make the class understand the values and limitations of the outline.

ROUGH DRAFTS AND ROUGH DRAFT WORKSHOPS

By distinguishing between early stages of prewriting used by some writers and the first attempt that can stand on its own as a draft, I do not mean to establish any absolute boundaries. When I write, for example, although there's lots of mulling over before I begin, I rarely use those techniques I've described, except, perhaps, for the last. I don't find I need them often: I'm warming up as I write out sentences in a rough draft. But practiced writers can take short cuts. Too many beginners I've faced spin out sentences with no prior thought and then submit those sentences, clearly only beginnings, for reading and evaluation.

Hence, you want to introduce the first draft as the next step *after* prewriting in the development of a page of prose. For those who produce lists or trees or scratch outlines, the first draft marks an attempt to lay out thought-clusters (which have been grouped somehow) in sentences that follow each other with clarity and logic. That's a key purpose of the entire writing effort, of course—but it's rarely fully realized in the first draft. Hence, you must insist upon keeping the notions of perfection and correctness off to the side. The draft is a starting point; it is the place that the writer needs and can benefit from help; and it is the place toward which you should direct creative teaching efforts. Toward these ends I urge the "Rough Draft Workshop" where, in one of several different settings, the writer receives guidance on his early attempts. Many instructors urge their students to rewrite papers *after* they've been evaluated, but beginning writers do not see much hope in revising papers already graded. To the student a scored paper is done forever. Of course errors on final efforts must be corrected, but the place to influence syntactic growth, clarity of expression, precision of words, mastery of form, is *before* the student submits a final draft.

A workshop, to be more than just a session of busy work, must have clear goals, and so before setting up any workshop in the classroom you need an exact sense of what students should do during the session and what they should have achieved at its end. It's not enough to have as a goal "to correct errors" or "to discuss papers"; objectives must be much more specific for a fruitful session when students bring their rough drafts to class. The best workshop, I believe, looks at the draft for its ideas and for its clarity of expression. Using the checklist developed earlier, readers can focus attention upon meaning: Just what is this writer trying to say? How well has he achieved his goal?

But there are many approaches to take in establishing the rough draft workshop. Some instructors teach specific sentence-combining techniques and then ask students to read their rough drafts with an eye toward more efficient expression. Some teachers deal with word choice and review concepts of specific and general language, asking students to seek out in their papers words which lack precision and to substitute more exact expressions. Although I believe that attention more to correctness than to clarity and logic is misdirected at the rough draft stage, some instructors focus upon a sticking error—sentence boundaries, subject-verb agreement, verb tense—and ask students to check their papers for that particular error. Whatever the goal, make sure students know *exactly* what to do during the workshop. Move about the room giving help where it's requested, offering suggestions where they'll have value. Without writing on the student's paper, ask questions about the choices he's made, suggest options he might want to pursue. It's unwise to cross out a student's words or to revise a student's sentence structure; instead, offer ideas which he might consider in order to expand his options. If a glaring error prevents clear meaning—even though the error might not be one the student has learned about—make note of it and point it out quietly. Try to avoid showing where the error is or how to correct it, saying instead, "You have a fragment in the first five lines there. Why don't you try to fix it?" Send the student to the text to see if he can figure out how to correct the error. If he fails on his own (keep a close check and don't let too much time pass), call him up to the chalkboard and explain the mistake. There's no learning that takes place so well as that which affects a problem on the writer's page, a problem that, if corrected, will improve the quality of expression. Achieving that for clarity's sake is the main goal for early drafts.

Class workshops to which students bring their rough copies may require writers to work alone at their seats, the goals for their activity clearly before them. Or, set up collaborative units where students can work in groups toward a specific end. (Groups need especially clear goals so that participants have a sense of purpose.) After discussing the particular word or sentence skill which requires attention, members of the group exchange papers and suggest possible alterations based upon instructions of the day. If the purpose of the workshop is to attend more to elements of content and organization than to syntax, another approach has students reading themes aloud while others listen and take notes which pertain to the specific goals set for the activity. If your goals are offered as questions—for example, "Which sentences could be condensed by means of subordination? Which words in the paragraph are too abstract?"—they are challenges for the group to work on together, one paper at a time.

Students working in pairs can also exchange rough drafts, even outlines or other prewriting exercises. After reading what their partners wrote, students respond to specific questions which may give the writer hints on how to clarify and expand ideas. Some teachers offer guide sheets to accompany this exchange of drafts. The writer attaches to his own draft questions he has about it, such as: "Is my topic clear? Where do I need more details? What is the one major strength in this paper?" The reader of the draft responds in kind on a separate sheet.

I see two essential qualities in good peer-evaluation sessions of these kinds, no matter what the particular workshop technique. First, I encourage students to read their papers aloud whenever possible. Speaking their own written words to others builds a commitment that is essential for beginning writers. Reading aloud also directs comments and questions away from error: listeners cannot easily attend to correctness and can direct their energies at clarity, logic, and deail, important concerns at this stage. Each writer reads his piece at least twice, the first time to give a general sense of the writer's purpose, and the second to allow closer attention to particulars. Listeners take notes as writers read; and then afterwards there's a give and take about the paper. "I didn't understand the point about your friend. What do you mean?" Response. "Well why don't you say it that way? It's much clearer now." The second quality I point to is, again, the need for a clear statement of goals as the blueprint for the workshop. I prefer less the general guide sheets for use on all themes than brief lists of goals prepared by you and the class for the specific writing activity. In most cases these lists of goals are just like those you agreed upon when you made the assignment, after you read student models and discussed them. But I spend time eliciting again the most important goals for this theme; with a list of them on the chalkboard, peer-evaluation sessions have a highly specific context and can offer real guidance in the preparation of subsequent drafts.

As an alternate activity to the workshop—especially when class time constricts toward the end of the semester—you might want to collect rough drafts in order to write questions, comments, and suggestions yourself that will guide work in the next draft. There are dangers here: you have to resist writing the paper by making suggestions that sound like edicts; and you have to avoid editing the surface features of the language. For the first: to guide the writer, raise questions or offer advice that can lead to new formulations and expanded ideas. For the second: make no corrections of run-ons, fragments, spelling, and the like. If those intrude upon the clarity of expression or if they are at epidemic proportions and are easily categorized, a summary remark at the bottom of the draft will guide the writer's proofreading in later stages: "When you prepare your next draft look especially for end mark punctuation. It's hard to follow here where one sentence ends and another begins."

If for some reason you cannot take classroom time for early stages of a writing task, you should at least collect a prior draft along with the paper submitted for evaluation. Even a quick glance from the final copy to the rough shows the writer's progression in thought—and, certainly, if he has progressed, whether or not he has used the draft as a starting point from which to move.

THE FINAL THEME COPY

Between the first draft and the final copy lie a quantity and rigor of performance that depend upon the writer alone. Hence, it is inaccurate to talk of *first, second,* and *third* drafts. Many writers make five or six attempts before a piece looks finished, rewriting pages to reshape sentences; other writers work over and over upon one or two attempts only, cutting and pasting, switching colors of ink, scratching out words and reconnecting phrases to arrange successive revisions. The issue, then, is not the number of times the writer copies over his paragraph; it is instead the fact *that* he has made sufficient discrete efforts. Few writers ever feel that their work is truly finished even when they've decided to stop, so at best that sense of closure is tentative even among professionals. Share that observation with students; explain that as they move through several efforts at revision they will grow more and more aware that the process could go on indefinitely unless something inside, no matter how haltingly, insists "That's enough!" Most beginners have never heard that voice, however, and your labor with drafts is to get students to see how ideas often need time and space and fresh attempts in order to grow clearer, but that at some point work must end.

What experienced writers actually do when they revise their efforts is of course complex. The eye and the ear and the pencil are changing word and idea not only for meaning and clarity and sound, but also for correctness, often both at the same time. Separating the process of revision to shape and to clarify ideas from the process of revision to meet the conventions of correctness is wise nonetheless for beginning writers because as I've suggested before their attemps to revise tend to concentrate exclusively upon error, and especially upon spelling. Activities in class with beginners' rough drafts until now emphasize revising to make clear. But, of course, as one deals with syntactic changes and with precision of words, the boundaries between Shaughnessy's "territory of choices" and "territory of givens" can blur. Still, beginners should approach the rereading-revising of their drafts with different and limited purposes. You've helped students revise for meaning; now you need to help them learn to revise for correctness. (You may find it helpful to reserve the word *revising* for changes made in thought and meaning, and to use the word *editing* for changes made in the surface features of language.)

There are at least two places in the draft process at which writers need to open wide the editorial eye and to close at least halfway the "meaning" eye that looks at thought and style and clarity. First, revision for correctness plays its most significant part just before the writer decides to copy over his piece into a final draft for someone to read easily. Revisions for meaning and clarity over, correctness takes center stage. Second, after the final draft is completed, writers again check over their pages for minor errors that might either have slipped by or have developed in the recopying. Unfortunately, beginners even after instruction in proofreading tend to read for correctness only at this stage. What started out as a final manuscript turns rapidly into a draft. Make students understand that major changes on a completed manuscript make it unfinished, requiring further recopying.

At these two stages, then, proofreading is an important skill to teach, and practice needs classroom supervision. Talk first about what proofreading is and how it differs from the usual kind of reading people do every day. Proofreading is an activity that involves slow and patient examination of words on a line. Most other reading is quick, eyes often skimming across a page in order to take in as much information in as short a period of time as possible. An effective way to demonstrate these differences is to present a familiar statement with one or two words repeated. Write the statement out in a box like this; make a transparency; ask several students to read it aloud.

> Ask not what
> your country can
> do for you but
> what you
> you can do for
> your country.

Many students will miss the repeated word in line five. Why? Explain to the class, first, that they are probably reading quickly. Next, explain that they are reading familiar words. As with Kennedy's statement, when they reread their own papers for error, students are so familiar with what they meant to say that they often miss mistakes, often read words that are not on the line, often omit words that are on the line, often look at one word and see another. Writers must learn how to slow down their reading when they proofread. Here are some suggestions for students:

1. Read slowly. This is not a job done by skimming. Look at every word. Read aloud what you've written.
2. Use a ruler or a blank sheet of paper below each line. This will help you avoid reading too swiftly. The fewer words you examine at a time the easier it is to find spelling errors. Check doubted words in the dictionary.
3. Try pointing to each word as you pronounce it to see if it's correct.
4. Be aware of your usual errors. Check your last theme to see what corrections your instructor pointed out. If you're a chronic run-on writer, look especially for run-on errors when you proofread.
5. Proofread at least twice—once before you write your final draft and once after you write it.
6. If your final draft paper looks too messy after you've proofread it, you might have to recopy it. Don't hand in a paper that does not fit usual manuscript requirements.

For practice in reading skills, provide a sample loaded with many obvious errors of the kind inexperienced writers make. Here's one students can work on:

Even when i was in the fourth grade of washington elementary school, I was insecure and unsure of myslef. Once I had to in front of the class to read a composition. Its frightening to stand in front of other childrens. All I could thing about was my squeaky voice I was scarred my friends would laug at me even thought they new me. So many brown a blue eyes starring at me made it worser. Although my Teacher kept shouted, "speak up, Ellen!" I just remained quite.

But the best exercise is the one which encourages proofreading in class as students check over the draft before the final one. To dramatize the effectiveness of the skill when it is properly applied, ask students to use a pencil or a different colored ink as they proofread for corrections. Go about the room watching for overcorrecting, occasionally asking a student to explain reasons for making a particular change.

In regard to the final manuscript, it is a service to suggest a positive outlook toward the shape and appearance of this copy. Faced with students who are tense about their writing, instructors often are permissive in regard to proper manuscript form—long yellow sheets, small thin-lined loose-leaf paper, pages ripped from a spiral notebook, are all accepted for evaluation as final efforts. Yet our own writing tasks and the tasks students will face when they leave college demand much more careful attention to form. In the basic writing classroom you must ask for proper manuscript appearance. Require 8½-by-11-inch paper. Express hope that the papers can be typed. If they cannot be, insist on regularly lined paper upon which the writer: leaves wide margins; writes a title, properly punctuated, at the top of the page; leaves space at the bottom; uses blue or black ink; observes the conventions of neatness and correctness. Offer written guidelines like those on page 42.

Provide good final copies for the class to examine, using the opaque projector to contrast themes. Make the point that the guidelines you're offering students are exactly the kinds of guidelines you have to follow yourself if you want someone to evaluate your writing.

The day you collect the first formal manuscripts, hold up individual papers (masking the author's name) and ask for comments on appearance and fidelity to manuscript requirements. At the end of class return any paper seriously in violation of the standards you've set and ask the student to rewrite.

What Your Final Copy Should Look Like

	If it is typed	*If it is handwritten*
Paper	8½ x 11 inches, white unlined, sturdy, not corrasable.	8½ x 11 inches, white, wide lines.
Ink	Use a black ribbon.	Use black or blue-black ink.
Spacing	Double space.	Use ruled lines.
Margins	Leave at least 1 inch at top, bottom, and on each side.	Use ruled margins at top and left. Leave 1 inch on right. Skip two or three lines at the bottom.
Name and Date	Top of page 1, on a title page, or on back of page (as instructor directs).	
Title	Center on page one, 1½ inches from top, or on title page. Do not use quotation marks. Do not underline. Skip line after the title.	
Paragraphs	Indent five spaces.	Indent one inch.
Page Numbers	Use Arabic numbers (2, 3, 4, . . .). Start numbering on page 2, placing number at the top center or top right-hand corner.	
Neatness	Avoid strikeouts, cross-outs, ink smudges, and erasure tears.	Use a plain, readable handwriting. Avoid crossouts, ink blots, and erasure tears.

IN-CLASS PAPERS

For better or for worse, most basic writing programs require formal themes written under classroom supervision and collected and evaluated after a single period's duration. In typical placement or competency exams the student sits in his seat, exam booklet opened; he reads an assignment from a handout or from the chalkboard; he writes for a full period; he submits his paper for evaluation. The pedagogical weaknesses inhering in such a task are obvious and require mention only in passing: few writers work under hour-long deadlines; all our instruction in process flies out the window when we demand for our most important evaluations tasks that seem to *circumvent* process; tensions generated by controlled writing prevent fluent, accurate products; in-class writing is an unfair measure of student growth and progress—there are others certainly. Yet the need for a controlled impromptu writing experience both to certify the student's own work and to establish finite, shared conditions for performance is an instructional expediency and has many supporters. This is especially true in large school systems where only comparative evaluations can reasonably measure minimal achievements, each paper assured a reading that adheres to agreed upon standards of judgment. Certainly for establishing minimum competencies controlled writing is here to stay (more on this in Chapter 5).

And yet it is not thoroughly indefensible when you consider the kinds of writing that students will do throughout the academy and after they leave it. The writing exam in other courses is no doubt a more pernicious form of deadline writing than in-class themes, and yet we readily accept an hour's biology final written in a sweat as part of the *rite de passage*. At a desk with a supervisor's breath hot down the neck, employees pen under pressure reports, letters, memoranda. People who work at law, advertising, editing, management, write with an eye on the clock too.

I'm for explaining all this to students. Different writing assignments arouse their own special problems not only
through subject matter, but also through conditions of performance, which writers cannot always control. The point for
successful instruction, though, is to help students manipu-
late the process you've been teaching all along so that it
serves the broadest possible range of tasks. A reasonable
formula for breaking down writing time is, roughly, 20 percent for planning, 60 percent for writing, 20 percent for
rereading, revising, and repairing. Thus, in 50 minutes, a 10–
30–10-minute breakdown works well.

Prewriting for in-class essays, then, is no less important
than for any other kind of writing exercise. Certainly it is condensed, hurried, and unsatisfying; yet without thinking about
the assignment, without making random jottings, without attempting some organizational plan at least mentally (if not in
rough outline form on scrap paper), the writer risks incoherence. Practice these prewriting activities with the class
under high-pressured situations before you demand full-ses-
sion writing for evaluation. "I'm going to call out a topic,"
you might say. "You'll have five minutes for whatever kinds
of prewriting exercises get you going. After the five minutes
each person will explain just where he'd expect to take a
reader in an hour's time."

It's small reward to note that, condensed to five desperate
minutes or so, prewriting for in-class themes nonetheless
fares better than other important stages in the writing process. In fact, in-class writing does not reduce, but it eradi-
cates the draft concept. There is no final manuscript here
like the one you've insisted upon in previous general instruction. From the random jottings that steer thinking under
pressure, the writer prepares his first and only copy. Despite
the temptations of premature editing and of recopying first
efforts, you must discourage these as forcefully as you can.
For rewriting, one limited session is not enough. If time pressures interfere with idea development, they play havoc with
recopiers who leave out end marks, words, whole lines in

their race against the second hand. In exam booklets when writers skip every other line, when they leave wide margins, and when they write on one side of a page only, open space makes emendations possible and readable. Carets and arrows, clearly drawn, will guide the reader along.

The final fifth of composing time, as you see, has the writer reworking materials both for clarity and correctness. In the time reserved for this part of the effort at least a couple of editing efforts will help beginners separate the chores. The first rereading looks at meaning, detail, organization, and logic; the second scrutinizes the right-or-wrong features of the language. In teaching these operations you might offer to the whole class a page of in-class writing done by a student in previous years. Students in groups can rework prose in the two stages you're recommending.

INSTRUCTORS' WRITTEN COMMENTARY

There are many possible ways to develop a system of writing comments from which students can learn. In the final analysis a good method is one that suits the instructor and student both philosophically and practically. But certainly the best method is the one that always accents the positive features in a piece and that offers constructive comments upon which the writer can build in the next theme.

Some teachers feel that a bloodied paper, red scrawls all over the margins, is demoralizing and negative to students. Others approve of the psychology of the red pen because students take special heed of what speaks out in red ink. For still others, a lead pencil allows important flexibility so that the teacher can look at his own prose and can make alterations in it; the tentativeness of pencil supports the unfinished status of the early drafts and is expecially useful, many feel, for comments on rough copies. Whether you use red, green, or black ink or pencil, you can lessen trauma when you return papers. First use some word or symbol which stands for a positive comment that you can make in various places on even the poorest theme. An *x*, a check, the letters *Gd* (for good), will tell the student about specific words, phrases, or sentences that are alive, clear, and strong. Any word or sensory image may be pointed out in this way; so may any new attempts at vocabulary or sentence structure. A few brief words in the margin such as "I like this" or "Fine image" or "Good try" or "Wonderful" go much further than "Poor" or "Awful" or "Trite"—especially if the negative comments fail to indicate specific words or sentences. Furthermore, even on the poorest paper, the comment at the end is crucial. Try to start with some positive remark, no matter how brief: "I like your topic sentence, but . . ." "Your image on . . . is excellent but. . . ." Students respond much more strongly to comments that suggest improvements. And try to make comments do just that. Tell the student one or two things he can do to advance his writing, even suggesting a specific goal or two for the next theme. Perhaps the most stimulating marginal comments are those that pose questions to the writer. "Why didn't you combine these sentences?" "Why did you choose this word?" Encourage students to respond to questions directly on the page or in conference. I insist on responses before recording credit for a completed assignment.

To assure instructive statement on papers, some teachers affix a checklist to the student's final draft to guide their reading and commentary. With sections for remarks in several categories ("Thesis statement," "Organization," "Language," "Style," "Correctness"), checklists help focus comments and guarantee to the writer recognition of his efforts in the critical areas intelligent reading must acknowledge. I myself find checklists unwieldy—they offer yet another sheet that demands attention, and I'm constantly turning back and forth from theme to assessment page—but I note their usefulness in insisting upon the kind of information beginning writers need to help them move ahead.

In responding to student writing, you'd best avoid editing the prose. You can make suggestions or raise questions or present options, but it's inadvisable to cross out or to shift words or to correct them. After all, the writer has extracted with moan his page of prose, no matter what its weaknesses, and those halting words stand as products of creative effort. It is merely respectful, therefore (and not excessively romantic), to view them as inviolate by any but their creator, someone who may be led to produce change, but who, ultimately, must decide how (and if) the change suits his or her intentions. Editing student writing can create strong, clear prose, certainly—but then which teacher can objectively evaluate a sentence he has helped to build from a student's resources? Such partnerships are shaky at best. Occasionally, of course, a thorny sentence will require some editing especially on papers with second language interference, but if you indicate errors by using words and symbols in the margin, you can encourage self-sufficiency. Marginal notations make students read along the line in order to find their own error. Since that is what you are training them to be able to do without your help, it is practice for the next theme and for future themes. And students need to attempt correction by themselves. That often means reading textbook pages and learning new concepts in order to correct mistakes. Finally, if students try but do not know how to make a correction on their own, they will be motivated to come to conference for special instruction.

I've mentioned the use of symbols to indicate strengths and weaknesses in writing, but it's important to consider symbols as instructors' aids more than anything else. They're certainly not as helpful to beginning writers as clear, personal statements. Contrast "RO" with "You failed to separate or to join these two complete thoughts. Fix the run on." Still, it is impractical for the instructor to write out all words to indicate problems especially if they are repeated: in several sets of papers the time such a procedure takes would weaken considerably a grader's stamina and clarity of thought.

Symbols can work to make you a more efficient reader, but

not without planning. Class time before you return the first batch of papers must go toward explaining meanings and uses of symbols. One reason for the popularity of handbooks as texts for a writing course is that error symbols are keyed to sections in the book. Handbooks by their format imply that the student seeing *Frag* on a paper turns to the inside cover, notes that *Frag* means *fragment,* and then finds the page marked with that symbol in order to read an explanation of an error. Yet beginning students rarely use handbooks unless a teacher actually shows how to use them, how the symbol system works, how sections are keyed to certain symbols, and how writers can learn about specific areas of difficulty by going to those pages that a particular symbol on their graded papers suggests.

Whether you use a handbook or not, explain your grading symbols carefully. It's not enough merely to offer a list of your marking devices and an explanation of their meanings. Distribute a sheet of symbols complete with an excerpt from a paragraph containing errors. The whole class can work together on such a sample. Then students have not only a list of symbols, but also a concrete sample of errors that correspond to the symbols. Here is a suggested format for such a sheet:

Marking Symbols

CF—comma fault

RO—run-on sentence

Frag—sentence fragment

Agr—agreement of subject and verb

Dang—dangling modifier

Gr—error in grammar

P—use correct punctuation

Cap—use a capital letter

no cap—capital unnecessary

sp—spelling

WO—write out the word; don't abbreviate

T—wrong tense
Pro—reference of pronoun is unclear or incorrect
ms—incorrect manuscript form
W—wordiness and needless repetition
'—use the possessive
∧ —omission of words
¶—start a new paragraph
no ¶—don't start a new paragraph
US—wrong usage of a word

Sample from a Paragraph

no cap	College Freshman are
RO	adventurous they will try any-
Frag	thing once. Which sometimes
	causes trouble. Although ad-
sp, US	venture itself is alright, to
Agr	much excitement are not good
?	for a students nerves and can
Pro	interfere with their studies.

As for spelling, a few words of caution here: Don't rely only on your instincts. Keep a dictionary at your desk as you grade papers.

Though most teachers stress the idea of writing as a holistic activity, it is especially in the area of correctness that the student feels most strongly the injustice of this premise. On a paper the instructor indicates *all* errors, even those not yet covered in class. One alternative to the usual grading system on themes suggests that we look first at students' papers with an eye toward evaluating only those skills taught prior to the assignment, the skills from theme to theme cumulative. Errors and strengths in those areas you can indicate in the margin in one color ink; with different ink you can make comments appropriate to errors not yet explained. In this way you are saying: "I'm especially looking at the skills you have learned before this theme, even though I have pointed out other areas in which you need to advance."

I want to take some more time to discuss ideas for making appropriate comments on a writer's work. When giving advice on papers, teachers are as much fellow writers at that moment as they are tutors, and comments must stand on their clarity, on their acuteness of perception, on their succinctness, and on their ability to promote action. Ideally, your critique should be a model for the careful work you want from your students. I do not mean to sound unrealistic. Amid heavy course and student loads, precise, economical prose will often seem unattainable, I know; yet aiming for that goal will in the long run make you a more efficient grader.

There's not much research on what kinds of comments yield the best results for beginners, but I can offer some general guidelines that may help you design commentary on papers. First, you want to avoid excessively terse summary responses to the writer's effort. Neither "Good" nor "Weak" standing alone at the end of a theme takes the writer very far. The best approach, I believe, is to *describe* objectively what you see or do not see, sprinkling those descriptions with deserved praise and raising questions based upon your observations.

When you describe you offer verifiable propositions: "This topic sentence lacks an opinion"; "The image on line 3 makes a strong appeal to the sense of sound"; "The transition *yet* links sentences 3 and 4 smoothly." Certainly words of praise are not objective, but in the context of a descriptive statement they are also not gratuitous, and will bolster frail egos. And if your statements use the same language as the objectives you and the class established for the theme (objectives named, perhaps, in a checklist like the one I've described on page 74), you can reward an achievement the writer specifically aimed for. You want especially to resist offering negative judgments, ironic statements, or elegantly phrased insults. Trying to help the writer reach a high level of achievement in the next effort, you cannot risk interference from anger, resentment, or frustration directed at you or at your remarks. It's easy to crush a beginner with comments like "This is unacceptable" or "This is not a paragraph" or "You obviously did not work hard enough in this theme." A momentary release for the teacher who writes them, perhaps, those comments lead the student nowhere.

Finally, describing too much may result in a summary that rambles, so you want to be especially careful to target only major issues with your advice. Make some positive comments in which you highlight the strengths of the paper, then zero in on recommendations for improvement based upon conditions you have described accurately. Raising lots of questions alongside sentences as you read helps you gather straws easily in a summation at the end of the theme.

To frame your comments so they do the most good, I suggest you address them to this question: "What does the writer need to know most *right now* about this paper?" If you are reacting to a draft, the writer will have a chance for this assignment to act on your recommendations. (For that reason many instructors like to give their most comprehensive comments on the draft instead of on the final copy. But remember the caveats against editing, pointing out error, and offering advice that sounds like commandments.) If you comment on a final manuscript, writers should be able to use your remarks as guides for constructing the next theme.

On page 52 is a theme submitted by a beginner as a final draft for a paper in illustration (see also pp. 96–105). Instructor comments accompany it.

Those remarks are thoughtful and can help the writer progress. In the margins brief comments and questions point out specifics the writer can weigh. The *X*'s over *rushed* and *pushed* in sentences 8 and 11 commend their visual qualities. Each symbol in the margin (*RO, Frag, sp*) points out an error made somewhere in the line on which the symbol stands; students must, therefore, find the errors themselves. On a final draft the teacher is right to pinpoint errors in word use and syntax. Certainly, however, not every mistake demands attention.

Fears of being Alone

Story topic sentence. (Would it help to combine 1 and 2 with subordination?

(1) I usually feel uncomfortable and insecure whenever I have to go some place alone. (2) I often wish someone could always be with me no matter where I have to go. (3) For instance, when I first came to La Guardia. (4) I felt nervous and a little afraid I didn't know my way around, so I felt as if I were lost in crowd. (5) I wished I was home where every thing is more familiar to me. (6) After finally finding the room I was suppose to be in I felt some what relieved. (7) I didn't know anyone around me. (8) I sat waiting for it all to end, when it did I rushed out the classroom door in a hurry to get home. (9) Another time was when I had to go shopping for food alone. (10) It was my first time; I usually went with the whole family. (11) I pushed the cart quickly down the iles picking up items almost without looking at them. (12) When I got on line to pay for my groceries. (13) I felt a little impatient waiting behing two people who were also purchasing groceries. (14) When the cashier rang up my purchase. (15) I handed her the money and when she gave me my change I didnt even count it. (16) I just wanted to get out of there.

Frag

RO

∧

vb

RO

Good use of semi.

sp

Frag

sp

Frag

} Good transition

sp

what does it refer to?

x x

what items? Expand in an image

Closing? You've ended the subtopic but not the paragraph. See page 15 in text

It is pretty uncomfortable doing new things alone, isn't it? Your choice of topic suits the mode of illustration perfectly and your topic and first subtopic sentences help the reader understand your examples. (The sentence beginning "Another time" should state more exactly its relationship to the topic, though.) What a reader needs most here is detail. Which room made you feel uncomfortable? What images could help readers know what you experienced? In the supermarket (Was it one? You don't tell us!) what specific colors and actions might show your insecurity? What do people in the aisles say or do when you zip past? What do the people in front of you at the checkout do to make you impatient? How does the cashier react to your strange behavior?

You've got to work some more on fragments and run-ons. In a final draft they distract the reader. Fix yours; practice with pages 22–26 and 32–36 in your text; then see me in conference to discuss the exercises. Go to the Writing Center for more help.

The summary remarks on this paper can serve as a helpful paradigm for your own comments. The commentary first admits the valuable content offered by the writer. Students unconvinced that they have meaningful things to say need you to acknowledge their ideas and to react to them. Thereafter, comments can focus on structural elements, praising and suggesting improvement with the aid of questions. Reflecting goals established earlier, the instructor's remarks point both to detail and to areas of correctness demanding attention.

In regard to giving grades on papers, there are many procedures to consider, some more valid and more valuable than others. Some instructors score papers with grades for the last three or four assignments only, viewing the first several as experimental. Some grade all papers and allow students to drop their lowest score. Some instructors use numerical grades, others letter grades. Some assign two grades, one for content, another for mechanics and form, but there is little justification for this given the inseparable nature of form and content in writing. Others have devised grading systems on scales of 1–5 or 1–10, numerical scores quantifying specific criteria for form and content. Some teachers will grade 75 + 5, for example, where the 5 (or some other figure) will be added to the total grade if all corrections

are made. In all these procedures it is the grade that ines-
capably comes first, in both the student's and instructor's
minds.

On the whole, however, for beginners, letter or numerical
grades are not the best for evaluating a piece of writing. In
fact, withholding grades creates fewer problems than giving
them. First, forced to grade, you must often make arbitrary
decisions. When you wear the judge's robes, students have
trouble seeing you in your more important role, that of facili-
tator of better writing in the next effort. A "C" on a page can
say enough about it to preclude a thoughtful reading of your
comments. And students grow nervous at grades. There is a
finality about them that works against efforts to establish the
idea of progressive stages in written efforts. Without a grade
and with extensive comments a writer can move into another
phase of production. Certainly for advanced writers you
should expect a "final" draft to be just that (although no
writer is ever really convinced that his product is finished);
but beginners need practice, with your help, in deciding
when a piece most closely matches its potential for completion. Grades say "This attempt is over." Too much conference time is wasted in explaining, justifying, and defending
grades when that time should be used for discussions about
writing.

Though I prefer a system that avoids grades on individual
papers, I am not unaware of the demands on teachers for
final evaluations of students' work. However, at many institutions a mandated Pass or Fail grade in basic writing—a good
development so far as I'm concerned—means for teachers a
single judgment only once and in broad terms. There, and
for teachers in programs that insist upon final in-class
essays as exclusive measures of success in writing, instructors in good conscience can avoid putting grades on papers.
Even without such final essays, teachers required to judge
with a grade a semester's work for a beginner should not
think in terms of averages on papers written throughout the
semester. Writers grow from one effort to the next. To my

way of thinking, the question that leads to a fair grade at the term's end is: Given the goals of this course, where are students *now* in their command of the writer's craft? It may seem cruel to exclude considerations like how hard students work, how much they improve, how attentive or how motivated they are in class, but those deflect judgments that must be made about how the writer *writes.*

RETURNING PAPERS

When you return papers to students, especially the early themes, it is a good idea to have the best papers read aloud by the authors. Encourage reluctant readers with a circular seating arrangement so there's no head of the class. Reading can be done from seats. Some instructors do ask the author to stand up front and read to the class; others like reading aloud the most successful papers themselves. (Make sure to honor any requests for anonymity.) Direct the way the class listens to the papers by stating in advance questions you'll consider after the readings: "As LaVerne reads aloud, take notes on the outstanding features of her theme and especially on these three features, which we'll discuss when she's finished: the way she states her topic, the way she has developed images, and the way she uses transitions to connect ideas." You might even list those discussion points on the chalkboard to encourage active listening. Or, if you've prepared a checklist with the class before the assignment, now's a good time to turn to it, to renew the points that appear there, and to hold class discussion to comments on how the writer met the objectives everyone agreed upon. Just as in the rough draft workshops, these statements provide a framework for critical response to writing, a framework writers need for evaluating their own efforts alone at the composing table.

After each paper is read and you have asked members of the class to point out the strongest parts, ask for suggestions for improvement. Discussions in regard to improvement should focus on the skills already introduced to the class. Some instructors prefer to divide students into groups, each student reading his paper in smaller company. Relative merits of all the papers can then be discussed in these "reaction clusters." Representative papers from each group may then be read to the whole class.

On the day you return final drafts submitted for your evaluation, the more time spent on reading class themes the better. With the kind of careful planning you've been doing when you make assignments, you're bound to get many papers that will hold the class' interest. Hearing how their classmates dealt with a writing task and examining and comparing words and sentences produced by people in the room help underscore the elements of struggle and choice that underlie written activity. And in a community of effort, more opportunity for learning presents itself.

If possible, part of each session when you return papers should go to correction of errors. (It's perfectly all right, though, not to contend with error *at all* on the days you return the first few sets of papers. Look at errors at the next class if you're using full sessions for reading and discussing lots of different student themes.)

One method of examining simple yet gnawing mistakes is to follow Don Wolfe's advice in *Creative Ways to Teach English* and to dictate in rapid succession words and phrases written in students' themes. Here is a sample of such a rapid dictation drill:

1. Spell *occurrence.*
2. arrived too early. Spell *too.*
3. Write this statement: She said, "David works hard."
4. Write this construction: I bought a car. However, I really wanted a motorcycle.
5. the child's smile. Write *child's.*

To deal reasonably with error some instructors, covering students' names, use opaque or overhead projectors to present papers for class correction. Other techniques include duplication of errors for class correction (this is especially helpful in drilling one or two kinds of errors shared by many students); marking in brackets sentences or words on several papers and asking students to copy material onto chalkboards exactly as written in themes; dividing papers into groups based upon frequency and type of error and allowing students to work upon their errors within smaller units.

If there are one or two major errors on students' papers, teach or review those areas. Provide brief practice sheets so students can apply what they learned. Then *insist that graded papers be corrected* and collect them again to check on the students' understanding.

This is not as time-consuming as it sounds. If students use pencil or contrasting color ink to correct their errors, you can move swiftly through a batch of papers, noting which have not been properly attended to. Return those papers to students and insist upon corrections. Anyone who does not understand how to correct an error should be encouraged to come to conference. But it must be clear to the student that making corrections is as much a part of his responsibility as the actual writing of the paper itself.

Many instructors require full revisions of graded manuscripts. But with your active involvement in the preparation of writing at draft stages and with your expectation that writers learn to recognize a piece of work they've produced as finished, extensive revisions of final manuscripts you've already graded will probably not be necessary. Writers should focus their efforts at revision on intermediate drafts. Certainly particularly weak sentences or sentence clusters can be revised by writers on the blank reverse sides of their manuscripts, or in the margins if there's room. Instructors who do require full revisions of graded final manuscripts are best advised not to read them before checking to see that corrections of errors have been made. In revisions, rather than correcting a mistake, beginning writers will often avoid it by means of different words or structures.

Many classroom formats can serve you on the days you're at work helping students understand and correct their errors. Some instructors divide students into groups and allow consultations on the best schemes for correction. Others group students according to the kinds of errors made on their papers so that each group is working on one particular category of mistakes. In that way the instructor calls a small group up to the chalkboard and explains one error to a very attentive audience. When a student returns to his seat he has the information he needs to correct his own mistakes.

I see these sessions based on specific problems in student papers as different from other sessions on correctness, where you're often dealing with principles of grammar and usage that are a step or two away from the immediate needs of many people in the class. When you're giving formal classes on subject-verb agreement, for example, there are foundations you're building with the whole group, foundations that need reinforcement by means of practice activities somewhat distant from a student's particular error but designed nonetheless for mastery over it. But in a workshop setting, graded themes in hand, and with students alone or in groups working upon the errors that appear on their papers, there are highly favorable conditions for learning. By means of immediately acquired skills writers can directly transform into correct expression the errors identified in their prose.

From seating plans to talk of process, from framing and discussing assignments to supervising their production in stages, from commenting upon papers to overseeing corrections, the instructor's role in the writer's progress is active and rooted in careful planning.

2

The Paragraph as Rhetorical Model

A strong course in basic writing concerns itself with methods of developing ideas and with the quality of detail used to support them. As a unit of expression, the paragraph provides solid ground for experimentation, encouraging sustained utterances within a substantive dimension of form. Although both the sample course calendars (Appendix A) as well as the next chapter emphasize the need for instruction early on in rudimentary word and sentence skills, it is really inappropriate to approach assignments by beginners with the sequence traditionally offered in developmental courses: start with words, then sentences, then longer, more developed efforts. No writers construct ideas in that sequence. We take a thought and run all over the place with it, its shape much more a comprehensive element *like* a paragraph or several paragraphs than like words or sentences. Certainly, early instruction deals with word and sentence level skills, but staying exclusively in the territory of parts detracts beginning writers from the larger elements through which thoughtful writing proceeds. By encouraging the development of an idea through detail within a paragraph, you can easily avoid overwhelming an inexperienced writer. Once you acknowledge the writer's intent you can then look at the smaller elements and can evaluate their effectiveness.

The beginning course I find most successful requires experimentation with three methods of paragraph development, methods both accessible to beginners and meaningful in the acquisition of skills at composing: description, narration, and illustration (or exemplification). Though there are no doubt innumerable definitions of and concepts about the paragraph entity, I choose an approach to it less conventional than most. I am not interested in the short three- or four-sentence kind most obvious in popular newspapers and periodicals, nor even in the five- or six-sentence kind that frequently marks student writing. Rather, it is a paragraph that sustains an idea with substantial detail that lies at the heart of the course I propose. In ten to fifteen sentences of two-hundred, two-hundred-fifty, even three-hundred words, the writer develops his point within a one-paragraph theme. It is true that armed with other theories one might easily split the kind of paper for this course into several paragraphs, each developing a portion of the writer's idea with fewer sentences and details. In the illustration theme this certainly will seem very easy to achieve. For inexperienced writers, however, such splits and their concommitant demands upon formal elements (introductions, conclusions, sentence-long transitions) too often seem whimsical and difficult and add unnecessary complexity to instruction. At this stage of development the paragraph of substance is, I believe, the best way to teach required skills of invention, detail, and correctness within some structure that serves the writer's purpose. (I have written elsewhere—see the Bibliography—on the value of the paragraph, especially the single narrative paragraph, in teaching beginning writers about control of form and language, so I shall not detail here more extensive advantages I see for it over larger elements like four- or five-paragraph or open-length essays.)

THE PARAGRAPH ENTITY

Before I discuss some methods of approaching the paragraph exercises I stress in the course, I would like to deal with three structural features that one-paragraph themes ought to share at this level of production by beginners. By treating those features first, however, I am not urging their instruction all at once, for they require frequent and regular exploration throughout the term. Once introduced, what seem at first to be highly formal elements respond to experimentation. Ideally, instruction in rhetorical modes proceeds along with instruction in general paragraph structure, the two modifying and modified by each other.

PARAGRAPH PARTS

• The Topic Sentence

For advanced writers the topic sentence is an elastic entity, appearing here or there or not at all in a paragraph, especially if the paragraph is part of several in a long essay. For inexperienced writers, however, the topic sentence, which generalizes from the ideas the writer has gathered haphazardly on paper, is often the first formal attempt to impose order on random thought. Such a sentence has a central role in the development of the writer's ideas. In a one-paragraph theme I always urge the beginner to offer the topic sentence as the *first sentence*. There, it becomes a signal to the reader as to the writer's exact purpose right from the start. In that position it is also easy for the writer to locate when he looks back. And in checking back, by rereading the topic sentence frequently, writers can test the degree to which the detail they offer supports the topic idea without drifting off. (Inexperienced writers will often follow a digression which leads them astray.)

As an entity convenient to the creative effort of beginners, the topic sentence needs limiting right from the start. Students need to state the topic of their paragraphs—and they need to state their opinion, reaction, attitude toward, or judgment about the topic there too. Thus a topic sentence that reads in a descriptive essay like 1 below is merely a statement of fact in which the writer proposes no generalization to support. Hence he runs into trouble in developing a point. In 2, however, there is limitation and control right from the outset:

1	2
The room has black walls.	The room is dreary.

Students need to see the qualitative difference between topic sentences like 1 and those like 2. The word *dreary* helps the writer limit detail: all images in the paragraph—all supporting information—will advance the general notion of dreariness. With 1, though an experienced writer could order and control particulars with effectiveness, the beginner will soon be helplessly leaping from one physical feature of the room to the other, with no assertion allowing him to manage supporting details. After examining a sentence like 1 and one like 2 with the class, and after eliciting both a definition for and a description of qualities in strong topic sentences (stress the idea of statement of topic *and* opinion), look together at a list you've prepared of topic sentences of uneven quality. Let students explain poor paragraph starts. Which hinder control over detail? What generalization might the writer make? What word of judgment or opinion might he or she add to provide direction?

The sentence in 1 is far from adequate, of course, as a paragraph opener, though it is an advance over 2. With the raw material of stated *topic* and *opinion* you can propose sentence-building activities that will add specificity and detail so that the writer limits the topic even more as he develops his ideas. By adding elements of time, by naming specific places, you develop a sentence like this one:

On a cold Sunday morning at six o'clock the Corner Room on College Avenue is a dreary place to have breakfast.

Spatial and temporal limitations are not always possible—and certainly not always desirable—but in description and narration such statements of topic are a boon to the developing writer. Whatever practice you can suggest for the class to assert this skill—comparing sentences; creating topic sentences only (not whole paragraphs) on announced subjects; improving sentences that lack clearly stated topics, clearly stated opinions, and/or time and space limitations—will be helpful. A thoughtful topic sentence should allow a reader to predict the general nature of supporting detail: after one student writes an opening sentence, ask *another* student to jot down expectations based upon that opening.

Try to link guided practice in writing topic sentences with the specific theme for the week. In that way there is a context for practice. By advising the student in the preparation of a topic sentence, which might very well serve as the opening for his paragraph, you are directing him along a fruitful path. Later on, as writers learn to expand materials into themes of several paragraphs, the *introduction* takes over from the topic sentence as the means of stating the generalization that details will support. Although more expansive, the introduction nonetheless often presents the objective of the essay in a single statement not dramatically unlike the topic sentence in a one-paragraph theme. Hence, practice in writing topic sentences is practice that subsequent and more advanced writing exercises will draw upon.

• The Closing Sentence

The closing sentence in a single paragraph theme is less formal and less expansive than a *bona fide* conclusion in an essay of several paragraphs, but the closing sentence is a precursor of that extended ending to the writer's topic. It is not accurate to say that a closing sentence *must* do things like summarize or "clinch" or tie things together because, as with conclusions, the paper itself generates its own conditions for closure. Consequently, some closings will indeed summarize; others will raise a new but related question; still others will recommend change. The point is to see that the single-paragraph theme requires a closing and that there are options for the writer who needs to write an ending to a paragraph.

Practice? There are several ways to teach this skill. Read aloud a paragraph, except for its closing sentence. How does the class feel about what you read? What would writers in the class do to make the work complete? List on the chalkboard several suggested closings generated by the class. Then read the closing the writer of the paragraph wrote. Compare it to the ones suggested by people in the class. Why did the writer choose the closing he did?

Once the class has examined and analyzed some closing sentences, ask for generalizations: "What are some possible features of closing sentences?" Make a list on the chalkboard. Which points do students feel are most important? Follow-up activities would involve writing different kinds of closing sentences for a single paragraph whose ending is absent; analyzing, in writing, closing sentences of complete paragraphs; small group discussions in which students examine paragraphs written by group members, focusing their discussion upon closing sentences. How does the closing sentence match the criteria established earlier? Is it suitable to the needs of the paragraph? Perhaps the writer's closing achieves something not enumerated on the list the class prepared.

You will want to make the point that in writing longer essays in subsequent writing courses, practice with one-sentence closings will provide a starting point in learning how to write *conclusions*. Point out, further, that in an essay of more than one paragraph, the elements within each are less formal and that readers may not be able to identify in every paragraph the closing sentence as an entity that suits some exact criterion. However, even within longer pieces, readers can usually recognize some movement toward closure in the final sentence or sentences of a paragraph—despite the fact that in paragraphs of an essay each closing must often anticipate subsequent paragraphs, as well as draw together its own internal elements.

• The Title

As the first signal to what lies within, the title is an important feature of the theme, however long it is, however many paragraphs it contains. Aside from problems most writers have with titles—attempts to make them too clever or cute, to make them excessively long or unduly general for the thrust of the theme, to make them too formal or informal for the tone of the paper—basic writing students need to consider two other particular complexities in regard to titles.

The first is that titles are *not* starting sentences of papers. Too many beginning writers present a reasonably effective title (which often states a topic and a reaction to it); and then they will use a pronominal structure to refer to a subject or object in the title as if it were an integrated part of the theme. Thus a title "My Most Embarrassing Moment" might be followed by this as an opening sentence: "It all happened on a Tuesday last spring"; a title "My Father's Temper" might be followed by "This always shows when I come home late." One sure way to avoid this problem is to insist that titles be written on top of the theme as the *last* set of words the student writes. You might even require that no title be written at home; as soon as students come to class with a theme ready for submission, ask them to write their titles right there under your supervision. Since most of us do title our essays after we've done everything else, we're really setting ground rules writers normally follow.

Next, titles are usually not complete sentences. Here is an opportunity to review (or to introduce) the fragment (see pp. 141–53). It is perfectly legitimate to write only a piece of a sentence as a title, and students will enjoy the liberty of incompleteness that the title allows. Yet here is your chance to explore contrasts and to drive home the need for sentence completeness in the paper itself. Why are fragments acceptable as titles? Why are they not acceptable within themes themselves? A good activity in titles and fragments combined is to ask students to examine headlines from the local newspaper: Which are incomplete grammatical elements? How do the titles compare to the "topic sentence" in a news story? What different functions are served by titles and by topic sentences?

THREE PARAGRAPH MODES

• Description

In most forms of writing, description of one kind or another has a major role. For beginning writers assignments in description allow you to introduce both the idea of detail and the qualities of language that make detail lucid and precise. Thus, though a student may never, either for a course or on a job, describe a room or a person with the high level of sensory concreteness demanded from the beginner in descriptive exercises, such exercises nonetheless have value.

Just why should a student learn how to describe a room? Because with a vivid, accessible theme topic like this you can lay the foundation for concepts that guide writers in all their writing: the value of expressing a generalization early in a piece; the importance of concrete, relevant, detail; the effects of precise language, fresh and clear.

For any writer working in the descriptive mode there are problems which must influence the way an instructor makes the assignment. For beginners these problems are particularly acute and require careful attention. Inexperienced writers will choose vague and imprecise words with greater frequency than will more advanced writers. This, of course, is partly a vocabulary problem—students don't know enough words and so have limited options—and therefore part of any work with description involves extensive practice with words. (More on this on pp. 110–14.) You'll need to anticipate a range of vocabulary that a particular assignment in description will call into play; and you'll have to set up situations in which students can exercise that vocabulary. For example, if the first assignment asks for a description of place, deal with vocabulary of size and shape; increase the students' store of sense words which identify sounds; review the language of spatiality.

If telling instead of showing is a problem in description that plagues even more advanced writers, that problem is obviously worse for beginners. They are just as apt to use interpretive adjectives, for example, but their supply is sorely limited to a group noted for vagueness: *good, cute, interesting, nice, a lot, important, higher, lower, less, worse, many, much, hard, easy, bad.* By means of exercises in careful observations and in the recording of observed phenomena in sensory language, you can help the writer develop trust in his own sensory perceptions. You have a good deal of work to do in distinguishing between *concrete* and *abstract* terms and between *general* and *specific* terms and in distinguishing those pairs from each other. Also, you need to show *levels* of concreteness, especially when you deal with imagery.

The writing of clear, precise sensory images is the heart of the matter, of course. It is a skill that *any* student can learn, even if he can demonstrate his skill only intermittently at first, so it is well worth concentrated effort. You can show students how images grow, starting with a general term, replacing it with a concrete one, and then adding details until no reader misses the exact picture the writer attempts to convey. You need also to deal with *denotation* and *connotation* here. On pages 110–14 there appears a number of activities designed to build these and other skills in sensory diction.

Developing a sense of selection of detail is another important goal for writers, a sense nicely taught and practiced within the descriptive mode. Thus, a student must not only generate sufficient details to support a description, but he must then also choose details wisely and prune those that are not relevant. Right from the start, therefore, and in the spirit of the suggestions offered for the development of topic sentences (pp. 63–65), encourage the writer to locate in his own responses some attitude toward the place he is describing. Suggest the use of that attitude as a controlling mechanism for the development of the paragraph. Seeing a room as *ugly, cheerful, busy,* or *depressing* imposes an automatic principle of selection upon detail. Do not, of course, insist that this dominant impression be stated before details are gathered, though it might be, certainly. Some writers will choose to list random details and then to determine some controlling attitude suggested by them. But any image the student offers up to support his description must relate to that attitude. The writer's subjective responses, therefore, become an organizing, controlling, selecting principle for the development of the description.

Dealing with selectivity of detail requires an attention to excessive modification. Frequently, students interpret insistence upon "showing" not telling and requests for concrete sensory detail as a commandment: "Thou shalt use adjectives." You need to offer repeated practice in selection of *le seul mot juste,* the precise noun or verb that, because of its exactness, requires little modification. You need to show alternatives to piling up adjectives before nouns: "the tall, blonde, blue-eyed, long-legged, banking executive's son." The poor noun is smothered by the modifiers, keeping readers farther and farther away from the object described rather than bringing them closer to it.

In order to overcome problems in establishing point of view, try to limit within the assignment the specific location of the narrator. The use of first person identifies the speaker right from the start; a statement early on by the writer about his physical position relative to the object helps draw the reader in.

After you have introduced and encouraged practice in concrete sensory detail and imagery—and have offered activities such as those described on pages 110–14—there is no more successful assignment for beginning writers than a description of the classroom at one particular moment. Having laid the groundwork for concrete sensory detail with previous activities, you are now ready to require sustained sensory responses. The classroom is a strong model for description because it offers an immediate sensory experience. In this environment you can guide and develop writing about a scene everyone has shared.

Now you want to be sure to stress when you make this assignment that writers should aim for a *personal* description, one based on their active, subjective responses to the classroom during one defined period of time. This is not a tract for an insurance inspector or for an architect, not a "factual" description in the sense that it needs quantifiable data to make its point. The writer's purpose here is to show clearly what he thought about the room and, by means of original detail, what made him think so. Without an understanding of this reason for writing, students struggle to offer accurate, objective, even scientific descriptions, which ultimately *lack* purpose. (I'll have more to say on objective writing later.) What I am suggesting here, obviously, is the need to deal with audience, purpose, and situation; yet I am reluctant to urge a full scale treatment of those concepts for beginning writers. I advise that, rather than explore them with all their options, you address audience and purpose in your assignment and encourage beginners each time they write to look at their readers as being the teacher and the other members of the class.

Instructions might run as follows. "Today each of you will write a one-paragraph description of this classroom. You remember our work on the topic sentence for this assignment: You'll have to state the topic clearly and you'll have to indicate your attitude toward that topic, which is, of course, the room. How do you feel about this room? Is it noisy? Is it attractive? Is it depressing, busy, quiet, or tense? Once you have determined a reaction this room arouses in you, you'll then have to think about the features that cause that reaction. Is it the walls? the furniture? the ceiling? the lights? your classmates? Your task in this assignment is to use color, action, sound, smell, taste, touch—in short, all of your sensory responses—to convey your impression of the room to me and to the students in the class. Write only about details that support your opinion. Leave out any details that do not back up your attitude toward the room."

Armed with those directions, students can choose any of the prewriting tasks you've introduced. Or, if you want to assure practice in a variety of prewriting activities, suggest that for this assignment everyone in the class try one particular approach you've singled out. One especially helpful technique for description is a variation on free association. I suggest for this descriptive writing task a "sense chart" in which four or five ruled columns allow the writer to record snatches of imagery, each image rooted in a particular sense:

What I saw   *What I heard*   *What I smelled*   *What I felt*

As the writer fills in each column with eight to ten images, he records for later use the details which his own sense of form will incorporate into a paragraph. The advantage of the sense chart at this early stage of the writer's development is that it combines the freedom demanded by prewriting with an orderly means for recording data.

Working inductively, have students record as many images as they can about the room. Then, looking over this list, a student can generalize from it and can afterwards return to the images, crossing out those excluded by the generalization. In an alternate activity divide the class into four groups, each group exploring the classroom for images that appeal to a single sense: sight (color and action), sound, smell, touch. Each set of images prepared by a group must relate to some dominant impression about the room that the group can agree upon. Or, *create* a dominant mood or impression in the classroom with special techniques: dim the lights, draw the shades, use records or tapes, movies, slides, and so on. After students experience the mood you have created, elicit images that could support that mood. Help in the selection of detail: "Does that image contribute to the overall mood?"

To add an exciting visual component, the camera that develops pictures instantly is an effective method of involving students reluctant to perform verbally. Someone taking pictures during the writing of the assignment can then compare a portrayal of the room with a verbal description. Adding a tape recorder (unknown to the writers in the class) can later help test the authenticity of student responses. The recorder can also lead to a solid discussion of compression and selectivity of details and of the accuracy and value of written expression. (See Chapter 4 for other suggestions about the use of media in the classroom.)

Read aloud several good descriptions of a classroom, perhaps even one you have written. Before you read, pose questions to the class to direct their listening and to focus attention on those areas of achievement you will look for in the writing. Here is a final draft from a freshman with good skills:

A Few Minutes To Go

Sitting here in this basic English class on a rather warm Monday morning, my fellow prisoners probably feel the tension of doing their first writing. The free people on the outside of the classroom are shuffling about rather aimlessly as the period is coming quickly to a close; but inside there is much tension. On my left sits Rocco, tapping his polished chrome pen nervously on his red and yellow notebook. A look of blankness and fear sits on his face. When his eyes meet mine they drop quickly down to his empty sheet of theme paper. On my right I can see Barry in a dark blue shirt. He holds a tight sweaty grip on his pencil and tries to get in a few inspired sentences before the time allotted for the period expires. Suddenly an amusing smell lightens our discomfort as it disturbs my trend of thought. A passerby ambles in front of the door with a cupful of golden French fries from the truck that sells them near the main gate of the college. Taking a quick look at the clock on the wall, I see the hands have almost reached their destination with only a few minutes to go. The ruffling of papers becomes more pronounced, in fact, deafening to this supposedly silent classroom. My mind goes blank as all these distractions seem to be growing and growing in strength. Consequently, I will put a period at the end of this sentence to end my misery.

—Lawrence Skibicki

After the class has considered and discussed the assignment and after some good sample themes stimulate discussion, prepare with the class a specific list of objectives. As I pointed out in the last chapter, if the class has understood the terms of the activity and has at least on a basic level some sense of what makes memorable description, a list of helps and pointers is a fine way to review all the principles developed to date. Here is a sample of a checklist which one class prepared.

A Checklist of Requirements: Theme 1

1. Write a topic sentence that includes an opinion and tells what your topic will be. Make sure the topic is properly limited.
2. Tell time and place as early as possible in the paragraph.
3. Use at least three words that appeal to the sense of sound. See class notes for new "sound" vocabulary.
4. Use at least three colors in different places throughout the theme.
5. Mention two people in the class by name. (If you don't know the names of people you want to write about, ask them. Show each person performing some action.)
6. Give the reader an idea of your surroundings by describing parts of the room. Try to make details suit the opinion word you stated in the topic sentence.
7. Use concrete words; avoid general ones.
8. Check your theme for your usual errors.
9. Don't jump too quickly from one item to another within the room. As you mention a person or a thing within the classroom, take two or three sentences to show clearly what you see before you move to another.
10. Use words like *up front, to my left, nearby, across the room, far away, above, beside, in the corner,* to help you move from one thing you wish to describe to another.
11. Use a variety of sentence patterns like those we practiced in class.

Such a list or chart has a number of advantages other than those I've already mentioned. First, the student has before him concrete goals to inform the success of the paper. Next, readers and evaluators can respond to particular aspects of the presentation, grading and commenting according to the student's degree of achievement. In this way you are really objectifying what a student often complains are subjective reactions to his papers. Now you can say, "You've not included enough images. Where are your word pictures that use sound or smell?" Last, the checklist can guide students into practicing what they've learned whether it is basic grammar or basic rhetoric. An efficient way to test understanding of a concept is to ask for a demonstration in the writer's language. If you teach about sentence completeness, for example, and you show how certain words often force inexperienced writers to miss sentence junctions and to run sentences together, you can then require that somewhere in a given paragraph the student use one of those "danger" words. Students often run together sentences when conjunctive adverbs (like *then, however, therefore, suddenly*) or subject pronouns (*I, he, she, we, it, you, they*) stand at sentence boundaries. After the class can recognize these words easily, you can integrate them into the checklist for the writing assignment: "Use one of these to open a complete thought: *however, therefore, then, suddenly.*"

Now, the description of the classroom is only a *suggested* first assignment in description. The community, the urban or suburban scene—any experience which grows naturally out of the student's environment suggests valuable theme topics. You might want to send teams of students to different, busy parts of the campus, and on a sense chart such as the one I've already suggested, require the groups to record the most intense images that could recreate the place for someone who did not see it at that moment. This could be done individually, as well.

Whatever the exact nature of your assignment, you need to point out several important considerations for beginning

writers of description. They should look at the place at only one specific time. They should identify that place as soon as possible. They should name the time of day and year during which they are making the observation. Writers should suggest or state some dominant impression about the place, an impression they can support with adequate detail. And writers should use intense images that appeal to the sense of sight, sound, smell, touch, taste.

To introduce the description of some place other than the classroom, rely on active class discussion so that the group can hear each other's ideas take shape (see pp. 21–25). For group work, set students discussing rooms or outdoor places that have some focus. "Each of you in the group describe a *noisy* place you've been to. Make sure you describe what features of this place make you believe it's noisy. Of course, you'll want to name some details of color and action as well."

After your discussion session, move into other prewriting activities. One might argue that discussing topics in advance is somewhat artificial since most writers struggle alone with a topic and have little opportunity to discuss their writing beforehand. But as I have insisted before, for the inexperienced writer it is critical to see how others think through instruction, so varied and unpredictable is the inventive faculty. After discussion is time enough to move into those inner activities writers perform, the brainstorming, the writing down of haphazard notes, the grouping of materials according to some plan. (You might want to review in the previous chapter the section on prewriting for some precise suggestions on approach.)

After this prewriting stage, you want to ask students to come to class with a rough draft—their first attempt at gathering and developing the ideas of their themes in complete consecutive sentences in a paragraph. Here's the chance to offer a rough draft workshop (pp. 33–37). Make sure to suggest clear aims as students try to improve the quality of the first draft. Will they try to improve imagery? Will they attend to new sentence structures the class needs to practice? And, it is important to decide on a format for the workshop. Will students work in small groups? Will each writer work alone as you go about the room making suggestions and offering help with good questioning techniques? Perhaps students will work in groups of two, one reading aloud while the other listens and takes notes using the Checklist of Requirements, the guide for individual comments and suggestions. The management of this first rough draft workshop is critical: students must come away having tested the notion that sentences must be changed and moved around, that ideas need refining, that words must be eliminated and added. Especially with one or two clear objectives can that goal be achieved.

Workshop ended, require the final draft to be submitted very soon after. The discipline demanded by meeting deadlines is something all writers need to develop; and you don't want the student's energy and interest to flag over too much time spent writing. When students submit their themes for your evaluation, they should follow correct manuscript form, which is described in this resource book.

When you grade and return papers, follow the suggestions and guidelines I described on pages 55–58. Devise some specialized follow-up activities so when students again write description they can build upon corrected problems. Here is a good opportunity to examine images from student writing and to compare the unspecific image with the specific or to compare the over-modified image to the more economical, yet exact, one.

Describing a place asks for the application of such important skills and is such an accessible writing activity that you could without risk of redundancy make a similar assignment for the next theme. However, describing a person is an equally good (though somewhat more complicated) task, one worth asking the class to perform. Here again students can try their hands at sharp sensory language, which selectively develops a topic in time and place. Because learned skills should be cumulative and because writers should demonstrate competence in skills already taught, in preparing the checklist of goals for this theme, you want to take into account all previous instruction in rhetorical and basic language skills. If you have taught sentence completeness, make the absence of problems in sentence structure (or their relative absence) one of the requirements of success on this theme. If you have taught about specific language, you can fairly expect a more effective use of such language in this theme than in the last one. And you are again insisting that the student focus in description on a single point in time to help him limit and direct his writing.

Discussion and prewriting activities here should help students explore ideas for description of people. Begin by listing a number of personality traits—friendliness, selfishness, anger, unhappiness—and then ask students to describe how people look when their behavior manifests such traits. Stress the idea of how a person's face is a miracle of expressions and feelings, a face sometimes predicting the personality that lies beneath. Ask students to bring in pictures of faces which express some quality the student understands, feels, appreciates, or hates. Does the face express *pain, delight, fear, shame, love, pride?* Go around the room asking each person to name the impression the face gives. Then ask students to name and to describe the features that give that impression. Are the eyes soft or fierce? Are the lips heavy or thin and pale and do they contribute to the sense of sadness? Do the eyebrows or the slant of the chin create important impressions? How does the clothing or the suggestion of action contribute to the impression?

As another warm-up activity, ask students to think of some person they know well whose face conveys a strong impression. Then, using rich sensory details, students can describe three or four features that contribute to that impression, each image appealing to sight, sound, touch, or smell. Because this is an informal "prewriting" activity, it is an effective way for students to explore the topic. Here is one set of responses:

My Father: Peacefulness During a Nap on the Couch

1. eyelids lifting up and down
2. quiet breathing and whistling
3. unwrinkled brow
4. square chin dropping with each breath

As part of the prewriting activities provide vocabulary options. What are some words used to name judgments about people? What words describe physical features?

Perhaps the best formal assignment to make for the one-paragraph description of a person is the description of a fellow classmate. Though there is much value in this assignment, its main importance is that you can again help the writer limit his focus to one controlled object at a single point in time. This is not a description based upon observations made over a long period: it *is* a description of one person at one place at one time.

With good planning this can be an extremely successful activity. Pick the model carefully. Select someone with a lively personality, someone dressed colorfully, someone who is animated in movement. Ask this person to stand in front of the room and to speak about himself while the class takes notes about him. Let the class ask questions so that the model continues to speak. With time spent in prior discussion about the kinds of details writers should be looking for— details of face, clothing, speech, action—there will be a clear focus for the notes. Provide a chart of suggestions such as this one or a better one that you prepare with your class' help:

Hints for Successful Paragraphs About a Classmate

1. Mention in the first sentence time, place, and the single impression you have of the student.
2. Use some details of setting, naming a piece of furniture perhaps.

3. Use only those details that contribute to the single impression. Leave out any details that do not help create the impression.
4. Mention the person's size, the color of his hair and eyes, his clothing. Use images of sound, color, and touch.
5. Write a sentence that tells what the model says.
6. Toward the end of the paragraph, describe the one feature of the person's face that best gives you the impression you have.

Read a good sample aloud before students write, one by a former student, one you have written yourself, or failing these, one written by a professional writer, a description that demonstrates achievement of the same goals you're looking for in student writing. If you require the student to quote exactly some line of spoken conversation by a model, you can easily evaluate the student's mastery of quotation marks and can determine whether or not to offer formal instruction in that skill. Here's a strong model from a very good freshman writer in a course more advanced than the basic writing course:

Richard

Richie Fries sits confidently atop the brown desk before us on this English theme day in late November. He speaks immediately, brown eyes sparkling at his audience of fellow classmates. His pressed blue shirt stresses his tall straight posture as his hand motions express words. He scratches his neat black hair as if in thought. "Next question!" he says. "Gotta wake you up. Ya look like you're falling asleep." The class watches his every expression, but there is no sign of nervousness in Richard, not a drop of sweat falling from his brow. "Look at me," his apple cheeks shout. "Look at me," his smile says. "Look," his position at the edge of the table screams. "Look at me. This is my moment of glory." His actual words race by at record pace. "My father tells me I should think in seventy-eight and talk in thirty-three," Rich speedily adds. Susan asks him to smile and change his position. Propping himself upon his elbow, he leans back on the desk. "Hey, why isn't this guy in Hollywood?" I think to my-

self. His eyes dance. They illuminate when he talks and glow
softly when he is silent. His exciting brown eyes hold the class in
a strong grip. They are only brown, same as so many other eyes,
but they twinkle and they bubble and they look squarely at their
audience without so much as a nervous blink. His eyes smile
even when his lips fall. The girls like him: he is lively, has a
good physique—I suppose it is understandable. Michelle asks
where he goes to meet girls and the class giggles squeamishly.
After a long, funny answer, Richie leans back, the edges of his
lips pushing his cheeks up. His brown eyes now stare at no one.
Everybody is writing. He takes a deep breath. Then, in a sudden
leap from the table, Richie returns to his seat like a conqueror.

—Debbie Osher

Here from a beginning writer is an effort to describe someone she sees. You can see how the instructor will have to
tend to some of the issues we've discussed. But despite the
over modification, the imprecise generalization, the tendency to cliché, this is a notable achievement.

A Person to Know

He was known for his features. His shiny slick forehead, and thin
curly black hair surrounded his sheek mustache, and mul-
ticolored beard which was mostly gray. His peachy skin and
smoth creamy lips centered perfectly on his round plump face.
He had sky blue eyes which sparkled like marbles, but his right
eye was injured and is unable to use it now. The tight short
sleeve cloroxed white shirt was pressed up against his large
tummy with an expensive silver pen clipped to the shirt pocket.
He had faded away baggy wrinkled blue jeans, and rough soled
brown leather shoes that he wore in his appearance. His strong
and sensious hands were very firm, and his clean fingernails
were nicely shaped. The tiny dark black curly hair on his arms
were quite noticeable, and his legs are as bow legged as can
be. His deep mild voice and warm smile brought out a pleasant
sense of humor. He's the kind of person you would really want to
know.

—Julie Crawford

Once students have their notes for writing before them, you have a rich opportunity to reinforce what you taught earlier about prewriting as a key stage in the composing process. Ask that the ideas be grouped or outlined and that the writer produce a topic sentence which names the topic, locates the model in time and place, and expresses some attitude toward the topic. Supervise the preparation of the rough draft: go from desk to desk as students generate their ideas. Stress the notion of flexibility, that sentences must be shifted, expanded, condensed for more accurate expression. Remind the class of exact word choice. For a session soon after ask that final drafts be submitted—and check whether or not students remembered what you taught about proofreading by reviewing and by supervising a brief proofreading effort, each student examining his own paper. To check further on students' comprehension of process, collect the rough draft along with the final draft. Comparing them will give you insights into how students are accommodating the various steps demanded by the written activity.

Of course the classroom model is only one of numerous possibilities for describing people. But the key to any strong description of a person is the faithful recording of detail about him or her at one place at one time.

Descriptions of people and places are fruitful exercises for the development of skills early in a writer's career. However, without much more intensive preparation, the description of an object is not an assignment easy to manage at this stage. First, an object does not easily engage all the writer's senses, and so from the start sources of detail are limited, unless the writer expands the scene in which the object stands. To describe an egg in its shell, for example, a writer could avoid calling upon sound or smell or taste in order to reproduce the egg through images. And because objects are frequently static—the egg certainly no exception—even the visual dimension constricts sharply. There are no actions to capture in crisp, clear language unless the writer draws in surrounding elements. Details therefore develop around precisely measurable data—"It is a white oval two and a half to three and a half inches from tip to tip"—that do not easily hold a reader's interest. Often these limits on detail push the writer to caricature, a much more highly complex type of writing than students can manage successfully now.

Though some people argue that describing a thing gives good practice in *objective* writing (without making a judgment the writer simply records sensory responses), I do not find this to be the case at the level of instruction we're considering here. Even without conscious awareness a writer is exercising some insight for selection of details—why leave out *this* bump on the eggshell, why describe that one?—an insight often difficult to articulate as a generalization. I don't believe that objective writing exists as a precise enough category for instruction. Certainly in all descriptions of objects I can think of, even those based essentially in "factual" or scientific information, writers exercise selectivity when they present detail. Perhaps they do not highlight this selectivity by means of an expressed attitude about the object; nevertheless by some process of evaluation they record some details but not others.

I'm not minimizing the importance of describing *things* as opposed to places and people. Surely much writing for science and technology involves the careful description of an object. But I am thinking out loud about the kinds of problems you would need to anticipate if you chose to make such an assignment, and about how instruction without care might deflect students from a slow but steady build-up of skills. Perhaps a short warm-up exercise for describing an object in three or four sentences that reflect close, intense observation of measurable detail might help students practice with precise language. From there, and anticipating the difficulties I have enumerated, you might ask for an object described amid its surroundings so that writers' options for sensory data are not severely restricted.

• Narration

You are right to expect the writer's skill in using concrete sensory language to advance as he explores the narrative mode. Because of its daily application in speech, narration is familiar to the developing writer. Problems of rambling, undirected narratives are easy to trace to spoken forms, but it's the rare student who cannot breathe life into a brief and significant flash of time. An instructor's main role in teaching narrative is getting students to select for expansion what Don M. Wolfe calls a "moment." You are not interested in stories that stretch out over a month, a week, even a day or an hour. You are searching for a short temporal span which, because of its indelible impression upon the writer, he can recall clearly and can find language to expand. In fact, the problem beginners often have with narrative develops from inattention to appropriate time frames: students attempt to narrate too many events and, hence, fail to focus them adequately.

The exercises for beginning this assignment again rely upon class discussion before writing. Through prewriting exercises you want to direct the selection of a moment which by its nature has some compelling, internal drama easy to capture with clear detail. Encourage the student to speak his narrative informally before he writes, and with thoughtful questioning tease out images to support the narrative frame. Here, too, insist upon a statement of the writer's opinion, attitude, and judgment about the narrative so that he can control the selection of detail.

In narration you need to teach the unravelling of events in a clear march of scene. That means that you are not only asserting the importance of chronology, but you are also teaching the vocabulary of time, a vocabulary beginners often use indiscriminately. *After, later, prior, former, latter, subsequent, suddenly, before*—these have nuances that urge discussion. Narratives that violate chronology need examination so that students can observe the damage in careless sequencing. You must also teach *against* flashback, a dangerous and ungratifying technique for reader and inexperienced writer alike. Even for proficient writers flashback has its pitfalls. For novices it is a sidetracking from main event that carries them off too frequently to a loss of command over their own point.

Because of its accessibility to students as writers, the narrative mode should serve more than one assignment. In fact, a narrative as the first formal in-class exercise (see pp. 43–45), coming after an at-home narrative, is a fine opportunity for students to progress by reading comments on their earlier papers and by incorporating suggestions on the first effort into the next. In both assignments the student taps his own experiential resources: these are expansions of real events in the student's life. With the second theme in narration, students will, further, practice writing a final draft under the pressures of classroom time. After the class understands the assignment, students will come in with notes or outlines and from those materials will write under your supervision. (This will offer some practice similar to final achievement themes demanded of beginning writers at most institutions, themes for which there is *no* advanced preparation.) However, having practiced during rough draft workshops, students will not find writing in class thoroughly strange.

In thinking through narrative assignments you must select topics carefully. One of the most successful ways to arrange valuable prewriting for narration is to select some general discussion area to which the writer may bring to bear his specific experiences. This general area will depend certainly upon the interests of students in the class.

There are a number of possibilities which have shown excellent results for men and women at many age and interest levels:

- *a moment with a relative.* Here the writer discusses a significant moment in which a relative reveals himself as a "real" person with problems, strengths of character, or weaknesses.

- *a moment of discipline.* What particular moment does the writer remember in which his mother, father, grandparent, aunt, or uncle disciplined him? Direct your students to select the most indelible experience.
- *a moment at sports.* What special moment as participant or spectator does the writer recall?
- *a moment with a teacher.* What incident at school stands out in the writer's mind because the moment was strange or funny or sad or unpleasant?
- *a moment of friendship.* What special incident in the writer's life demonstrates friendship? Did the writer or his friend make some sacrifice of deep (or superficial) significance?
- *a moment of danger or fear.* What single incident can the writer dramatize to illustrate a time he felt frightened or endangered?
- *an "automobile" moment.* What incident that revolves around a car can the student expand with detail into an interesting narrative?
- *a moment of prejudice.* What moment can the writer call up to show when he experienced prejudice?
- *a moment of learning about death.* What particular episode can the writer expand to illustrate the impact of the death of some person (or animal) on his own life?
- *a moment of loneliness or solitude*
- *a moment of travel*
- *a moment of triumph or defeat*
- *a moment of love*
- *a moment of pride*

Many of these topics will tap deep emotions. Assure anonymity to the writer who wants it if his paper should ultimately be read aloud. No doubt nothing deeply revealing will emerge in class discussion (though this is not always true), but in the privacy of his own thoughts as he prepares to write, and with the ideas explored by his fellow classmates to set him thinking, the writer often turns to moments of raw feeling.

The discussion my take many forms. Write up a list of unfinished statements which revolve around the topic. Using chalkboard or overhead projector, present the statements to the class; allow some thinking time, then go around the room asking each student to select a statement to complete. With carefully constructed sentences you can direct attention to a single narrative moment. For a theme about recalling experiences at school, for example, here are some sentences which can evoke particularly lively completions:

- When I played hooky, I . . .
- The time I got in trouble, I . . .
- My teacher lost his temper when . . .
- My teacher understood when . . .
- I was embarrassed at school when . . .

Responses to these questions know no ethnic nor cultural bounds; events in every student's life find application to some of these questions. If your students respond too briefly, prod them with questions. Make students fill in details of background, of time and place, of action, thus setting the stage for the writing. You will notice how the sample sentences above entice students to focus at the outset on a brief moment.

It is worthwhile here to take up the notion of the *moment* as an entity for students to consider.

- A moment is a memorable instance in the writer's life that illustrates some opinion or idea he wants to write about.
- It is limited as much as possible in time, a brief span of minutes sharply recalled.
- The writer must make this "moment" as vivid for readers as it was for him when he experienced it. In order to do this, he needs to fill in details with concrete sensory language.

- What kinds of details does the writer need to make the moment come alive? He should try to show some images of the setting (where the moment occurred) through color, smell, touch, and sound; to describe the people who participate in the moment, their faces and actions; to use bits of important dialogue that people speak as the moment develops.

Another approach to prewriting that helps students to release ideas and to explore this stage of invention is to divide the class into groups with clearly defined discussion goals. Set a single question around a general theme topic. For example, in dealing with a moment in which a parent disciplined a child, ask each group to consider this question: "What moment when your parent hit you or scolded you or otherwise disciplined you stands out most in your mind?" Although older students will draw easily upon their own experiences as children, some parents in the class might prefer to describe a moment in which they disciplined one of their children. Students question each speaker about details of time, place, and setting. One person in each group makes a list which *briefly* summarizes the topics stimulated by the general question. Each recorder then recites the list for the rest of the class. This exchange will also expand the writing possibilities for students.

Or you might prefer to begin with a visual activity. Select some photograph or painting which captures one moment in time. Better, get several pictures to allow work individually or in groups. First, ask students to identify the main purpose of the photo or painting and to state some attitude or impression that the visual entity conveys. Then ask students to name the various details that contribute to that impression.

Once there is sufficient discussion, the class is ready to consider the challenges which narration offers to the writer. Here you will deal with the notion of chronology and of completeness. Beginning writers will often omit some step in the narration or will fail to mark adequately the movement through proper time sequence. In the language of chronology students need considerable practice. What do those words that signal chronology mean and how does one use them? I am talking essentially of vocabulary here, and inexperienced writers need to work with words that show time and sequence. Shaughnessy suggests that we give students jumbled blocks of sentences and ask that the sentences be reassembled in correct sequence after we introduce the appropriate vocabulary for signaling structure. She also describes an excellent activity by a teacher who has devised a controlled assignment that requires the student to incorporate time words into a partially constructed narrative.

When discussion is over, read some samples of narrative. Remember to direct the class' listening: "When I finish reading this paper, I'm going to ask you to evaluate the topic sentence. What does it say about the topic? What opinion does the writer express? I'll also ask you to pick out what you think are the liveliest and most original images, the best examples of sensory language in this paper. Take notes as I read."

It is especially important to review here the notion of the topic sentence. In the narrative assignment students will often revert to vague beginnings which subvert their goal of telling about a clear, indelible moment. One characteristic opening sentence you might meet is:

It all happened one day last year.

Such a beginning is a plague to the inexperienced writer. Aside from its ordinariness—how many times have you read such openings in the popular press? how many times in student themes?—it offers no direction for the reader; and worse, at least at this stage of writing development, it offers no direction for the writer. With that kind of opening sentence the inexperienced writer is all over the place, following a rambling tale often deadened by flashbacks that remove readers further and further from the main event.

Here are two student samples of narratives with vivid openings.

The House Didn't Catch Fire

Because of my grandmother's bravery, the September night in New Jersey our brown wood house didn't catch fire is one night I will never forget. I remember those moments clearly. There was a full moon outside my window, floating on white clouds in a blue velvet sky, an unusually quiet and chilly night. I sat spellbound by the fire in the fireplace; it cracked and popped as it burned the wood. And the orange, red and blue colored flames danced in the darkness of my room. Suddenly, precariously, my window lit up from an enormous fire a few miles away. The moon no longer floated on its puffy clouds. When flames danced up the trees and caused the wood to crackle like the fire in my fireplace, I screamed for my grandmother from the next room. She rushed in and quickly took my hand and we ran out of the house. I held tightly to her as she stood looking at the fire and felt the soft cool flannel of her yellow gown. Grandmother looked up into the flaming sky as though she was praying to God, while lines of worry and fear grew deep in her dark brown skin. The fire looked as if it sped in our direction as my grandmother dashed around the side of the house. I felt cold and afraid standing in front there all alone. Soon grandmother returned with two wooden pails of water from the water tubs. When she threw water on the house and dashed back to the tubs, I ran to the water also, grabbed a handful and threw it on the house, because I was seven and too small to carry a wooden water pail. We threw water on the house and the earth nearby until they were completely soaked. By now the fire had grown closer and nearly encircled the house. We ran inside to wait for the fire either to die down, or to kill us; the heat outside was too much to bear. My grandmother held me close to her again. As the night grew into day, I grew tired and went to sleep. I awoke to find the fire had stopped within yards of our home, leaving the earth burnt and bare for miles around. But my grandmother's courage and quick thinking kept our house standing.

—Odessa Harris

Jungle Boy

A suppertime conversation one fall evening several years ago shows how both my parents can join forces to make me feel worse than I already do. My mother slammed the knives and forks upon the table with a startling clatter and stormed back to the sink. A bright yellow tablecloth with red roses did nothing to counteract the tension that hung about our usually cheery kitchen. Quizzically my father glanced at me but I lowered my eyes quickly and labored at my grapefruit until I squeezed it dry. My brother solemnly leaned over his lamb chops and string beans. The large black, yellow and blue marks on his arm stood out, the result of a fight with me that afternoon. Again mother stalked to the table, her brown eyes moist, the glass salt shaker clenched in her hand. She let loose her rage in a violent burst of words. "Are you crazy? Do you want to break your brother's arm?" I slouched lower in my chair, taking a piece of broiled meat in my mouth but unable to swallow it. My father looked at me through steel grey eyes. "I told you never to raise your hands in anger in this house," his voice boomed. The words echoed in my head as I felt my face warm. My mother shrieked at the top of her voice, "Why can't you get along with your brother the way your cousins do? They laugh together and play together, but not you, not Allen of the jungle, you have to fight and punch your brother." Quietly, sternly, my father said, "I've never hit you, Allen, without first discussing the situation with you like civilized people have I?" I stirred uncomfortably in my chair and murmured an acknowledgement. My father's words weakened the wall that I built to fight my mother's assault. "I've brought you up to respect your brother and him you. We won't speak about this again, but in the future you'd better think before raising your hands." Feeling ashamed for my childish behavior, I excused myself from the table and tramped off sullenly to my cave.

—Allen Zuckerman

Once the class discusses the themes, an excellent way to summarize your findings and at the same time to provide a concrete set of objectives for writers is to prepare together a checklist of goals. Once again, remember that this checklist is a hedge against criticism that instructors' judgments are too subjective. When you score the student's paper you can say, "Has he included this? Where is that structure I have suggested? Does the use of detail and chronology reflect the standards the class has set?" Here is one checklist developed for a narrative theme that asked students to write about a moment with a relative. You can adapt it to your students' needs. Notice how you can call attention to mechanical skills within the framework of the assignment.

A Checklist of Objectives

- Write a topic sentence that states a limited topic through some opinion or attitude.
- Tell of only one moment in which your relative revealed his personality.
- Try to include time and place in the topic sentence. If you find this impossible, tell time (month, part of the day, or season) and place (a special room, some street whose name you mention) as soon as possible.
- Use several colors in various places in the paragraph. Allen Zuckerman says "steel grey eyes"; Odessa Harris writes "our brown wood house."
- Show the relative about whom you are writing as he or she performs some action. Use a lively verb; Odessa Harris shows a vivid picture of her grandmother dashing from the water tub to the house.
- Show the face of your relative as he responds to the situation you're writing about: "lines of worry in her dark brown skin"; "her brown eyes moist." The eyes are particularly easy to write about if you combine color with another sense like touch (moist, hard, soft, etc.).
- Use several word groups that appeal to the sense of sound. "Jungle Boy" includes "slammed the knives and forks upon the table with a startling clatter."
- Show details of the scene in which the moment occurs; use a detail of touch and one of smell.

- Write one quotation sentence which gives someone's exact words.
- Tell your story in clear chronological order.
- Check your theme for your usual errors, especially the fragment and the run-on error.
- Give your pargraph a lively title.

Provide as many topics as possible, topics which narrow the general theme you and the class have been discussing. If the assignment asks students to explore a relative's personality in a single moment you might try one of these:

My Brother's Temper
A Good Uncle
My Husband's Bad Mood
Working With My Wife
When I Appreciated My Father
When My Son Made Me Mad
An Unjust Moment
My Son, the Pest
Family Battle
An Unforgettable Beating
My Father and My Date
My Wife Understood
Asking For Money
My Father (Husband, Wife), the Boss
Grandmother Helping Out

With careful discussion and preparation, students are ready to confront other elements of prewriting, this time on their own. By directed classroom discussion, you have been simulating the kind of interior dialogue students must learn to carry on before they write. You'll have to review again the private prewriting stage by talking about the need to sit and to think; about ways to get the juices streaming; about the need to make lists and to jot down information as it flows; about the need to get up and to walk about to clear the mind. Explain the importance of arranging idea lists into

some order that best advances the topic; of preparing outlines, if they help; of writing rough drafts. Show how to improve rough drafts by combining sentences and by trading
general words for concrete ones; by correcting serious errors; by preparing a second draft; by writing a third or fourth
draft, if necessary; by proofreading for errors at two critical
stages. A rough draft workshop in connection with a narrative assignment allows you to select some specific skill in
language growth or in correctness to explore with the class,
a skill which students can then accommodate in their writing.

   After examining the papers, review the elements of good
narrative. Look at the checklist developed by the class and
have the best themes read aloud, guiding the listening. To
focus on some special skill that needs reinforcing (based
upon predominant errors on students' papers), use any of
the techniques I described in the section on returning papers.

   Before assigning the second exercise in narration, highlight the major strengths in the first set of narrative papers to
encourage replication and the major weaknesses to encourage improvement. This second narrative assignment is a
good place to give students practice with the special considerations of writing under pressure in class. (There are reasons other than a final essay to recommend in-class themes,
despite complaints against them; I've discussed both sides
of the issue on pages 43–45 and will touch on them again in
the chapter on testing later on.) I'd use this first, formal, in-
class theme to help cross the divide between the kind of
high-pressured, impromptu writing at a required place in a
sharply limited time span, and the more expansive leisurely
writing at home in elected surroundings and under more
generous temporal conditions.

   For this theme, therefore, you want to announce the topic
in advance as you would for an at-home paper. After discus-

sion both about the topic and about in-class writing, ask students to come to the next session with notes either in outline form or in some other arrangement of ideas. Don't allow drafts. For this in-class writing activity the rough draft is eliminated as a formal stage in the composing process, you remember, simply because there's not enough time for a draft. However, working from notes, inexperienced writers are less shocked at having to skip a draft than they would be if they had to write at this point on some previously unannounced topic. Despite the absence of the rough draft, you can assure a reasonably careful effort on the paper the student prepares in class by apportioning writing time. Because prepared notes are before them in a fifty-minute hour, students should write for only forty minutes, the remaining time spent on rereading for clarity and correctness. Insist on that time and supervise its use. Even if some writers do not finish within the allotted time frame, a portion of the session must be reserved at the end for proofreading for error, for infelicitous phrasing, for omissions and extraneous material. (For later impromptu efforts, actual writing time should drop to thirty minutes, the remaining twenty split about evenly for planning and for rereading. And you can adjust this breakdown to suit time given to your session by following the rough formula I offered on page 44.) For this in-class theme make dictionaries available during the proofreading activity but discourage their use while students are building sentences from notes. Spell words on the board if anyone asks for help. Wander about the room; offer suggestions at the writer's invitation. Try to make this first experience in "pressure writing" as comfortable as possible.

As with descriptive paragraphs, narrative is a highly accessible form for beginning writers. It allows for the continued development and practice of skills in the use of detail. By moving from description to narration you help students sharpen earlier concepts and you build upon the ability to frame images that are sharp and strong and appropriate as detail.

• Illustration (Exemplification)

In the theme of illustration the writer works with more complex techniques than those called for by modes practiced earlier. Illustration requires support for a generalization by means of *several* examples. Thus, with the topic "embarrassment," a descriptive paragraph could show with clear details someone's appearance at an embarrassing time; a narrative paragraph could tell the story of an embarrassing event; but a paragraph of illustration would offer details of three embarrassing moments, say, or of as many different physical changes as embarrassed people might display. Certainly description and narration do critical service in illustration's command, and they will support dramatically topics developed through exemplification. Yet there are more sophisticated problems in organization here than in the other modes, and those problems require attention early in your instructional plan.

You have first to deal with order. How will the examples be arranged. Spatially? Temporally? By importance?

Next arises the notion of connecting ideas. How does the writer move smoothly from one example to the other? Transitions frequently present problems in meaning, and students must experiment with the vocabulary of connectives.

The ability to select detail needs honing if the illustration theme is to succeed, and so you want to help advance the skill you introduced when you presented description. Which details does the writer exclude in a given example? Which example gets the most comprehensive treatment? The student's expressed opinion about or attitude toward a chosen topic helps focus and limit the details here too, so you are again concerned with a clear, concise statement of purpose somewhere in the paragraph as a guide for the reader and writer.

In illustration the student again taps his experiences in terms of sensory impressions. He is writing to offer illustrations selected from his own life, illustrations which demonstrate a principle he wishes to support in written language. You are reviewing, therefore, the power of the sensory image, of words that name sounds and actions and colors.

Since this assignment asks the writer to offer more than one example to support an idea, topics should allow for easy development in the illustrative mode. In discussion you can again offer unfinished sentences for students to complete. The selection of some general theme upon which to base sentences offers a common ground for exploration of idea. One successful *general* topic for this theme is "the memory thread." Here the student searches for one dominant trend in his personality, behavior, actions, preferences, weaknesses, strengths, and so on, and provides three or four examples to support that conclusion about himself. Here are some unfinished sentences which start class discussions and open the door to instruction in techniques of illustration:

- The times I played hooky I . . .
- I lose my temper when . . .
- The things that frightened me as a child were . . .
- I'm easily embarrassed when . . .
- I can always please my children when . . .
- I can always annoy my wife by . . .
- My insecurity shows when I . . .
- My childhood was unusual because . . .
- With men (or women) I don't know, I always feel . . .
- My confidence showed when . . .
- I disliked some of my teachers in secondary school because . . .
- I remember learning about death when . . .
- Happy memories of my adolescence were . . .
- When I returned to my old neighborhood, I . . .
- My basic personality trait is . . .

Another approach encourages discussion on the nature and role of emotional and physical responses in the lives of children and preadolescents. What kinds of experiences do students feel linger into adulthood: experiences of fear, pain, sorrow, loneliness, love, hunger, anxiety? What kinds of experiences help determine character, for better or for worse? What specific experiences relating to any of those emotional responses can students recall?

Other instructors play the "association game" in class. Name an emotional experience—love, fear, anger, pleasure—and have students write down three specific incidents in their youths, incidents that the mention of the word makes them think of. If papers are anonymous, have them shuffled up and redistributed. One student at a time (before the class or in groups) can read the paper before him and comment on the appropriateness of the supportive examples.

These oral activities insist upon the application of more than one supporting illustration to a discussion topic. In each case, students will undoubtedly be relating narrative incidents as examples, and that's just fine. Students should note that when they write this theme they will have to compress detail much more tightly than they have previously. A paragraph about one single narrative moment is much richer in detail about that incident than a paragraph that offers several incidents of illustration. Therefore, the quantity of detail for each of several illustrations is considerably lower, though the paragraph itself would not show much difference in length.

Once students see illustration as an important kind of writing—discuss its purpose, its value, its distinctions from straight narrative and description—provide activities that focus upon problems writers have with this mode and that allow practice in solving the problems.

When you teach arrangement of the illustrations a writer will offer, remind the class that usually the theme on this level provides two options: arrangement through chronology or arrangement through importance (though occasionally a spatial arrangement is possible). Demonstrate this principle visually by selecting several newspaper photographs of an important personage engaged in different activities. Pictures of the President performing various functions of state would be effective. Label each picture clearly with the date of occurrence. Mix the pictures up and then show them to the class. What order would students suggest for arranging those photographs? In most cases, the preferred order will be chronological. Then ask for an alternate order. Someone might suggest that the photos could be arranged according to where they happened: those events in Washington, those in the President's home state, those in other states; or even those on the streets of Washington, those in the White House, those in the Capitol. Elicit further the idea of arranging the photographs according to an idea held by the arranger that some of these events are more or less important than others. Which photograph shows the most important event of the day? the least? If students were to present these photographs in their order of importance to someone who wanted to know what a president did, which picture might go first? last? Help establish the idea that in arrangement by importance the most significant illustration usually goes last so that the viewer (or reader) comes away from the experience with the most important idea clearly in mind. In a sense the other examples are preparatory for the last, the most significant in terms of the writer's purpose.

After the visual activity, illustrate the options in arrangement of written details. Ask students to suggest three pleasant (or unpleasant) events that can face a student at your institution. List them on the board. Discuss the possibilities: Which event occurs first, second, last? Which event is most pleasant and least pleasant? It is important to point out that though one event might precede the others chronologically, if it is the most significant, the writer would probably want to discuss it last. In some cases, of course, the chronological arrangement is exactly like the arrangement by importance.

Now offer some individual practice. Ask students to list several instances that might illustrate topics you provide. Then ask for an arrangement of details in their order of importance. You can see how related this activity is to goals for prewriting: first the writer jots down the haphazard elements that relate to a topic; and *then* he concerns himself with order. Or, you can present completed topic sentences that stimulate students to suggest supporting examples. Here are some topic sentences you might want to provide:

I always loved living in a big city.

The guidance counselor in my daughter's high school helped her more than anyone else.

At our last assembly in my high school senior year, the principal made several startling announcements.

High schools should grant many new freedoms to students today.

For a topic sentence like the third one above, there's good opportunity to review again the differences in effect resulting from chronological arrangement as opposed to arrangement by importance.

The notion of order established, provide the vocabulary of transition for this particular assignment. The class has been talking about transitions all along as they pertain to each specific theme assignment—transitions have not been taught as an entity in isolation—but this theme assignment makes its own special demands for smooth connections. Here, help establish several kinds of options in the use of transitions for beginning writers who attempt illustration:

• *Connecting through "time words."* Students might have discussed this in connection with narration. In any case, go over words like *next, later on, today, afterwards, before, earlier, former, latter, in the past, first, second, third,* and so on.
• *Connecting through coordination.* Go over the use of *and, but, or, for, nor, yet* as idea connectors.
• *Connecting through repetition.* Note how repeating an idea either at the beginning or in the middle of a sentence helps join ideas together smoothly.

- *Pronouns as connectors.* Show how the use of pronouns to refer back to nouns serves as a unifying element in a paragraph. (If the class responds well to practice in this activity, here is a fine place to talk about correct pronoun reference. Remind students that the pronoun refers back to the closest noun in gender and number; that will prevent problems later on.)
- *Connecting through degree.* Comparatives and superlatives like *more, most, less, least,* help establish degree and provide a means for joining examples through importance.

In discussing these connectors, illustrate them with solid examples—either brief selections from professional writers or from students' own papers. And make the point that overuse of any transitional device (students are especially fond of *too*) weakens a paper.

Because of the number of choices and options that the assignment in illustration presents, spend ample time on the structure of this paragraph. Though I discourage strongly any formula writing, there is value nonetheless in showing the skeleton of one kind of paragraph of illustration. This skeleton is perhaps more rigid than most in that the writer restates the topic each time he offers a new illustration. But such instruction gives beginners a starting point from which to move off on their own. I call those topic restatements *subtopic sentences.* The term is helpful for beginning writers (certainly you ought to explore the definition of the word by referring to its parts—the prefix *sub,* the word *topic*) because it reminds them about the need for a clearly stated topic. The term also suggests that within the paragraph the writer ought to gather ideas together, to reassert his intention, to remind himself and his reader of his purpose.

Begin instruction of subtopic sentences by reminding students of the need to unify examples used to illustrate points. Experiment with a topic sentence that allows for the use of illustrations to support the writer's idea. Here is one example:

As a child I learned many important lessons from my brother Tyrone.

The topic will deal with selected events which show what the writer learned from his brother. His attitude toward those events is that they were valuable. The next sentence in the paragraph might be: *He taught me about sportsmanship.* What similarities do students note between this sentence and the topic sentence? How does this sentence limit further the topic stated in the topic sentence? Lead students to explain what they would expect to see in the three or four sentences following that statement of subtopic: an explanation by means of concrete sensory detail of a lesson on sportsmanship. The writer will probably offer a brief narrative, although the option of naming and briefly describing two or more situations to support the idea of sportsmanship is his. After developing that thought group, the writer might write a sentence like this: *I also learned from him about the value of money.* The words *learned from him* (note the repetition of idea and use of pronoun) refer to the topic as it is offered in the topic sentence. The words *about the value of money* introduce another part of the topic, another limited aspect of it now awaiting support. The word *also* serves as a transition, too, an "adding" word, one among many students have to learn to use. After the subtopic sentence about the value of money, the writer would offer an event to support his contention and would use concrete sensory detail in its presentation. After this thought unit ends, another subtopic sentence might appear: *But most of all he taught me respect for people less fortunate than I am.* Which part of this sentence, you would ask, goes back to the topic sentence? Which words suggest the limited avenue the writer will travel? Which words work as transitions? Which words help the writer make a choice of order clear to the reader?

Once students see the way these subtopics operate, draw

up a working definition of the *subtopic sentence.* Why may a writer choose to use it? Then, offer some topic sentences on a variety of topics so that students may practice writing subtopic sentences. Offer a schematic diagram of *one* approach to the illustration theme:

```
XYZXYZXYZXYZXYZXYZXYZXY.
XXXXXXX ∿∿∿∿∿∿∿∿∿∿∿∿∿∿∿∿∿
∿∿∿. ∿∿∿ (T)YYYYYY ∿∿∿∿∿∿∿∿∿
∿∿∿∿∿∿∿∿∿∿∿∿∿∿∿∿∿∿∿∿∿∿∿∿∿∿∿
∿∿∿ (T)ZZZZZZZZZ∿∿∿∿∿∿∿∿∿∿∿
∿∿∿∿∿∿∿∿∿∿∿∿∿∿∿∿∿∿∿∿∿∿∿∿∿∿∿
∿∿∿ XYZXYZXYZXYZXYZ.
```

In such a scheme the topic sentence, represented by XYZs, suggests the need for an opener that calls for illustrations to support the topic idea—here, three. The first subtopic sentence, represented by Xs, indicates that the writer has selected one aspect of the topic suggested by his topic sentence and has presented it for the reader. The wavy lines represent sentences of support, sentences rich in sensory detail. The subtopic sentence (T)XXXXXXX indicates that the writer has selected another aspect of the topic, an aspect stated or implied by the topic sentence; the T in parentheses indicates the probable need, but at the writer's option (hence the parentheses), of transition. Again, wavy lines equal sentences of supporting detail. The representation (T)ZZZZZZZZZ is pretty much the same, covering the third and last illustration the writer wishes to offer to support his topic. The final representation XYZ again reminds the student of the need for a closing to the paragraph. Many inexperienced writers will either omit entirely the necessary closure or will close off only the last of the illustrations, thereby diminishing the effect of the paragraph.

At one point or another discuss emphasis and proportion. Remind students not to get carried away with their details: if the last illustration is the most important, the writer must make sure to reflect that significance through language. The temptation is often to develop only the first illustration fully, but that will weaken the paragraph.

After preparation like this, read sample paragraphs and direct the listening. "What illustrations does the writer offer to support the topic? How are the details arranged? Make a list of the transitions—or pick out the topic sentences if there are any." You might want to use this model as you accumulate your own from those prepared by students in your classes:

Horrors and High School Math

I will never forget my math teachers because I disliked most of them throughout my high school years. I remember my eleventh year math teacher vividly. She was a short, dumpy woman with a straight nose on which a pair of gold-rimmed glasses sat tightly at the end. Before each lesson began, she compelled me, her worst student, to erase the long white columns of algebraic figures from the chalkboards. Each day she gave pages of homework, expecting us to hand in our assignments during the very next class. I hated those pages of math, so I just ignored them. In the end, of course, my reward was a fifty in red on my report card. Next, my geometry teacher stands out in my mind. Although Miss Carpenter was no more than twenty-five, she acted like an old witch of a hundred. She wore the same dingy green dress each day. Sloppily, mousy brown hair hung in her eyes, and throughout every lesson she scooped strands and curls off her forehead. Her voice, high-pitched, would screech across the classroom and down the hall. "Julius," I can still hear her squeak, her lips pinched in a little pink circle, "If you don't know about diameters, I'll have to fail you." Everything about that teacher was awful! But of all my math teachers, I disliked most the one who taught me algebra. A tall, lanky man weighing a mere hundred-or-so pounds, this teacher had an angry temper that kept most of us from asking questions. Once a short girl in the last row asked timidly, "Will you explain that again please?"

As Mr. Gilian's face grew scarlet, he plunged his hands in his black pants pockets. "Try paying attention," he barked, "and then you won't have to bother me with ridiculous questions." From my past unpleasant experiences with math teachers I have grown to dislike them all automatically; is it any wonder that my math grades never rise above C's and D's?

—Julius Passero

Here are some topics that lend themselves to development through illustration:

- how you used to get in trouble at school
- some peculiar dates you had
- the fun you had with a local team or gang
- jobs you enjoyed
- the responsibilities you have at home
- a teacher or some teachers you liked (or disliked)
- three of the worst rules you have to obey
- the time(s) your mother had to come to school
- how a special person taught you some important lessons
- the fear(s) you had as a child
- the early heroes you had as a child
- the time(s) you did something you knew was wrong or bad
- the job you dislike most at work

The illustration theme with its insistence on examples connected clearly by the writer demands a kind of control over form that narrative and descriptive modes require to a much lesser degree. Ending the beginner's course with practice in illustration brings to a fine point the growth of skills in detail and structure for the beginning writer.

Larger rhetorical dimensions aside, I'd like now to look at skills with words and sentences, skills any instruction for the novice must include. Much of the attention you pay in the classroom to words and syntax will fall into place as important practice elements, while you prepare the class for theme assignments. In other cases, skills that are drawn from conventions of correctness take the spotlight only after students develop a rhythm—no matter how irregular—as writers.

3

Word, Sentence, and Punctuation Skills

The approach any teacher takes toward helping students to improve syntax and to avoid common errors is rooted in what he or she knows about grammar and how to use it effectively in the classroom. Unfortunately, the research is inconclusive about which grammar system—if any—works best for teaching students what they need to know about language so that their writing can improve, and so there's no need to take sides on whether traditional, structural, transformational, or "non"-grammar is the one teachers must learn. (We know that underlining nouns and verbs in someone else's sentences does not help anyone improve writing skills.) Advances in the last twenty-five years in our thinking about grammatical systems impose upon writing teachers a need for familiarity with different courses in language study. This is not to say that formal grammar instruction should demand class time. It says, instead, that the *teacher* must know grammar systems in order to teach students how to use language wisely. After all, what the instructor can best adapt to classroom purposes is what's good; and only a flexible, eclectic approach will assure good instruction. You need to take some material from traditional grammar and some from modern grammar, but the point is that you must have, to begin with, the resources upon which to draw.

To help expand the writer's power over language you should look at word and sentence skills in two ways. First, you need to suggest new options, new possibilities for words and the legitimate ways people have of putting them together in sentences. Next, you must look at the issue of correctness: How can a writer, given his own linguistic system, adapt his language to meet the conventions of Edited

American English? One approach is an opening of new passageways. Another is an act of refining, clarifying, and correcting what is on the page so that it meets a reader's expectations. Instruction in these areas is often related, working at similar purposes.

SPECIFIC LANGUAGE

The beginner's main disadvantages in vocabulary are both a frequent inability to remember forms and definitions of words *and* a lack of judgment in using words appropriately. Shaughnessy suggests three kinds of learning when the student approaches vocabulary: learning about words; learning words; and learning a sensitivity to words.

In learning about words, the student needs experience with word parts—with suffixes, prefixes, and roots—so that he can learn to observe the make-up of words that he meets when he reads or that he generates when he writes. To practice this the student should build lists of words with similar prefixes and suffixes. He should be able to make predictions about unfamiliar words and should be able to practice word-class shifts in the context of phrases and sentences.

In teaching about words themselves you have many options. Because you cannot possibly present in one term all the words students need to learn, you want at least to introduce techniques for learning words so that students will have an *approach* to take when they confront vocabulary. Further, you want to *teach* words in the context of the theme assignment so that the writer can apply new language directly to his writing. In this guidebook there are suggestions in the discussions of paragraph modes on how to achieve this end.

In teaching a sensitivity to words, you work first on the notions of general and specific language. Set up categories which move from general to specific:

food→ meat→ steak→ sirloin
plant→ flower→ rose

Then ask students to name specific words for general ones you supply; or ask that lists of words be arranged in their order of specificity.

You need to explain denotation and connotation. Here you supply words in sentences, substituting for a key word another with similar definition but with different connotations:

The *doctor* treated my mother.

The *physician* treated my mother.

The *specialist* treated my mother.

How does the meaning of the sentence vary with the change in word?

Once you have established the need for specific language and for attention to shades of meaning, you can teach what is to me one of the most basic—and, sadly, one of the most neglected—areas of instruction: the use of specific detail to support observations. Beginners must learn how to generate language that evokes the senses as a starting point for command over concrete diction. Probing the experiential world—the close-by physical environment of the room itself (as suggested on pp. 70–75)—the student works with concrete sensory language and imagery to build detail. Explain the way the mind acquires data through the senses and how good writers attempt to turn what they perceive into language that evokes those perceptions for a reader. Review the storehouse of words that name sensations: *hot, rough, bumpy* for touch; *smoky, sweet, dusty* for smell; verbs like *clatter, thud, whisper* for sound or *plunge, hobble, creep* for actions. Show how colors establish immediate visual recognition for readers. Make lists of sense words organized into appropriate categories. Ask students to supply most of the words after studying examples.

Once you have established the writer's dependency upon sensory language and, earlier, upon the need for specific words and for attention to shades of meaning, you can teach imagery, sustained sensory pictures that capture time. Start by comparing words with images of different levels of concreteness, at first without attention to complete sentences:

1	2	3
a car	a green Ford	a green Ford rattling to a stop

How has the writer in 3 achieved a high level of concreteness? How does 3 compare with 2? With 1? Which word adds color? Which adds sound? Which words could the class substitute for the color word, the sound word, even for the highly specific noun? Experiment with turning the image in 3 into a sentence that paints an even more exact picture:

4

At dawn a rattling green Ford halted in the snow on High Street.

At a red light on the corner of Broadway and Eighth a rattling green Ford sputtered to a halt.

Ask students to suggest their own images for familiar objects and then to build those images into full sentences. (Here is a means of assessing early on the class' sentence sense without a formal lesson in grammar.) When building sentences, students should draw upon the lists of recorded sense words, or words like them, especially those that state specific actions. Offer sentences with vague verbs like *walk* and *is,* requesting substitutes of strong verbs that name actions clearly. Next select a short paragraph alive in sensory language and take away all the sense words, leaving blanks. Under the blanks, signal the kind of sensory appeal the writer aimed for and ask students to put in their own words. Then compare the two, the student's effort and the original.

After you have taught about sensory detail, you need to devise exercises which help students avoid over-modification. Frequently a student learning about sensory language will fill his prose with adjectives. How could the class change this—*The tall, thin-legged, nervous, red haired woman rushed away*—so that the adjectives do not cluster before the noun? Sometimes a different, more expansive, structure provides flexibility; sometimes a more specific noun will do it. An alternative like this one might be more useful:

> As the wind blew her red hair, a tall woman rushed away nervously. Her thin legs wobbled as she ran.

Practice like this in converting the smothered-noun image lays foundations for later activities in sentence expansion, foundations that require no extensive grammatical brickwork.

Exercises in growth of vocabulary will help the student to overcome basic weaknesses in language use: the preponderance of vague nouns and pronouns, a dependence on weak verbs, and an absence of modification. If the context for vocabulary study is application—"Learn these words, learn about these words, because you may need them for this theme"—students will make the always difficult effort to incorporate new vocabulary into their own supply of language.

Despite clear instruction, and despite a student's ability to write strong vocabulary in classroom exercises, be prepared for a slow incorporation of imagery as an element of supporting detail. A set of sentences like these, for example, prompts an instructor to encourage expansion:

1

> The city has many problems. One problem is the bad transportation. It's terrible. Another problem is sanitation. . . .

After having learned about supporting detail and imagery, and after having practiced them successfully in class, the student, revising, generates these sentences which to her meet the request for detail:

2

The city has many problems. One problem is the subway. The trains are dirty and unpleasant. The floors are filthy. Another problem is . . .

Now that's an improvement. Naming *subway* and *trains* the writer moves into the territory of concreteness. And she attempts to create an atmosphere: *dirty, filthy, unpleasant*—although they are too general to evoke a picture and are examples more of telling than of showing—take the writer somewhat beyond the realm of unsupported assertion that appears in 1. Still, no clear details draw the reader into the writer's mind.

Redoubled efforts, more work on expanding pictures with sense words, repeated instructions to individualize a scene may in time yield sentences like these, much more consistent with the goals of writing rich in supporting detail:

3

The city has many problems. One problem is the subways, which are dirty and unpleasant. Yesterday on the Flushing local cigarette butts and crumpled pages of *The Daily News* lay everywhere. Streaks of black and yellow paint covered the windows. On the only empty seat in the car sat a paper bag wet from cola that dripped to a brown puddle on the floor.

It takes a while to bring a beginning writer along so she can produce a few consecutive sentences such as those in 3. But to view those in 2 as a good enough end point for achievement in the use of detail is no service to the reader or to the writer. True, there is an attempt at exemplification, but it is too insubstantial to be judged as a finished effort.

DICTIONARIES

Writers at this level have no clear sense of the usefulness of a dictionary. Some will chain themselves to one and as they write a rough draft will look up every third or fourth word that finds its way onto the page. Others will avoid the dictionary at all costs, not understanding how, if one cannot spell a word, the dictionary can offer any help. Many look at the symbols and markings in a typical entry as so many hieroglyphics.

The main objectives of teaching a lesson on the dictionary are to explain what is available there and, more importantly, to encourage its use during those stages that can benefit from it. Most beginners probably have had *some* sort of dictionary practice and are vaguely aware that the dictionary contains the "meanings" and spellings of words.

Before you can do anything at all with a dictionary, of course, you need to make sure that every student has one. Announce to the class on the first day that writers need a dictionary (a pocket edition is good for the beginner) and remind them repeatedly until you see that they each have one. Design a brief session that covers the main points about what students can find in their dictionaries. Make the class aware of the various kinds of dictionaries that exist and why they are used.

Probably the easiest way to show students what is in the dictionary is to give a sample entry and then to dissect it in class. Select a word like *run* for example: it can be used as a noun and a verb; it has a variety of definitions (well over a hundred), many with fine distinctions that make for good discussion; it contains many of the common symbols the user of a dictionary needs to know. Type whatever entry you choose so that the print is easy enough to read, and then label the main parts with arrows so students can follow your instruction. The overhead projector is excellent for demonstrating a typical dictionary entry. After you discuss the word as the dictionary presents it, offer an exercise which calls upon students to use the various parts of the entry. Here's an exercise devised for the word *run*.

1. Identify the meaning of *run* in each of the following sentences:
   a. A child *runs* across the floor.

   b. My old Chevy doesn't *run* right.
   c. My brother Charlie is always on the *run.*
   d. My teacher *ran* her eyes over my exam.
   e. All the colors will *run* if you use bleach on that shirt.
   f. What a *run* of good luck!
   g. He *ran* second in the marathon.
   h. The storm *ran* them ashore.
   i. David will *run* for class president.
2. What does *v.i.* mean? How is it different from *v.t.?*
3. From what languages did the word enter the English language? In what order are these languages listed in the etymology?
4. Pick out the pair of guide words that would appear at the top of the page containing the word *run:*
   runagate–ruralize
   ruff–rumble
   rumbly–runabout
   runaway–running board
5. *Would run-off* appear before or after *run?* Where would *rune* appear, before or after *run?*
6. What does the symbol û indicate? What does the symbol ǝ indicate? Where can you look to find out?
7. What does *syn* mean? *Ant?*
8. Why does the dictionary give examples for some definitions and not for others?

    Other words you might want to use as your sample entry could include those which change pronunciation as different parts of speech (*separate,* for example) or which have interesting etymologies (like *assassin*). Try to avoid words that would be completely unfamiliar to the student.
    Part of what you are illustrating is that even for everyday words the dictionary is a goldmine of information for the precise use of language.
    Another part of this unit should include practice in the general use of the dictionary. Activities should require the quick location or words with the aid of guide words at the top of the page. Also, there should be practice in using the

dictionary to discover pronunciation. Exercises should offer, further, activities which allow students to distinguish among meanings of words, to alphabetize, and to discover special spellings (plurals or alternate spellings).

Here you can also start to work on spelling problems by showing students how they can use the dictionary to look up a word that they have no idea how to spell. Give them a particularly tough word that they probably haven't seen (e.g., *misogyny*), take suggestions on possible spellings, and work through the looking-up process together. Then you can divide the class into groups and have students work on a list of tough words as you dictate them.

When you're holding a correction workshop after you return a theme, have students use dictionaries to check spelling and usage errors. Dictionary work is also valuable as part of the rough draft workshop when writers do their first and major proofreading job before preparing final copy.

SPELLING

Any reader of Shaughnessy knows immediately the enormous range of spelling problems affecting beginners. But he also knows how to approach those problems with intelligence and with hope. The first obstacle in working with students on spelling is getting them to believe that good spellers are made, not born. Armed with that encouraging news and a dictionary, students can start working on particular spelling problems.

As Shaughnessy notes, the best approach is one that compels writers to observe themselves as spellers. In order to do this, demonstrate that errors in spelling tend to fall into categories on individual papers. By reducing the nine spelling errors that may occur in a particular theme to *three kinds* of errors, you can reduce spelling anxiety.

Shaughnessy describes eleven kinds of errors:

1. long vowel sound
2. short vowel sound

3. final consonant or consonant cluster
4. silent *e*
5. homophone
6. suffix
7. prefix
8. double consonant
9. missing letter of syllable
10. word confusion
11. letter reversal

Students should understand basic terms like *accent, compound, consonant cluster, silent e, homophone, prefix, schwa, suffix, syllable,* and *vowel,* and should be able to sound out written words, to understand the main diacritic marks, and to divide words into syllables.

With a student who has a major spelling problem there is usually a poor conception of the relation between written and spoken words; that is, he has trouble pronouncing the sounds of written English as he reads them in words on a page. In working with such a student, have him read his paper aloud, making him pronounce each word as he has written it (rather than as he thinks he has written it). This procedure is helpful for students who leave letters out of words (*whih* for *which*), or who substitute other words inadvertently (*the* for *that*). During the practice, get the student to read each word individually, perhaps by blocking out the rest of the line or by having him read the line from the last word to the first. Of course, sometimes the problem is that the student spells as he speaks ("he use to go"), and thus the problem is not so much getting him to proofread aloud as it is getting him to recognize certain characteristics of the language. You must be able, too, to distinguish between spelling and syntactical errors.

My colleague at Penn State, Bob Zeller, helped a student prepare this chart of spelling errors from a single paragraph theme. It follows Shaughnessy's plan:

word	misspelling	letters or syllables involved	type
1. personality	1. personaity	I/-	1. missing letter
2. being	2. beening	e/een	2. long vowel
3. activities	3. activitys	ie/y	3. suffix
4. a	4. an	a/an	4. word confusion
5. completely	5. completly	e/-	5. silent e/suffix
6. length	6. lenght	gth/ght	6. final cons./clus.
7. your	7. you	r/-	7. final cons.
8. them	8. then	m/n	8. final cons.
9. their	9. there	eir/ere	9. homophone
10. extreme	10. extream	eme/eam	10. long vowel

By suggesting to this writer that he concentrate on final consonant sounds (and by giving him examples of words to look out for), an instructor provides a reasonable and important goal for the student's own writing. In the pattern that shows itself on the chart above, two kinds of mistakes account for half the errors.

Another kind of error chart asks the student to come up with an original method of remembering the misspelled word. With some handy mnemonic or even an absurd sentence that highlights the problem areas of the word, writers can fix in their minds the correct spelling of one of the "demons."

word	trouble spot underlined	a way to remember
abundance	abun<u>dance</u>	Have <u>a</u> <u>bun</u>; then <u>dance</u>.
dilemma	dil<u>emma</u>	<u>Emma</u> is in a dil<u>emma</u>.
parallel	par<u>all</u>el	<u>All</u> lines are par<u>all</u>el.

Whatever the method you recommend for charting spelling errors, help students prepare the charts during correction workshop or during conferences. Your goal is to get students to take such spelling inventories on their own and after each paper. (Some instructors collect the individual spelling lists each time the student submits a corrected theme.)

Shaughnessy recommends that you begin with misspelled words susceptible to correction by application of rules. Such rules can often be put in the form of a series of questions. For example, here is the rule for doubling the final consonant:

Does the word end in one vowel, plus one consonant?

Is the accent on the final syllable?

Does the suffix begin with a vowel?

If *yes* to all three questions, double the consonant.

Finally, in trying to help chronically bad spellers, provide word lists that demonstrate how to spell certain sorts of words. For instance, if a student has a problem with the final *ch* sound, supply a list like *watch, match, teach, clutch, sandwich, reach, brooch, ditch,* and so on, and encourage a search for patterns. The practice in seeing words correctly spelled in groups should help. Then examine the plurals of the words. Change tenses of the verbs.

Of all problems in the written language, spelling is the most visible to people who will examine the writer's product later on. No matter how minor instructors may think spelling is as a required skill, students' competence as writers will often be judged primarily on their ability to spell. In any case, spelling problems can be attacked systematically, and you must try to involve the student in looking systematically at the kinds of spelling errors he makes.

DIRECT AND INDIRECT QUOTATIONS

It's not that quotation marks warrant early treatment in the course because they are any more important than other punctuation; but students describing and narrating in early assignments will turn to snatches of dialogue as supporting detail. Here, then, is concrete connection between a specialized skill and the writer's needs at the moment: teach the conventional use of quotation marks so that students can use them correctly and without frustration when they write.

With quotations you want first to explore conceptual levels: the notion of quoting is one that confounds inexperienced writers. The similarities we recognize with ease between quoting someone's spoken words and someone's written words escape beginners, mystified both by the concept and by the plenitude of marks required to set off quoted material. Here, I suggest that you overlook for the moment the specialized demands made upon writers who borrow other *written* material. Later on (and maybe in another course) you will have to connect techniques of quoting someone's spoken words with techniques of quoting someone's written words. In the meantime establish the idea of quotation as a way for a writer to set off words he attributes to somone else from his or her own words. Examples you offer should be spoken words that writers intend to capture for their readers. Sometimes those words are exactly what some person said or wrote; other times the writer wishes to use his own words to tell what someone else said.

Shaughnessy recommends as an introduction to quotations that a student should examine passages cast in dialogues—interviews, hearings, or plays—where quotation marks are not required. He can then try his hand at writing dialogues or interviews on his own. Another good approach is to look at strip cartoons in the local newspaper, cartoons in which more than one character talks. The bubble in which the words of each character appear helps establish the idea of setting off spoken words.

When you introduce the punctuation of a direct quotation that names the speaker and a manner of delivery (*he said, she whispered thoughtfully*), it is helpful to distinguish two parts of the sentence. One part tells who is talking (this may be called the conversational *tag* or *label*) and the other tells what he is saying. To impress upon students the different marks called for, present a clear chart with labeled parts, the tag appearing at the beginning, at the end, or in the middle of the sentence. Here is one kind of presentation: see how arrows point to essential punctuation and to places in the quotation where students are likely to err.

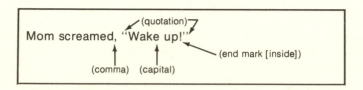

Offer similar charts with the tag in different positions. Remind students that the verb that indicates the action of the speaker is never capitalized; that the first spoken word always is; that if the writer attributes to the same speaker another sentence right after the first, no quotation marks appear between the two. (Mom screamed, "Wake up! You'll be late.") Point out that when the spoken words come first in the sentence (before the tag is offered), the writer requires before the tag and before the end quotation mark either a comma *or* some end mark (other than the period), not both.

"Wake up," my mother said.

"Wake up!" my mother screamed.

In this kind of sentence writers also need to remember not to capitalize the first word *after* the quotation unless a proper noun succeeds it.

For the quotation in which the tag breaks up a complete sentence, take time to explain on the chalkboard or with the overhead projector each convention of puncutation. Colored ink or chalk for the different marks will help the class follow more easily.

Students should practice each type of quotation sentence one at a time. Ask the class to take one of the comic strips examined earlier (or one of the dialogues written before) and to practice writing the sentences with the "he said's" in different places. Suggest that each student keep a log of ten sentences he heard someone speak at home or in the dorm or on the way to school. With the list of these sentences in class the student can write quotation sentences with the tag in different positions.

After students demonstrate mastery of direct quotations offer these sentences:

1. My mother said, "Wake up."
2. My mother said to wake up.
3. My mother said I should wake up.
4. My mother said that I should wake up.

How does 1 differ from the rest? Explain *indirect quotations.* Why, in 2, 3, and 4, would writers not use quotations or commas after *said?* Put quotations around the elements after *said* in 2, 3, and 4. How do the quotation marks alter— even violate—the writer's meaning? Many inexperienced writers will use quotation marks in those places, so move slowly in discussion. And students have often been taught that the word *that* is the only way of signaling an indirect quote. It is sometimes an effective signal (as in 4), but not always. For practice ask students to change an original direct quotation to an indirect quotation, offering suggestions about changing verb tenses and pronouns in order to weave the quotation into the writer's own sentence.

With enough class time available and convinced that students can manage quotations of spoken words and can distinguish indirect from direct quotations, you might consider instruction in quoting someone's written words. You'll have to work with the word "says"; students take this word too literally when we teach a quotation as what someone else *says.* Saying can be achieved in written language as well as spoken, and to use somone else's written words in a paragraph a writer must set them off from his own in the same way he sets off spoken words.

Show a page from one of the required textbooks used at

your school. Be sure not to select prose that itself quotes another writer—that would get you unnecessarily into the labyrinth of quotes-within-quotes. As you look at sentences from this textbook, show the class how you would incorporate the writer's words into your sentences. Start with the first sentence and illustrate the direct quotation as it would appear in your paragraph. Ask students—alone or in groups—to write correct sentences of their own that incorporate the borrowed material.

SENTENCE CONCEPTS AND MANIPULATIONS

The purpose of grammar instruction in the class for beginning writers must be to help them write correctly and to help them edit what they write. Although many instructors insist on extensive formal instruction in grammar, I have yet to see how teaching about nouns and adjectives and clauses and nominative absolutes helps the novice in any significant way. I'm pretty fond of grammar myself, and perhaps with a class of well prepared writers, grammatical instruction might well be an end in itself in the composition classroom. But after spending more time than I care to remember in trying to force terminology and the concepts caught up in it into students' minds, I'm convinced that language information required by beginners is best taught with as little terminology as possible. As you might have expected, I don't intend to suggest a grammatical "system" because I don't have one; and what I do is not without contradictions—I'll teach subjects, verbs, predicates, objects, and pronouns when I try to refine students' sentence sense. Further, I don't intend to back off from my earlier assertion that whatever works is good. But you've got to be convinced that what you think is working is working toward helping the student improve as a writer.

The most remarkable truth, and the easiest one to forget, is that native speakers of English already have a well-developed sentence sense. Most students know a fragment when they *hear* one; they know a complete sentence when they *hear* one. Yet the errors in their writing seem to prove otherwise: run-on sentences, comma splices, and fragments abound.

To help teach about sentence error you can take advantage of this native sense by first of all making students realize that they have it; and then by helping them listen to the sentences they write. Oral exercises to develop the concept of a sentence are a solid beginning because they give students a sense of confidence about their language ability. Returning often to such oral activities reinforces that confidence and helps it develop.

• Subjects and Predicates

An oral activity can set the stage for instruction in the nature of subjects and predicates *and* in expanding and contracting kernel sentences. Offer two lists (asking students to add words to each), one of subjects, one of verbs, with some of the verbs being verb phrases. Ask students to make sentences by selecting an item in the first list and an item in the second.

1	*2*
A child	hate
The woman	fell
people	was drawing
a tree	flew
the bird	sings
————	————
————	————

Example: The bird flies.

A child sings.

Ask someone to record on the chalkboard sentences offered by members of the class. What makes the word group a sentence? What workable definition for a sentence can the class suggest? (Here are definitions to consider: "A sentence is a group of words containing a subject and a predicate and expressing a complete thought." "A sentence is a group of words naming a subject and telling something about that subject.") Students will probably be able to identify within sentences the words in 2 as verbs and the words in 1 as subjects. Build upon that ability: How do we know that the words in B are verbs? What distinguishes verbs? Show how some verbs require more than one word. To test completeness of doubtful sentences on their own papers, students may occasionally need to identify subjects and verbs, so this is important practice. For the verb offer the traditional definition—and then some hints like these for finding and recognizing the verb:

1. Verbs can show tense. If you're trying to find a verb in a sentence put *yesterday, today, tomorrow* at the beginning of the sentence. The word that changes in order to give a sentence that makes sense is the verb. *For example:*

   He ran away.

   Tomorrow he *will run* away.

   Ran changed to *will run. Ran* is the verb.

2. Verbs work with subjects. If you want to test a word you think is a verb, use *I, he, she, it, we,* or *they* in front of the word. If the combination makes sense, your word can be used as a verb.

Example	*Test*	*Verb*
speak	I speak, they speak	Yes
olive	I olive?	No
desk	I desks?	No
dance	You dance, she dances.	Yes
ran	They ran, he ran.	Yes

3. The auxiliaries and modals are worth memorizing because they are instant clues to verbs and verb phrases.

Of course, the tests don't work all the time. Some words can be verbs as well as other parts of speech (*light, like,* and so on), so students need to see that it is on the basis of the use of a word in a *sentence* that they determine a grammatical label. Yet these tests, along with any definitions you offer, expand the student's ability to recognize the verb.

In dealing with subjects you need to discuss nouns and pronouns and to help students find subjects in original sentences. Once the verb has been found, students can ask *who* or *what* before it: the word(s) that answers that question is the subject.

• Simple Expansion and Embedding

Once students can recognize simple subject and verb combinations, you need to expand several of the brief sentences generated from the lists you examined earlier. Your early instruction is just to encourage students to make observations on the ways in which words or phrases get attached to (or embedded in) kernel sentences. Verb completers (objects, complements), for example, might be introduced here as one means of expanding the predicate part of the sentence. You can offer several complete simple sentences in which objects might be added:

The child sings (a song)

The actor spoke (his lines)

The woman ate (an apple)

People hate (murderers).

The objects in those sentences refine meaning; in these, the complement is essential for sense:

She was (tired)

That man is (a carpenter)

These new sentences with expanded predicates may themselves serve as starting points for further expansion and embedding.

For teaching embedding, Shaughnessy suggests a focus on position (single word adjectives and appositional forms); on suffixes signifying attachment (*-ly, -ing, -ed*); and on words that achieve embedding (*wh*-words, *that, if, although, whatever,* etc., *prepositions*).

Illustrate possibilities for expansion and embedding in a number of ways. One approach is to provide blanks with questions under them so that students may make their own responses:

The _____ _____ bird flew _____ _____ _____
     What   What   Where?   How?   When?
     size?   color?

Some instructors who rely on labels will name grammatical units that should fill the blanks, although I find students intimidated by the terminology even here:

The _____ _____ bird flew _____ _____ _____.
    adjective adjective   prepositional adverb participial phrase
                      phrase

Such fill-in-the-blank sentences might yield these responses:

The tiny red bird flew away swiftly yesterday.

One large brown bird flew over the trees slowly each morning.

A large white bird flew into the clouds swiftly, flapping its wings gracefully.

Different skeletal sentences will produce many original results, embedded phrases for expansion varying in form and length. (Point out subject and predicate sections of these expanded units and remind writers about the verb as the critical part of the predicate and the noun or pronoun as the key word in the subject section.)

You can ask that students write a second and third sentence to one you supply, suggesting that the new sentence provide information about the subject already named. Thus, sentences reading across in columns 1 and 2 can be rewritten, as in 3, to demonstrate different types of embedding.

1	2	3
The tiny red bird flew away swiftly yesterday	It is a robin	The tiny red bird, a robin, flew away swiftly yesterday.
,, ,,	It whistled softly.	Whistling softly, the tiny red bird . . .
,, ,,	,,	The tiny red bird who whistled softly flew away swiftly . . .
,, ,,	,,	Although it whistled softly, the tiny red bird . . .

Asking students to contract long sentences also helps develop sentence recognition skills. Select narrative sentences from folk legends or well formed sentences from student papers, avoiding complex or highly unusual structures. A sentence from a popular song also serves well in this exercise. If you've defined a sentence as a group of words naming a subject and telling something about that subject, ask students to extract subject and verb and to examine the remaining parts.

This introduction to sentences, to subjects and predicates, you want to offer students early in the term. You are not striving at this point for mastery in embedding, expanding, or combining. You are not trying to label numerous grammatical units nor to make students skilled in grammatical terminology. Here, the intent is to offer simple language by which students can talk intelligently about sentences; to explore sentence possibilities; and to demonstrate what writers can do with and to sentences.

In later sessions you will want to provide practice exercises in different kinds of embedding, teaching relevant punctuation with each operation but not expecting mastery of restrictive-nonrestrictive punctuation when you deal with relative clauses. The works of O'Hare and Mellon (and in textbooks the work of Strong in *Sentence Combining*) suggest many different activities; it's good to have those books available when planning class sessions. Individually or in groups students should add sentence elements where logic and syntax allow. Thus, the relative clause may be embedded after the subject *and* at the end of sentences; appositions, after subject and at sentence end; participial phrases, before the subject and at the end of a sentence. Whenever possible students should generate the kernel sentence, the element for embedding, or some other part of the sentence they are writing for practice. (One problem in O'Hare's and Strong's approaches is that these teachers supply the basic sentence patterns in language not typical of inexperienced writers.)

• Coordination

When you consider coordination, illustrate first how *and, or,* and *but* link elements within the sentence—subjects, predicates, complements, prepositional phrases. (Here is a good place to explain the idea of elements linked in series and to teach the use of the comma as a replacement for *and* between items—between all except the last two.)

Then look at the process of coordinating sentences with *and, but, for, or, (nor), so,* and the semicolon. Ask for definitions of those connecting words, students often using *and* and *but* interchangeably as sentence bridges. Demonstrate the effect on two separate sentences of the use of various coordinators.

Students must see that coordination joins elements clearly belonging together, and must be led away from overuse of coordination. For practice, offer sentences with coordinators named, students supplying one of the coordinated elements. Or, ask students to offer pairs of sentences that might be combined logically. Point out the use of the comma before the coordinator when complete sentences are joined.

Shaughnessy tells us to help students to see "that the comma before *and* has the significance of a period—that is, it signals the end of one sentence and the beginning of the next. . . . With the comma the writer has a chance to prepare his reader for a new sentence." It's also a good idea to mention that *and* is a perfectly legitimate word to start a sentence if its purpose is to move the passage forward or to end it:

> I watched Earl crying bitterly as the train pulled away. And that was the last time I saw him.

• Subordination

In teaching *subordination* examine the word with the class. What does it mean? Suggest several kinds of subordinators; ask the class to name others. In many cases students need to learn the meanings of words like *although, because, since.* Also point out that some subordinators have meanings similar to coordinators, and so there is sometimes a choice. It is not so much a denotative sense that the student lacks but rather a sense of the implications for the use of subordinators on sentence meaning. Relying too heavily upon simple coordinate structures, basic writers should learn how subordination compresses *syntax* and how it affects meaning:

> The wind blew wildly. The sparrows hid between buildings.
>
> Because the wind blew wildly, the sparrows hid between buildings.
>
> The sparrows hid between buildings because the wind blew wildly.

What differences in meaning do students perceive? Suppose (with appropriate changes in verb) the subordinator were *after, before, if, while* or *when?* What happens to the sense of the sentence?

Students should also compare two sentences joined by

coordination *and* by subordination. Which do students prefer? Why? What are the merits in using subordination? In using coordination? Another thing to do in class is to have students use subordination and coordination to create sentences at different levels of complexity. Yet another exercise asks students to switch the position of the subordinator in order to alter meaning:

> The fire started when the police arrived.
> When the fire started, the police arrived.

Students should see how completely different the sense in each of these sentences is. During these early lessons on subordination, and not in separate instruction on punctuation, is the time to teach the comma as a means of separating introductory dependent sections from main sections.

In working with relative clauses ask for additions to a list of such clauses begun on the chalkboard. Then, from simple kernel sentences prepared by the class, students can select one sentence and can embed the relative clause in key positions. (As was suggested earlier, oral activities offer helpful starting points for practice in these skills.) You can also provide completion sentences like these:

1. The man who _____ _____.
2. I brought the package to a house that _____.
3. A student whose _____ should _____.
4. The coach brought his little daughter, who _____.

In dealing with punctuation of subordinate elements in different sentence positions, bring up the idea of fragments, explaining the reasons an inexperienced writer might use a period after *house* in sentence 2 or after *daughter* in sentence 4. You would be wise not to subject beginners to the complexities of restrictive and nonrestrictive elements as they dictate comma use. But here is a good place to discuss the stylistic use of fragments by analyzing newspaper headlines, advertisements, or professional prose that use fragments skillfully.

• Embedding Participles and Infinitives

For embedding with participial or infinitive phrases students need first to recognize the suffix signals -*ed* and -*ing,* and the *to* marker for the infinitive. (Those markers are enough to help the student locate the structure in examples you offer, so don't force the terminology.) Then students need to practice making appropriate verb forms. Afterwards you can encourage practice with expanded structures in different sentence positions, working with the verbals one at a time. For practice with the -*ing* form supply—or ask students to generate—simple sentences to which participial structures are added. Here, a writer selects items from each of three columns and embeds the new structure.

1	*2*	*3*
		(a *word group to*
	(*one word to tell*	*tell how, when,*
(*-ing word*)	*how, when, where*)	*where, why*)
trembling	gracefully	in the sky
glowing	noisily	below the hill
soaring	clumsily	near me
blasting	there	through an open
speeding	yesterday	window
moaning	above	in darkness
creeping	innocently	on a warm summer
dancing	swiftly	night
cheering	today	with a whine
speaking	slowly	beyond the gray
drifting		mountains
slipping		at noon
		beneath a pale
		cloud
		across a stream
		from their seats
		at the campfire
		beside an old oak

Sentence: The boat moved along.

Speeding noisily, the boat moved along.

The boat, *drifting slowly,* moved along.

The boat moved along, *slipping gracefully across a stream.*

Students should experiment with the participial structure as a means for combining sentences to compress ideas:

I stared out the window at an ugly gray cat. I saw a German shepherd sneak around the corner.

Staring out the window at an ugly gray cat, I saw a German shepherd sneak around the corner.

Provide similar activities for past participial structures and for infinitives. Explain what happens when the writer uses a modifying element that dangles and try to prevent this error. Remind students that the first two or three words after the participial or infinitive word group that opens a sentence must tell *who* or *what* is performing the action of that participle or infinitive. It's probably best to identify the participle each time you discuss it rather than to rely upon students' abilities to identify grammatical concepts through the labels ordinarily used. I call the structures *"-ing* words" or *"ed* words."

With participial openers the comma is a good clue: it is often right after the comma that succeeds this opening word group that the writer must name the person or thing performing the action of the participle. Thus, in

Speeding noisily, the boat moved along

boat is the word that tells what was speeding and it is placed soon after the comma. In the sentences above, too, the word *boat* by its correct placement in the sentence clearly names the performer of the action suggested by the participle. Later on, offer practice correcting dangling modifiers which appear in student writing.

It is this practice in combining and embedding that helps turn around the attitude Shaughnessy reports: "Beginning writers tend to experience their sentences as unmanageable streams of words which, once set in motion, cannot be turned back." Explanations of process and adequate practice rather than direct grammatical instruction are valuable ways of improving syntax.

• Sentence Boundaries

Again, it is Shaughnessy who has helped us see that no matter how unconventional a student's punctuation appears to be, it is worth studying for the insights it gives into his perception of sentence boundaries and of specific punctuation marks. Many students, though they would say that periods are used at the ends of sentences, perceive sentences as rhetorical units that are longer or shorter than what we call the grammatical sentence.

Run-Ons and Comma Faults (or comma splices)

Beginning writers often show little grasp of convention for ending a sentence: they frequently use a comma and period interchangeably as a terminal mark, and frequently use no marks at all to help the reader separate one idea from another. Your earlier efforts at familiarizing students with the sentence as a grammatical unit and with methods for enlarging simple sentences by expansion and embedding will help inform judgments about sentence boundaries. To look at errors beginners make, present to the class a set of sentences like these:

> They arrived late to class the teacher looked angrily at them then he looked away

Ask one person in the class to read aloud while the others listen carefully. Most readers will stop after the words *class, them,* and *away.* Why? Convince students that they have a natural sense of what a sentence is although as writers they may not be marking off sentences according to convention. The writer who offered the sentences above failed to indicate closure in three places. How should he signal the ends of sentences? Elicit the names of the end marks (period, question mark, exclamation point); draw them on the board; ask someone to explain when to use them.

Someone is bound to suggest a comma either after *class* or after *them*. Describe the comma fault. Explain the difference between the comma and the period as a boundary marker. Students will have a sense of the comma as a signal of minor pause and a sense of the period as a signal of major pause, but will need practice in reading aloud and listening to the quality of the pause. At the end of a declarative sentence the voice usually stops and drops. Train students to listen to their own voices by offering short, simple passages with all punctuation removed and by asking different people to read aloud. Using a cassette recorder will convince even the most uncertain student of his or her ability to recognize closure. Play back a recording of that person reading several consecutive sentences stripped of their end marks.

The most frequent kinds of run-on or comma fault errors occur when an adverb, a conjunctive adverb, or a subject pronoun opens a sentence that is closely related to the previous sentence. Thus you read:

The teacher looked angrily at them, then he looked away.

She offered me a sandwich, however, I was not hungry.

The bracelet was expensive I bought it anyway.

Shaughnessy explains that students at this level need to learn how to use the logical connectives, which help skilled writers avoid comma faults. Her list of six types is helpful in teaching the vocabulary to students:

Logical connective	Similar connectives
furthermore	also, besides, in addition, likewise, moreover, similarly, or other words suggesting an addition
however	despite this, instead, nonetheless, nevertheless, on the other hand, still, and other words that reverse the logical direction of the sentence
therefore	as a result, accordingly, because of this, consequently, hence, thus, and other words suggesting the last link in a chain of reasoning
for example	for instance, to illustrate
that is	namely
then	afterwards, eventually, later, meanwhile, presently, sometime, soon, subsequently, thereafter, or other words suggesting a time relationship

After considering these words, students need to learn how to use them. Ask individuals to generate a sentence following a specific connective:

Women have more opportunities today; *however.* . .

Women have more opportunities today. *Therefore* . . .

Here is a good place to demonstrate the use of some of these connectors as interrupters:

I thought, <u>however</u>, that he was married.

They knew, <u>therefore</u>, that we would not be on time.

Apples, for <u>example</u>, are a major crop in New York State.

Why does the sentence require commas before and after the underlined words in the last three sentences? Stress the idea of the connector used as interrupter here. And how does the use of the underlined word differ from the use of the underlined words in the two preceding sentences? Instruction in the correct use of commas after the connective used as an opener would also be effective here. (*Nevertheless,* speak softly.) For an oral activity ask one student to offer a sentence and another to select a connective and then to speak a complete sentence after it. A third student suggests adequate punctuation. Also, provide sentences with the connectives removed and ask the class to fill blanks with logical word choices and correct punctuation.

In these exercises you want to introduce and explain the

How to Find Run-Ons and Comma Splices

1. Read your writing aloud. When your voice stops and drops you probably need a period.
2. Read your writing from the last sentence to the first sentence. See if each word group names a subject and says something about that subject.
3. Look for subjects and predicates to test sentence completeness.
4. Count your sentences. If you do, you'll be looking for end marks; and if your total on a given theme is low you might have run-on errors or comma splices.
5. Learn to recognize the words that frequently cause writers to make comma faults or run-ons:

Connectors	*Pronouns*
then, now	I
however	you
finally	he
suddenly	she
there	it
consequently	we
moreover	they
therefore	who

semicolon, not so much as a way of correcting run-on errors or comma splices but as a means of stressing a close relationship between sentences. You need, further, to discuss the use of the capital letter to signal the start of a new sentence and to explain why after a semicolon a capital does not follow: semicolons are connectors, periods are separators. And first you need to demonstrate how students can find run-on errors and comma faults in their own writing; and, next, how to repair those mistakes once identified. Most students can correct a run-on once someone points it out—the difficulty is in locating the error on one's own. Students having severe problems with run-ons might find these boxed suggestions helpful.

Demonstrate these various methods of correction by referring to a set of run-ons and comma splices on the chalkboard. Several exercises will give students practice in spotting and correcting run-ons and comma faults.

How to Correct Run-Ons and Comma Splices

Depending upon which method makes sense for the meaning you want to convey:

1. Use an end mark between sentences. Use a capital letter for the word after the period.
2. When the two sentences are closely related, you might want to use a semicolon between them. Start the word after the semicolon with a small letter.
3. Use a conjunction:
   a. if you use *and, or, but,* or *for* use a comma right before it
   b. if at the beginning of a sentence you use a subordinator (*because, although, while, since, when,* and *so on*), use a comma at the end of the word group that begins with the subordinator.
4. A comma does not work alone to separate two complete sentences.

1. Duplicate errors from student themes and ask the class to correct them.
2. Provide passages with all end marks removed and ask students to punctuate correctly. Select from newspapers, magazines, textbooks.
3. Provide practice with the words that often cause the errors:
   a. Ask students to generate their own sentences in response to your specific instructions: "Write two sentences about the weather. Start the second sentence with the word *it*"; "Write two complete thoughts about watching television. Separate them with a semicolon. Open the second sentence with the word *however*."
   b. Offer sentence clusters with blanks where words that might cause run-ons or comma faults should go. Ask students to insert the word you have indicated and to correct punctuation as required:

      (1) It was a long trial _____ it ended.
                              (finally)
      (2) College students need spending money _____
                                                (therefore)
          they take part-time jobs.
      (3) The large gold watch broke __ fell on the rocks ___
                                      (it)   (how-
          I think it can be fixed.   ever)

4. Direct one proofreading activity specifically at locating run-on and comma fault errors.
5. Dictate brief passages with "run-on traps"—let students copy and punctuate correctly.

In my discussion of the run-on sentence here I have deliberately avoided reference to grammatical concepts (even basic ones like subject and predicate, terms I use with my students) to illustrate the possibilities in instruction devoid of terminology. Admittedly, grammatical concepts can be helpful in some of this teaching—especially as options during individual conferences when you are helping students with serious problems to understand tests for sentence completeness. However, it is highly impractical to recommend the subject and predicate test for *each* sentence students write. Attention to a sense of completeness based on sentence meaning pays more reliable dividends.

Sentence Fragments

If the run-on and comma fault show the inexperienced writer struggling against closure, the fragment is, as Shaughnessy believes, an indication of his "caution about losing control of the sentence by allowing it to become too long" and his "difficulty with holding written sentences in mind when they contain more than one predication or even when one predication contains a compound subject or verb."

Previous instruction in the concept of the sentence and practice in embedding and combining provide a good frame of reference for instruction in fragments. Since the kinds of fragments inexperienced writers produce may be roughly divided into two main groups (and since means of recognition and correction of sentences in each group vary), it is wise to concentrate on one group at a time.

Fragments with no subjects, no verbs, or neither subject nor verb
As with their ability to spot a run-on or comma fault isolated from surrounding sentences in a paragraph, students can usually differentiate between a fragment and a sentence. Build upon that skill at differentiation by offering a list of fragments like these:

1. Over the curb and into the street
2. Rushing noisily through the trees
3. Just to play his radio quietly
4. Usually dressed in a blue woolen sweater

Let students talk about these word groups. What do people in the class sense? Someone will doubtless identify these groups as fragments; define the word, establishing a concept of *incompleteness.* What would make each of the word groups complete? Before turning to grammatical explanations, discuss the reasons why fragments disturb readers; remind the class of those structures that signal combining or embedding operations; and then point out the value of locating subjects and predicates as key units.

In 1 readers have no idea of *what* the writer wants to talk about nor do they know what *he wants to say* about it. What is being done "over the curb and into the street"? Who is doing it?

In 2 the writer doesn't tell who or what is rushing. Even if he did—let us say he adds the word *birds*—he would not make much more sense: "Birds rushing through the trees" does not do much more to complete the thought. The word *rushing* is only part of a verb; if it is to be the verb in the predicate it must have a helper.

In 3 readers again have no sense of who the writer is talking about. And as in 2 there is no complete verb in the predicate section; *to play* is an infinitive.

The words in 4 offer no notion of *who* is dressed in the sweater. Further, the word *dressed* (a past participle) alone may not be the verb in the predicate section. Depending upon the meaning he wished to convey, the writer might need a helping verb like *is* or he might need a completely new verb so he could use the participial structure as a modifier. Those options, incidentally, would apply to 2, 3, and 4 as well.

After discussion let students summarize. What do these pieces of sentences have in common? What do they all lack? Establish a working definition for *fragment*. Without introducing rules or complex terminology, encourage people in the class to correct the fragments aloud. Provide an exercise of several word groups, some fragments such as those introduced, and some complete sentences. Ask students to put checks next to complete sentences, X's next to fragments. Have each word group read aloud; ask students to suggest possible changes. Also, ask students to make up their own exercises which they then exchange with other people in the class. Each person makes up ten word groups, at least four of them fragments; another person marks off the fragments and says how he would correct them. Students might also analyze newspaper headlines or titles of songs and movies and books to distinguish sentences from nonsentences.

It's not especially difficult to recognize and to correct isolated fragments. Surrounded by other sentences in a passage, however, the fragment confounds inexperienced writers. Thus, you have to show the fragment as part of an idea cluster produced by a writer. Present to your class the segments on the left below. The explanation alongside will help focus discussion on key elements:

Fragment	*Explanation*
1a. In a square of pavement down the block a small dog played with a rubber ball, but it rolled out of his reach. b. He rushed after it. c. Over the curb and into the street.	Here a student might think that the subject *he* and the verb *rushed* in sentence b would also be the subject and verb in word group c. But that is not the case. Word group c is a fragment because it lacks its own subject and verb. The capital letter in *over* and the period after *street* indicate that the writer thought the sentence a complete one.
2a. A winter day like today is never pleasant. b. Everywhere I can hear the howl of the wind. c. Rushing noisily through the trees. d. There is also too much snow along the streets.	Here, a student might think that the word *wind* in sentence b would be the subject in word group c. But word group c must have its own subject. Furthermore, the word *rushing* is not a verb: if *is* or *was* appeared before it, or if the word were *rushed* instead of *rushing,* it would be a verb. But as it stands, word group c is also a fragment because it lacks a verb.

Fragment	*Explanation*

3a. It is important to understand that teenagers often require privacy.

  b. For an hour or two a boy wishes to be left alone in his room.

  c. Just to play his radio quietly.

Here, it is possible that an inexperienced writer would imagine the word *boy* in sentence b to be the subject in word group c. But word group c must have its own subject to be complete. In addition, *to play* is no verb. The word group needs a word such as *wants* or *likes* before the infinitive. Sometimes the infinitive can be changed to a verb: *plays, played,* or *is playing.* But as it stands, word group c is also a fragment because it lacks a verb.

4a. John Callahan, six feet seven inches tall, is easy to recognize on campus.

  b. He towers over everyone around.

  c. Usually dressed in a blue woolen sweater.

  d. John braves the cold without an overcoat.

Here, the writer gives no subject in word group c. Furthermore, *dressed*—as it is used—is only a part of a verb. It must have *is* or *was* or some such word before it. So, word group c is also a fragment because it lacks a verb.

You will want to point out in connection with 3 that some connectives often serve as warning signals, yellow lights that fragments might be coming. Words like *just, especially,* and *for example* will often cause an inexperienced writer to follow them with word groups that fail to include subjects and verbs.

Practice in identifying—not necessarily in correcting at this stage—fragments within sentence clusters will be valuable. Make up an exercise modeled after examples 1–4 and work on it in class.

After students show some skill in identifying fragments, review the features of the fragments currently being considered. These either have verbs and no subjects, subjects and no verbs, or no subjects and no verbs. One's options for correcting the error depend upon those conditions. With the overhead projector or with colored chalk provide strong visual clues—arrows, labels, boxes, or charts—as you explain different methods of correction. After each suggested method offer practice so that the writer tries all the possible options.

How to Fix Fragments

1. Add a subject and a verb to make the sentence complete.

Correct This Fragment

This Way

Over the curb and into the street.

The dog jumped over the
curb and into the street.
(added subject)
(added verb)

Rushing noisily through the trees.

It is rushing noisily
through the trees.
(subject)
(word added to make verb)

It rushes noisily through
the trees.
(-ing word changed to verb)

Just to play his radio quietly.

He just wants to play his
radio quietly.
(subject)
(word added to make verb)

He just plays his radio
quietly.
(infinitive changed to verb)

(subject)

Dressed in a blue woolen   He is usually dressed in a
sweater.   blue woolen sweater.

(word added to make verb)

2. Another way to fix the fragment is to connect it to the
   sentence that comes before it or after it. In that way you
   legitimately give the fragment the subject and verb it
   needs by using words of another sentence.

Correct the Fragment   *This Way*

(small letter)

He rushed after it.   He rushed after it over the
Over the curb and into the   curb and into the street.
street   (no period)

(no period)

I can hear the howl of the   I can hear the howl of the
wind. Rushing noisily   wind rushing noisily
through the trees.   through the trees.

(small letter)

For an hour or two a boy   For an hour or two a boy
wishes to be left alone in his wishes to be left alone in
room. Just to play his radio his room just to play his
quietly.   radio quietly.

(no period)

(small letter)

3. A fragment may be effectively corrected by attaching it to
   the sentence that comes after it.

Correct the Fragment   *This Way*

Usually dressed in a blue   Usually dressed in a blue
woolen sweater. John   woolen sweater, John braves
braves the cold without an   (comma)
overcoat.   the cold without an over-
                              coat.

Hearing the photographer talk about her travels through Alaska. Audiences responded with enthusiasm.	Hearing the photographer talk about her travels (comma) through Alaska, audiences (small letter) responded with enthusiasm.

Hint: When you open a sentence with a fragment that contains an *-ing* verb part or an *-ed* verb part, follow the fragment with a comma.

Students ought to be able to help prepare simple charts to review methods of finding and of correcting fragments. Here, as with run-on and comma fault, writers must learn to recognize the error in their *own* writing. Charts like these will summarize approaches:

How to Find Fragments

1. Read aloud. Listen for incomplete thoughts.

2. Look out for *-ing* words, especially when they start sentences.

3. Look for subject and verb in each sentence.

4. Read paragraph from last sentence to first. Stop after each sentence and ask: Is it a complete thought?

How to Correct Fragments

1. Add subject, verb, or both.

2. Add fragment to sentence that comes before or sentence that comes after. Make sure final sentence makes sense.

3. Change an *-ing* word to a verb by using *is, was, are, were, am* in front of it. Or, change *-ing* word to a verb.

4. If you put an *-ing* fragment or another "verb part" fragment in front of a sentence, use a comma after the fragment.

How to Find Fragments	*How to Correct Fragments*
5. Know some fragment danger signals: just especially for example also mainly for instance like such as	5. Change an infinitive to a verb by removing "to" and by using the correct form of the verb. Or, put one of these verbs before the infinitive: *like(s)*, *want(s)*, *plan(s)*, *try* *(tries)*, *is, was, were, are, am.*

After the class has considered the various "no-subject, no-verb fragments" and has seen how to discover and how to correct them, provide exercises for mastery. List sentence clusters with key words removed and ask the student to insert the word with proper punctuation:

1. The ball hit the branches _____ them hard.
   (smacking)
2. The ball hit the branches _____ them hard it looped
   (smacking)
   across the road.

3. He offered to help ___ any means.
   (by)
4. He offered to help ___ any means he could he would
   (by)
   support his candidate.

5. We wanted the use of the car ___ drive to Allentown.
   (to)
6. We wanted the use of his car ___ drive to Allentown
   (to)
   presented no unusual difficulties.

Offer brief passages with all end marks removed. Supply exercises with sets of sentences, a fragment or two in each set; ask students to correct the fragment in the most logical way, but encourage a variety of approaches to the errors. The best exercise is one that asks a student to generate sentences in his own language. Give the class a list like this and ask students to use each word group to open or to end original sentences:

Lifting her book

Not allowed to leave the dorm

Waving to his friend

Beyond the hill

Arriving at registration late

Require students to use "fragment danger signals" in sentences of their own.

Subordinator fragments (subordinate clause fragment, dependent clause fragment)
Writers who have practiced sentence embedding and who understand the vocabulary of subordination have a good foundation upon which to build a sense of sentence errors caused by another kind of premature closure. The look of the subordinate or relative clause will be familiar as an element for embedding in a complete sentence.

Refresh the class' memory on dependent units by asking that these word groups be read aloud one by one:
1. When an empty shopping <u>cart</u> <u>soared</u> down the aisle.
2. <u>Who</u> really <u>looked</u> ridiculous.
3. Unless our food stamp <u>program</u> <u>receives</u> much more publicity.

Why are these not sentences? The opening word in each group forces the reader to anticipate some condition which *must* be named in the sentence, some situation (though the writer failed to indicate it) upon which the material in these segments depends.

In 1, the reader wants to know what has happened when that empty shopping cart soared down the aisle. In 2, the reader wants to know who it is that looked ridiculous. In 3, the reader wants to know what will happen unless the food stamp program receives more publicity.

It is true that each of the word groups does contain a subject and a verb (they are underlined in each case). However, the use of the subordinator means that connection to a complete thought must be made for a correct sentence.

As with the other group of fragments we considered, these, isolated from surrounding sentences, are easy to spot. And some students even at this point will offer suggestions on how the fragments might be corrected. But be sure to show the class how the fragment looks within its context (left hand column, below); and elicit from students the explanations like those alongside.

1a. Parents should leave their children at home when shopping must be done.	The word *when* here is a subordinator. It must connect all the words that follow it to a complete sentence.
b. One afternoon at the A&P I stood minding my own business at the corn counter.	Since word group 3 is standing alone, and is not connected to a complete thought, it is a fragment. The reader needs to know, within word group 3, what happened when an empty shopping cart soared down the aisle.
c. When an empty shopping cart soared down the aisle.	
d. I know some little brat was to blame.	
2a. All the children in the third grade danced in snowflake costumes on the auditorium stage.	The word *who,* as it is used here, is a connector. It must join all the words that follow it to a complete sentence. In addition the sentence that uses the word *who* must also identify the person that *who* refers to. It's not enough to use Tyrone at the end of sentence 2. Since word group 3 is standing alone, and is not connected to a complete thought, it is a fragment.
b. Over to the left stood my cousin Tyrone.	
c. Who really looked ridiculous.	
d. He was covered with a big white sheet and he moved more like a hippo than a snowflake.	

3a. The government's latest attack on hunger is doomed.
   b. Unless our food stamp program receives much more publicity.
   c. In every ghetto countless people will go on starving.

The word *unless* is a subordinator. It must connect all the words that follow it to a complete sentence. Since word group 2 is standing alone, and is not connected to a complete thought, it is a fragment. The reader needs to know, within word group 2, what will happen unless our food stamp program receives much more publicity.

In each case, the signal for the fragment is an embedding word, one the student has examined in earlier class sessions. With extensive practice those words will stick in the mind as a way of predicting an upcoming fragment (Some students will choose to memorize the subordinators to make recognition of fragments easier.)

In turning attention to ways of correcting the subordinator fragments, explain (and demonstrate) the various options one at a time, instructing in the use of required punctuation. It is also wise to provide brief practice in each mode of correction before moving on to the next. In many cases the methods recommended to alter the subordinator fragment are the same as those presented in connection with fragments without subjects or verbs. Thus, examining those three subordinator fragments and their surrounding sentences, students should attend to these possible methods of correction:

1. joining the fragment to a previous sentence (in 1 and 2 join b and c; in 3 join a and b);
2. joining the fragment to the sentence after (in 1, join c and d; in 3 join b and c);
3. add a new subject-verb word group (in 1: When an empty shopping cart soared down the aisle, I (subject) leaped (verb) aside. I knew some little brat . . .);

4. remove the subordinator and add words required for meaning: 1c. An empty shopping cart soared down the aisle. 2c. He really looked ridiculous.

Lead students to see these as options for exercise only if the logic of the sentence in its context allows it. Thus, joining the fragment to a previous sentence might correct the grammar but violate the meaning; and the removal of the subordinator might destroy causal balance important for the writer to maintain.

After exploring methods for correcting fragments, offer hints for finding them. Reading the sentences aloud; reading sentences from the last to the first; learning the familiar subordinators as danger signals for possible fragments; frequent practice with embedding subordinate elements in kernel sentences—these will help the inexperienced writer recognize sentence completeness.

Practice exercises for the subordinator fragments should be varied and frequent. Select from these possibilities:

1. Provide fragments from student themes and ask for varied corrections.

2. Ask students to write subordinator fragments: ask other students to embed them in proper constructions in original sentences.

3. Provide an exercise which requires students to generate their own sentences, sentences which use structures that frequently cause fragments. Thus you would say: "Write two sentences that tell what you see each day on the way to class. Use the words *that I see* correctly in your response."

4. A review of the *two* groups of fragments together (no-subject, no-verb, and subordinator types) should also be used for practice.

After students show some skill in dealing with the fragment, introduce the stylistic use of fragments in writing. Refer back to earlier discussions of newspaper headlines and of eye-catching advertising copy. Why do newspaper stories and ads use fragments? Again provide samples of deliberate fragments by accomplished writers. What effects do the writers achieve by using pieces of sentences? Ask students to write brief descriptive passages that contain fragments; require the writer to mark each fragment with an asterisk so you know he can identify it easily. And after examining stylistic uses of sentence pieces, students should convert the fragments into complete sentences.

• Agreement of Subject and Verb

The range of problems students encounter with agreement is as extensive as the causes of these problems, causes nonetheless worth seeking out for each individual writer if you are to provide meaningful instruction. Only a careful analysis of individual students' difficulties can determine the kind of study to encourage. The discussion in this section covers a large range of problems, some only quirks in or exceptions to the dynamics of subject-verb agreement. Frequently it is only in conference with one student who misunderstands that you need to explore this material.

A command of agreement requires so many different skills that one feels obliged to present everything at once—and yet there must be a logical starting point for the introduction of the concept. The principles explained here suggest a general approach and do not take into account the highly specialized needs of students with radical problems in subject-verb agreement.

Although most mature speakers inflect correctly most of the time, those who frequently violate the system of agreement will require instruction in the differences between the -s or -es inflection for the verb and for the noun and will need to develop a sense of when to use the -s inflection on the ends of verbs. A good syllabus provides instruction before this in subject-verb recognition so you have a foundation in key grammatical concepts upon which to build.

A strong approach to agreement for those with severe problems is to look first (and briefly) at the notion of tense.

Offer on the chalkboard or projector these three simple sentences:

The boys <u>laughed.</u>
The boys <u>will laugh.</u>
The boys <u>laugh.</u>

Ask someone to explain the differences in the forms of the verbs. What does the verb in each sentence indicate? Why are there different endings on the verbs? Discuss *inflection,* offering brief examples from other languages, especially languages familiar to students in the class. Point out *ed* and *s* (or *es*) as critical inflectional letters in English. Put off a prolonged discussion of the *-ed* ending, although it is important to explain *tense* as a set of time relationships built into the verb system of the language. Students will explore later on how that system works.

Right now we are looking at the present tense verb system and how each present tense verb works along with its subject. In the sentence

The boys laugh

why is there an *s* at the end of boys? What does the *s* at the end of nouns usually indicate? What other plural words could students suggest instead of *boys* in that sentence? Without mentioning the concept of agreement write this sentence directly below the last one:

The boy laughs.

Why is there no *s* on boy? What concept of number is the writer trying to indicate? (Define *singular* and *singularity.*) Chart the sentences, asking students to name the parts and to fill in the first *three* columns below.

1 Subject	2 Singular or Plural?	3 Verb	4 Singular or Plural?
The boys	Pl	laugh	
The boy	S	laughs	

What does the class notice about the verb in each case? Why does the verb change? Offer several other examples. What general "rule" can students draw from the behavior of the charted subjects and verbs? When someone sees that the *s* (plural) on a noun subject demands a verb without an *s;* and that no *s* (singular) on a noun subject demands a verb with an *s,* introduce the concept of *agreement* as a way certain words link formally in a sentence to reinforce meanings. Go back and fill in column 4 in the chart above. Take time to show that a singular noun subject requires a singular verb: point out how the mark of the plural verb is that it (usually) does *not* end in *s* and that the mark of the plural noun is that it (usually) *does* end in *s.* Expect problems in introducing these ideas. Students need to be led patiently to see how the -*s* ending signifies singularity *as well as* plurality, depending upon where the inflection appears (native speakers will know about *s* as a signal for plurals but will not be consciously familiar with the *s* as a way of marking the third person singular verb). Here is where the value of different colored ink or chalk is apparent: green *s* for noun plurals, red *s* for third-person singular verbs, for example. And agreement patterns in other languages (especially in languages students may know) are excellent to offer for the class' consideration here.

Once the concept of agreement seems reasonably well established in the students' minds, offer practice:

1. Provide two lists, one of singular and plural nouns, one of singular and plural verbs. (Stay, for the moment, with nouns ending only in *s* to show plural.) Ask students to mark S for singular, P for plural.
2. Offer a list of words ending in *s*—some because the *s* shows singularity, some because the *s* is merely the final letter of the stem of a word (miss, this, glass, bus). Ask students to distinguish the function of the *s* ending in each case.
3. Provide a simple passage in which singular and plural nouns and verbs appear abundantly. Have students circle

all words ending in *s* as a mark of plurality and underline all words ending in *s* as a mark of singularity.

4. From the lists provided in 1, ask students to select a noun subject that works correctly with a verb and to offer an original sentence using the combination. Expand these sentences with the class as you have before; insert modifiers after the subject so that it no longer immediately preceeds the verb. Point out the separation, reminding the class that no matter how far one is from the other, subject and verb obey the rules of agreement.

5. Show how the form of a word often stays the same even if it works in different grammatical ways. Only its use in a sentence tells how it functions. (The *sneezes* shook the room. She *sneezes* when she smells roses). Provide exercises in which students must identify the part of speech of a word used first as plural noun and next as singular verb. Then give the class a list of nouns and verbs ending in *s*. Students must write an original sentence for each word and must mark *N* or *V* for noun or verb depending upon how the word has been used:

> They laugh noisily.   (V)
> The laugh echoed in the room.   (N)

6. Another valuable activity asks students to switch verb forms from singular to plural (and vice versa).

> The light shines brightly.
> The lights _____.
> His ideas sound clever.
> His idea _____.

Looking at a passage like the one suggested in 3, ask students to change all plurals to singulars and all singulars to plurals.

At this point a good summary will call upon students to suggest that plural noun subjects (ending in *s* or *es*) do not match verbs ending in *s*. The -*s* ending appears on subject

or on verb but not on both. Make charts with colored chalk
or ink and arrows:

SINGULAR SUBJECTS	+	SINGULAR VERBS	=	AGREEMENT
(which usually DO NOT end in *s*)		(which usually DO end in *s*)		
A writer		work*s*		hard.
That book		i*s*		torn.
The bed ↗		creak*s* ↗		noisily.
No *s* means singular noun subject		*s* means singular verb		

PLURAL SUBJECTS	+	PLURAL VERBS	=	AGREEMENT
(which usually DO end in *s*)		(which usually DO NOT end in *s*)		
Writer*s*		work		hard.
Those book*s*		are		torn.
The bed*s* ↗		creak ↘		noisily.
s means plural noun subject		no *s* means plural verb		

With these review charts on the chalkboard, on dittoed sheets, or on the overhead projector students should now consider the exceptions, situations in which the -s form of the verb does not work according to the general conditions you established:*

1. *Some noun subjects form plurals in ways other than by adding s. If a subject is plural do not use the -s form of the verb.* Show an example:

Children run.

Is the subject singular or plural? How do we know? How is this plural different from usual plural forms? If we use a plural subject what kind of verb do we need? Point out that the word *children* forms a plural by adding letters. What other kinds of special plurals do students know? Look briefly at subjects that change letters—*geese, women;* subjects that have foreign plurals—*bacteria, fungi;* subjects that are pronouns and have plural forms completely separate from the singular—*they* for he, *these* for this, *those* for that; subjects that are pronouns that can be either singular or plural depending on the words they refer back to:

The girl who reads will advance.
Girls who read will advance.

Supply exercises that allow students to apply the concepts of irregular plural information.

2. *The base word of some verbs ends in s, so it's possible that occasionally an -s ending may appear on a plural verb.*

A verb like *to kiss,* for example, might confound students without this explanation. In the sentence "The boys kiss the girls," *boys* is plural and *kiss* is plural. The *s* on *kiss* is not signaling anything about agreement—the verb just happens to end in that letter. Besides, looking at a singular construction, "The boy kisses the girl," you see that the verb adds the

---

*With her permission I am using here some of the statements Mina Shaughnessy lists as rules on pp. 147–49 of *Errors and Expectations.*

-s inflection to indicate singularity. Other such verbs?—*dress, hiss, bus, toss, pass, miss.*

3. *If the subject is I or you, do not use the -s form.*
Offer lists of inflected and uninflected verbs and with the class' help cross out those that do not work with these two subjects. From a list of infinitives the class should offer the correct forms of verbs used with *I* and *you.* Offer practice in listening to and writing first person singular verb forms.

4. *In the simple past tense do not use the -s form of the verb.*
Point out that only *was* and *were* of all the past tense verb forms follow the principle of agreement and that *was* violates rule 3 in the use of I (*I* was). Students should see that when a sentence demands the past tense, no -s forms are used. Shaughnessy supplies these examples in which students must cross out the incorrect verb:

Once, after school was over, it

starts
began
happens
happened

When I was a child I never

thought
was
wanted
dreams

5. *Do not use the -s form of any verb that follows a helping verb.*
Remind students of earlier instruction in verb identification—some verbs are of more than one word. (Some examples: *was told, will speak, has eaten, should have studied, might have been delayed.*) Review the concept of main verb and helping verb; and illustrate that the main verb gets no -s form.

6. *Do not use the -s form of the verb on the infinitive.*
Especially for students whose native language is not English, the infinitive is a mystifying sentence element, which, depending upon its use, seems to violate established principles of agreement. Explain what an infinitive is; then follow Shaughnessy in indicating the three forms a writer is likely to use when he writes an infinitive:

  a. to + verb stem (to play)
  b. verb stem (play)
  c. to + auxiliary + past form of verb (to have played)

Form a is easy: if *to* preceeds the verb, no *s* appears on the end of it. Form c follows exception 5 above: no *-s* form succeeds a helping verb. Form b is a problem because the *to* vanishes and it's hard for the writer to know whether he requires a stem form or an *-s* form:

He hears the bells (to) ring.
They let the child (to) wait.

When there is doubt, writers can test which verb form is required by trying to substitute *him, her,* or *them* for the subject of the verb in question. If the substitution works, the required verb form is the infinitive.

He hears *them* (to) ring.   Infinitive form
They let *her* (to) wait.   required.

7. *Learn the present tense forms of three tricky verbs—to go, to have, to do—and the present and simple past forms of to be.*
Because of their important role in spoken and written language, these verbs need special attention in the context of discussions about agreement. It's not that *go, have,* and *do* are any more or less irregular than other irregular verbs, just that their repeated appearance in a student's speaking and writing makes error with them more frequent. *To be* is so irregular that special treatment for the present tense forms and for the simple past (because of *was* and *were* and their demand for correct agreement) is bound to help.

8. *Know the singular and plural pronouns which work as subjects of verbs.*

Although the singular subject pronouns other than *I* follow generalizations about the *-s* form of the verb—*He* (singular, no *-s* ending) *runs* (singular, *s* ending)—the plural pronoun subjects, because they do not end in *s* the way plural *noun* subjects usually do, need special attention. You touched upon pronouns in the discussion of exceptions 1 and 3 to the principle of agreement, so remind students of that. After presenting all the singular and plural subject pronouns, distribute exercises that ask students to substitute plural pronoun subjects for singular noun subjects in sentences. Verbs will need to be changed accordingly. And depending upon the level of the class, provide a list of some of those peculiar pronoun subjects that seem to students to be plural but that are, according to formal English, considered to be singular. Words like *everyone, everybody, no one, anyone,* and *each* are worth mentioning, though any prolonged discussion is best reserved for later on.

9. *Remember that joining two singular subjects with "and" makes the subject plural.*

In the sentence

A desk and an old lamp stand in the room

the words "a desk and an old lamp" make the subject plural, despite the fact that there is no plural marker on either word. Here the marker is *and.* For the need for instruction in the tricky *either . . . or, neither . . . nor* connectors, assess the level of the class, but in general it's best to avoid much discussion of the principles governing these special cases.

10. *When sentences require "it is," "here is," "there are," "there were," look for the subject <u>after</u> the verb in order to determine which form to use.*

Offer sentences to illustrate these points. Ask students then to write original sentences that open with the constructions just considered—provide singular and plural nouns as required subjects for the sentences.

11. Beware of singular or plural words that appear between the subject and the verb in a sentence.
In this sentence

The rain on the rooftops disturbs me

ask the class to point out the verb. Ask someone to name the subject. Someone will say *rooftops:* immediately ask the student to comment on the verb form. If *rooftops* is indeed the subject (a plural one), why is *disturbs* singular? Lead the class to see that the subject is *rain.* Why did someone pick out *rooftops* as the subject? (Remind the class of an earlier exercise you did together, expanding a sentence by adding modifiers between subject and verb.) Students should see that usual word order in English sentences places the subject right before the verb and it is *familiarity* with a principle that works successfully in many cases that ultimately causes trouble for the writer. Here the student is being consistent but the *language* is not!

If the class is familiar with prepositional phrases, show how those structures frequently appear between subject and verb: when the number of the last word in a prepositional phrase is different from the number demanded by the subject and verb of the sentence, one can easily get confused. And, of course, the correct structure will frequently not sound correct to the student's ear. After pointing out that sound is not a good test, given most students' spoken language system, try to provide practice in speaking and in hearing these structures when they are correct. Ask the class to make a list of prepositional phrases (write it on the chalkboard) ending in singular or plural nouns or pronouns. Then offer several kernel sentences and experiment by embedding prepositional phrases between subject and verb. Or, offer a subject followed by a prepositional phrase whose object has different number from the subject; give the infinitive of the verb that students need to change to the correct present tense form. Students should then complete the sentences as in the examples below:

A plate of candies (to be) ————————————·
Three quarts of milk (to have) ————————————·

As I pointed out before, the needs of individual students in the class will determine the depth of study of these principles—and, in some cases, even *whether* the study ought to be undertaken at all.

From all the pages I've taken just to draw some of the boundaries of this particular concept, you can see how complex and extensive instruction will have to be for many students. Students' needs vary and are not completely predictable. For sufficient exercises to meet these varied needs, establish your own file of worksheets labeled according to their specific function in reinforcing elements in the concept of agreement.

When you provide extensive follow-up and review, it's useful to choose from among the exercises in Shaughnessy's plan:

1. verb selection that requires the student to justify each choice
2. substitution exercises in which the writer shifts from singular to plural
3. analysis of verb forms in increasingly complex passages
4. proofreading for erroneous forms in prepared passages
5. proofreading of passages written by the student on topics designed to elicit the -s form—"Write a paragraph that begins 'This is the way my friend spends his Saturday afternoons.' "
6. proofreading for subject-verb agreement. It's especially important for a student with serious problems in this area to pay careful attention to -s forms. He should proofread for one error at a time, focusing upon -s forms in one reading, then rereading for a different type of error common in his own writing. In reading for agreement students might number their subjects and verbs:

                1   2   2
The woman who lives next door has five children,
                3   3
but only one of them lives at home.

For many students, errors in agreement will be the most persistent, and its principles the most evanescent. The more you break down the separate elements of the agreement concept and the more you ask students to practice those elements in original sentences, the closer you'll bring the class to understanding.

• Dangling and Misplaced Modifiers

In an earlier introduction of the participial phrase (the -*ing* or -*ed* word group) as a syntactic option for compressing ideas, you were careful to suggest to the student the need to place the modifying element correctly near the word it describes. I suggested that you try to anticipate the dangling modifier. Despite this, however, the first group of papers in which students consciously strive to open sentences with participial structures will no doubt show a number of dangling constructions. You need to make clear that there is nothing obscene about such constructions, merely that they are sometimes unclear because they do not say what the writer wants them to say. The best reason to avoid dangling modifiers is that they distract careful readers who perceive them as clumsy and do not expect to find them in good writing.

Select from your students' papers two or three sentences with dangling modifiers. One sentence should, if possible, achieve a humorous or even an absurd dislocation of meaning because of the incorrectly placed construction. The other sentence or two, however, should not seem ridiculous because of the dangling modifier, but instead unclear, ambiguous, and distracting. All too often the dangling construction on the student's paper is not of the outstandingly humorous or strange kind (and often there is no real question about intended meaning), so instruction should not suggest that this error stands out always for its absurdity.

One approach to the problem of dangling modifiers is to present without comment the incorrect sentence alongside a correct one, a participial construction as the sentence opener:

1	2
Dressed in a new overcoat, a car brushed against me and soiled my sleeve.	Dressed in a new overcoat, I brushed against a car and soiled my sleeve.

What difference in meaning do students discern between these two sentences? Remind the class that, whether or not it is intended, the first noun or pronoun after the verb-part opener is automatically its subject, the word being described by the participial structure. Sentence 1 does not say what the writer wants it to say: there, the car is dressed in an overcoat.

After students see the ambiguity created in other dangling constructions, offer suggestions for correcting the error. Caution the class about stylistic losses that result simply from changing the participial phrase into a subordinate clause or some other structure. Participles enhance the clear expression of ideas; they offer an option for sentence variety; and they are not to be avoided, but simply to be used carefully. It is important to show how participial structures in sentence positions other than those at the beginning similarly need to stand near the word the writer actually *wants* described.

Students who misplace other modifiers will need instruction in how a word or a group of words placed in different sentence positions can alter meaning. After initial comments on the problems in clarity created by the misplaced modifier in general, try to find some pattern within each student's errors. Instructors must speak directly to the kinds of mistakes students make. During correction workshops, group several writers who do not place modifiers correctly and teach members of the group about their errors.

• Tense

You have already seen in the discussion on agreement how enormously complex the verb is for beginning writers. The brief comments there on auxiliaries illustrate one small area of the problem students face when they need to deal with tense. Add to those difficulties the elaborate tense network in English and the complications involving *mood* and *voice* (concepts beyond the goals of this course), and the verb is indeed a puzzling grammatical unit.

First efforts in dealing with tense in the classroom are to accept the distinction Shaughnessy makes "between the closed linguistic network whereby certain kinds of time relationships are built into the verb system (*tense*) and the larger experience of time that seems to begin with infancy and culminate in adult perceptions that are too subtle and various for us to describe or fully explain (*time*)."

With such a distinction it is easier to realize that you are not teaching students about time—they know about it quite well—but that you are describing in general how a specific tense system works by pointing out and listing the parts of that system; by guiding the writer to see how those parts are combined; by enumerating the irregularities in the system; and by building a sixth sense about the use of the less familiar tenses.

In learning about tenses writers need both to understand the formal system for producing tense changes and to develop intuitions for tense combinations in a range of situations. You can make few assumptions about the students' knowledge of grammatical tense; you cannot assume, further, that any set of concepts that seem easy is indeed easy for inexperienced writers. The -*ed* inflection for past tense verbs, for example, though seemingly simple, presents many problems. First, it frequently vanishes in speech. ("He laugh*ed* *t*oo hard.") It is redundant in sentences in which other words indicate time. (*"Yesterday* he laughed too hard.") Further, one does not find it particularly helpful to know the "regular" past tense formation since the language depends so much upon strong irregular verbs (*be, go, have, take, speak,* and so on). Finally, many different grammatical structures demand the *-ed* ending—all the perfect tenses for regular verbs, many passive constructions, adjectives.

Many students need to examine situations in which the *-ed* inflection is *not* required. To avoid structures like "She can laugh*ed*" you need to consider that modal auxiliaries (*shall, will, would, could, may, must*) combine with the *stem* form of the verb, not with the *participial.* But the range of individual misconceptions about verb forms within the tense system is impossible even to suggest with teaching strategies. The teacher's analysis of an individual student's errors with tense is the only workable means for approaching the problem. The teacher must, therefore, possess a grab bag of possibilities for good instruction: grammatical explanations, practice in speaking and writing, *time* to allow the complex features to sink into the understanding. Students' peculiar errors with verbs are often the result of *thinking* and not of carelessness or irrationality. Helping students master the verb system, Shaughnessy says, "depends upon being able to trace the line of reasoning that has led to erroneous choices rather than unloading on the student's memory an indifferent bulk of information about verbs, only part of which relates to his difficulties."

With such advice it is hard to proceed in offering even a rough program for specific lessons on tense, lessons that must be rooted in errors students make. However, you can teach some general principles of tense formation, can demonstrate the meanings certain tense forms impose upon verbs, and can drill in oral and written activities those verbs most often confused.

At the start of the discussion on tense, review the concepts developed when the class considered subject-verb agreement. Look at some sentences in which the same verb serves in different tense forms:

The boys *laugh.*	The boys *speak.*
The boys *laughed.*	The boys *spoke.*
The boys *have laughed.*	The boys *have spoken.*

Ask someone to comment on each sentence. What kind of information does each tense form offer? Tell the class that in order to explain more easily the tense system we call attention to some important parts of a verb, the parts that help us make all the tenses. Start with the infinitives *to laugh* and *to speak.* Define *infinitive,* perhaps as the starting point of the verb, the form that always has *to* in front of it, the form that allows us to make the parts that work in the tense system. Students have used infinitives before in activities of combining and embedding. Present examples from Spanish or French to show how the infinitive operates in another language. Then prepare columns, each column headed with an explanation. The traditional names of the principal parts appear below the more useful functional labels:

1	2	3	4	5
"to" form (*infinitive*)	base (present tense)	*past tense*	form used with *has* or *have* (past participle)	*-ing* form (present participle)
to laugh	laugh	laughed	laughed	laughing

Working with one column at a time, demonstrate in sentences the tenses formed from each part. Explain their meanings; ask students to create original sentences with other verbs in the same tense you illustrate. Make sure the class understands the range of meanings and uses for each tense before you move on to the next.

2
He *laughs* ⎫   Present (use the form of the verb from
They *laugh* ⎭   Column 2b)
I *will* (shall) *laugh*   Future (use *will* + the verb from
            Column 2b)
They can (*may, shall, will, must, could, should*) laugh (use one of the modal auxiliaries with the verb from Column 2)

3
He *laughed*
They *laughed*   *Past (use the form of the verb from Column 3)*

4
a. He *has laughed*
b. He *had laughed* before the show started
c. Before next week she *will have laughed* at all the silly jokes in the book

This group of continuing action tenses in 4 needs explanation—and it is probably a good idea to *avoid* those traditional complex names like *present perfect, past perfect,* or *future perfect.* The verb in a. says that the action began in the past but may go on into the present. This tense is formed by using *has* or *have* with the verb form from Column 4. In b. the verb *had laughed* says the action began in the past but ended before another action in the past. This tense we form by using *had* with the verb form from Column 4. In c. *will have laughed* says the action will be finished before some definite time in the future. This tense we form by using *will have* or *shall have* with the verb form from Column 4. Some students in the class may need drill on the correct use of *to have* in the present tense, so be prepared to offer it if necessary. In general, the perfect tenses are extremely difficult to explain, so you need to rely upon many examples in order to build a sense of when to use the correct verb. It won't help much to teach students all the conditions for use and then to expect easy compliance with them.

When someone points out that Columns 3 and 4 have

verbs with the same form, turn to other examples with *to speak*. Explain the notion of *irregularity* in the verb system, even mentioning briefly how a language assimilates forms and how words change through time. Explain that many errors students make with verbs often result from inconsistencies of the language, not from any lack of logic shown by the writer. Thus someone who writes

He has *ate*

They have *chose*

is using the past tense form (the writer is smart enough to know that the verb is irregular), which for *most* verbs is the same as the Column 4 form (the past participle). A writer who offers

We teached him a lesson

is trying to form a past tense in the way that past tenses are usually formed. In a sentence like

I sung a song

the writer *knows* that irregular forms exist for the verb *to sing* but just has not used the form according to the demands of the tense system. (Some verbs have alternate forms which are correct: *speeded* for *sped,* dreamt for *dreamed,* and *shined* for *shone.*)

Look with the class at a few irregular verbs and offer practice, which includes speaking, listening, and writing the tenses in original sentences. Don't go over all those irregular verbs listed in columns in the texts; do a few at a time or have different groups working with different sets of verbs, students planning their own practice exercises to exchange with other groups. Always ask students to use these forms in original sentences.

In discussing the *-ing* verb form, remind students of the need for auxiliaries made from *to be.* Perhaps a set of review charts based upon the kinds of helping verbs demanded by the forms of a main verb would be helpful.

"will" helpers + base of verb (Column 2)		*"has"* helpers + Column 4 verb	
will		has	
shall		have	
could	laugh	had	laughed
should	sing	will have	sung
might	+ tell	shall have +	told
would	drink	should have	drunk
may		could have	
can		must have	
must		might have	
		would have	

"to be" helpers + *-ing form* (*column 5*)

is		
was		
are		
were		laughing
will have *been*		singing
would have *been*	+	telling
should have *been*		drinking
could have *been*		
might have *been*		
must have been		

With these charts before them the class should propose original sentences using different tense structures with troublesome verbs.

Students whose first language is not English will require even more elaborate instruction and practice than those suggested by this overview. More good English-as-a-second-language textbooks appear each year; check those for varied activities you can adapt to the special needs of students in your class.

CAPITAL LETTERS

Another system that seems arbitrary and confusing to the beginning writer is the system of capitalization. Basic writers often do show a logic in their use of upper and lower case letters, but it is a logic that often runs counter to Edited American English. For emphasis or for no reason other than idiosyncratic handwriting style, the writer on this level usually uses a superfluity of capitals. One aspect of confusion is related, no doubt, to the students' misperceptions of the rules for sentence boundaries. Thus the capital letter works either alone or with commas to signal some kind of closure or new or tentative beginning for which the writer has not learned to adapt the demands of syntax.

Last year I hated school Now I like it.

Last year I hated school, Now I like it.

When the wind blows The Children go indoors.

Other errors show a misapplication of one or the other (or both) of the rules for using capitals with nouns or pronouns: the word *I* demands an upper case letter at all times (but not the other subject pronouns unless they open sentences); and names of people require capital letters (though not the pronouns that replace those people's names):

When You go to the Park i will meet You there with My sister.

And there is certainly confusion with this concept as it is usually taught—"Capitalize proper nouns"—when proper nouns are explained as the *exact* name of something. Thus the student is mystified about why *robin,* which is the exact name of a *bird,* is not capitalized while *Empire State Building,* the exact name of a *building,* is. Sometimes it is merely a favorite word or idea that the student will capitalize without reason.

As with all instruction in mechanical and grammatical aspects of basic skills, the best approach will seek to discover a pattern in the student's errors. Often, extensive instruction in all the uses of capitals is not useful to the student who does not understand the relationship between a period and a capital letter, or the student who capitalizes subject pronouns because he perceives them as people's names. Frequently, the program of instruction in capitals for many students will proceed successfully and through conference with the writing teacher or with the tutor in the Writing Center (see pp. 196–204). Often it is merely a matter of pointing out to the writer how distracting it is for the reader to be subjected to a peculiar pattern of capital letters; and simple practice in the conventions of handwriting will help the student see his errors in perspective.

Instruction in capitalization proceeds better by demonstration than by rule. One good way is to prepare a set of boxes that group similar applications of some feature of the system of capitalization, for example, geography, areas and directions, writing letters, titles, buildings, and organizations. Each title above a box names a category; the illustrations often show both the accepted use and exceptions or possible confusions for beginning writers.

Days, Months, Seasons, Celebrations	*No Capitals for Plants, Animals, Games*	
Monday	daisies	a vicious lion
April	sycamore tree	baseball
spring, summer, fall	an old oak	football
autumn, winter	bananas	swimming
Election Day	a bluebird	monkeys
Festival of Lights	six sparrows	apple
New Year's Eve		

An overhead projector is especially useful for this demonstration.

Explain each box one at a time, asking students to supply further illustrations from their own language resources.

Where convention demands exclusion of capitals, spend extra time—these are areas bound to trip up the writer.

Textbooks offer exercises which attempt to apply these illustrations: there will be practices that ask students to write in the first letter of words in a sentence——e bought a new ⸺hevrolet and drove it ⸺ast on ⸺llen ⸺treet ⸺uesday—and those that ask that corrections be made where capitals are incorrectly used—The Child sneezed when he smelled a Rose at the house on York avenue. (Students enjoy making up their own exercises of the type just considered.) Shaughnessy suggests providing practice in modernizing the punctuation of earlier writers. And rewriting advertising copy from newspapers or magazines helps students apply correct conventions of capitalization to eye-catching but irregular uses. But the most effective practice asks the writer to demonstrate with his own written language how well he understands the concepts. A dictated exercise like this will achieve that end:

- Write a sentence that names the bank you do business with.
- If you could fly anywhere, in which direction would you go? Write a full sentence.
- Write a sentence that tells your three strongest subjects.
- What is the name of your former school? Write a full sentence.
- In which geographical area of the United States would you like to live? Write a full sentence.
- Write a sentence that names your favorite flower.
- Write a sentence that names the street on which you live.
- Write a sentence that names your favorite sport and that tells something about it briefly.
- Write a sentence about a river that goes through your state. Name the river in your sentence.
- Tell in a sentence about your favorite television program.

POSSESSION

As with the -*ed* on past tense words, the -*s* inflection on nouns (for plural and possessive alike) is lost easily in speech, especially when the sounds—as in *desks* or *wrists*— are hard for the speaker to make. Add to that the fact that the distinction between plural and singular possessive is a function of writing alone (we cannot tell when someone speaks if he means *the boy's hats* or *the boys' hats*); that inexperienced writers somehow fancy the apostrophe and use it idiosyncratically when a word ends in *s* or when they wish to indicate plural (*three book's*); that the apostrophe serves another function, that of indicating omission of letters in contractions like *can't* and *it's*—and it is clear why the correct use of possessive forms seems such an extraordinary puzzle to beginning writers.

Though it may *seem* logical to relate instruction in possession to concepts of plurality and singularity, students are often unncessarily confused by that approach. In the presentation I have found most successful, when students consider the rule for possession they look *only* at the last letter of the word they need to convert into possessive form.

But first you need to introduce the idea of possession without suggesting that it's anything simple or pat. (And don't be surprised if some students do not know what an apostrophe looks like nor how to make it or name it correctly.)

So much of the use of possessive forms relates to aspects of genitive with unclear indications of ownership. It is hard, for example, to explain that the inflected noun in the word groups below really owns anything:

an hour's time

the world's problems

New York's appeal

two dollars' worth

Begin by examining the concept of possession as people understand it in English, using where you can other languages like Spanish or French or Italian for contrastive in-struction. Present to the class a few sentences that suggest ownership without apostrophes, sentences in which the noun may clearly be thought of as possessing an object or idea. Then show a sentence with the noun inflected to in-dicate possession.

It is the car of the lawyer.

It is the car owned by the lawyer.

It is the car belonging to the lawyer.

It is the lawyer's car.

Ask students to read the sentences aloud. What do they all try to indicate? How is the quality of possession suggested in each sentence? Make sure someone points out for each sentence the thing owned and the person who is owning it. Which sentence sounds best to the class? Most will reject the first as awkward. Though the second and third appear frequently they are not as economical as the last. Point out in the last that the *'s* on the noun shows ownership in the ways that words like "owned by" and "belonging to" do. Point out how, in the construction with the apostrophe, the owner is usually named before the thing being owned. (It is worth pointing out later on, when students have mastered the concept, this form:

The car is the *lawyer's.*

Did you see that car? It is the *lawyer's.*)

For the moment concentrate on two separate ideas that usually inhere in possessive constructions:

- somebody or something is the owner—that word will have an apostrophe;
- something or somebody is being owned—that word usually comes after the word with the apostrophe.

Before offering practice in recognizing owner and owned, provide an example of an inflected noun that is less clearly an owner in the sense you have defined it. Select from one of these phrases perhaps:

the <u>nation's</u> youth

<u>love's</u> pains

<u>day's</u> end

Why does the language demand a possessive form for the underlined words? How do those words differ in meaning from the inflected form *lawyer's?*

Now offer an exercise in which students identify in sentences or phrases both the word that shows ownership and the word for the thing being owned. Or, make two columns, one of words with correct possessive forms, another with words to indicate objects that could be owned. Ask students to match them and then to create their own sentences.

You are not yet ready to introduce the two basic rules for possession. It is first necessary to remind students about how apostrophes are *not* used. Since the most characteristic misuse of the apostrophe appears when writers make plurals of nouns, indicate that apostrophes have *no* role in plural formation. (The exceptions—pluralizing letters or numbers—are rare enough to exclude mention at this point.) Provide a typical error of this sort:

He earned two college diploma's.

The store sells pencil's and pen's.

Why are the inflected forms incorrect? What does the apostrophe signify? How does the meaning of the sentence present a possessive sense? Why have the writers used apostrophes? Now provide a mixed list of inflected nouns of two types—one, singular possessives; the other, simple plurals—for students to use in sentences:

child's   turkey's
boys   turkeys
boy's

Or, list sentences where apostrophes are used incorrectly to show plural and ask students to make changes.

The easiest way to teach the two basic rules for possession is to present them one at a time, to make the presentation as visual as possible, and to offer lots of practice before going on to the next rule.

The first principle of possession states that if the word that will name the owner does *not* end in *s,* the writer should add an *'s.* Show examples:

The gir*l*'s dress is torn.

The child*ren*'s bicycles disappeared.

A count*ry*'s strength is in its people.

Ask students to point out the thing being owned and the person or object owning. In each example call attention to the last letter of the word before it was converted into possessive form. Make clear that whether or not the word is singular or plural is not important (*children* is an uninflected plural form)—the point is that the word does not end in *s* and that the rule calls for *'s* if the word does not end in *s.* Drill the rule with exercises.

The second principle states that if the word that will name the owner *does* end in *s,* the writer needs to add only an apostrophe:

Mr. Harr*is*' fence broke.

The studen*ts*' holiday ended early.

In these cases the word, before it was inflected, ended in *s*—it doesn't matter that *Harris* is singular or that *students* is plural. The rule tells us to look at the last letter of the word that will show possession. Drill this rule, too, with exercises.

It's a good idea to point out (by way of review) the steps a writer might need to go through in coming up with the correct possessive form. In writing a sentence that sounded in his head this way—"The ladies' club met on Tuesday"—the writer would have to say first, "How many ladies am I talking about?" He'd have to know how to spell the correct plural form if he meant more than one lady. Then he'd have to make sure the word *required* a possessive form; once assured, he'd apply one or the other of the rules. Go through a few examples with the class in this way, tracing the steps one often needs to take for correct possessive forms.

Practice exercises should be varied. Dictation is excellent for building skills; offer some ambiguous possessives (like the *boy's hats*) so that students need to use their own judgments in making choices and need to defend their choices. Provide a list of nouns to which students can apply the two rules you have illustrated:

Word	*'s or '?*	*Example*
Doris	'	Doris' house
child	's	the child's toy
children		
lady		
ladies		
woman		
women		
person		
people		

(Some stylebooks insist that *singular* nouns ending in /s- or /z/ require an *'s*—and admit exceptions like *Jesus, Moses,* classical names, and so on. To the basic writer this would be unneeded fussiness and confusion. Though you might point out that other uses do appear, the two principles you have taught are both correct and easy to remember.)

Students will require special attention to these concepts in regard to possession:

1. *time* and *money* words. Explain the conventions of the inflected forms

    a *quarter's* worth
    two *days'* work
    three *dollars' worth*

2. *pronouns.* Consider the possessive pronouns, which to many native speakers are redundancies. In the use of pronouns apostrophes rarely show possession (*one's* idea, *anyone's* dream): when apostrophes appear with pronouns the mark of punctuation usually indicates omission of letters in a contraction:

> *It's* raining.
> *Who's* there?
> *That's* his.

After discussing these two special cases and before providing exercises for review, present a chart on this order:

REVIEW: IF YOU THINK A WORD NEEDS AN APOSTROPHE BECAUSE IT SHOWS POSSESSION:

1. See if you can figure out what is being owned.
2. See if the word in which you want to use an apostrophe is the owner of something. Usually, the thing owned appears in the sentence soon after the owner.

> Exceptions: It is David's.
> We ate at Carl's.

> Here the thing owned is not specifically mentioned, but understood.

> David's (book)
> Carl's (house)

3. Sometimes the owner is more than one. Make sure the word shows plural with the right ending.

> a. If the word does not end in *s*, add an *'s*.
> b. If the word does end in *s*, add an apostrophe.

> Example: a. You want to show that a boy owns books. The word *boy* does not end in *s*. The possessive is shown this way:
>   the boy's books (add *'s*)
> b. You want to show that many boys are the owners of books. The word *boys* ends in *s*. The possessive is shown this way:
>   the boys' books (add apostrophe after *s*)

COMMAS

Because you introduced the comma at each stage of instruction in embedding and expanding sentences, there is no need for elaborate lessons on the use of commas in all its positions. You have already dealt with comma use in these places:

- in series
- after introductory elements (logical connectives and subordinated elements including participial structures)
- with appositives
- with interrupters (logical connectives, subordinated elements, participial structures)
- with direct quotations

If the writer integrates the correct use of the comma with the particular sentence he is constructing, it makes it unnecessary to introduce complicated rules for comma use. Selecting those areas in which the class makes the most errors, review the principles which will help students see those errors. Again do not concern yourself with mastery of restrictive and nonrestrictive constructions, though you will want to point out how meaning is often seriously affected by the use of the commas within certain sentences. Perhaps you can offer a review chart for uses of commas not yet covered.

Some Familiar Places for Commas

1. In dates, after everything but the month:
   On April 17, 1970, my life began.
       (commas)

   On Saturday, May 7, 1971, Alexander's Department Store had a sale on men's suits.   (commas)

2. In an address: (comma)
   A riot occurred in Brooklyn, New York.

Atlanta, Georgia, has many qualities of Northern big cities.

(commas)

3. Before and after someone's title if the title comes after
   the name:
   Carl Berkson, Ph.D., practices psychology in Los Angeles.

   (commas)

   Dr. Smithers has retired.

   (no comma)

4. To set off someone's name, if that person is being spoken
   to in the sentence:
   Carol, why don't you do your assignment?

   (commas)

   I understand, Mr. Harrington, that you cannot pay this last
   installment.

5. In informal letters, after the opening words and the
   words before the signature:
   Dear Martin,
   Dear Carl,   (commas)
   Yours sincerely,
   Very truly yours,

   Hint: In a formal
   letter, use a colon
   after the salutation.
   Dear Mr. Porter:
   Dear Senator Byrd:

6. To set off a variety of numbers:

   (comma)

   six feet, three inches
   19,385 students

   (comma)

These special uses should receive no undue stress.

For review exercises in comma use, ask questions that
require students to generate their own sentence responses:

1. Write a sentence that you might speak to a friend. Use
   his or her name at the beginning of the sentence.
2. Write a complete sentence that tells your street address,
   your city, and your state.
3. Write a sentence that tells the name of some well-known

author. Use the words *a famous author* after the person's name.
4. Write two *complete* sentences about the kinds of classes you like. Use *and* or *but* to separate the sentences.
5. Write a complete sentence that tells *three* television programs you like to watch. Use the word *and* only once.
6. Write a complete sentence about some singer you enjoy. Use the words *whose voice I like* somewhere in the sentence.
7. Write a quotation sentence about something you said to one of your friends today. Use the words *I said* somewhere in the sentence.
8. Write a sentence about two things you like to do during the summer. Use *although, when, if, while,* or *because* at the beginning of the sentence.
9. Write a sentence of advice to someone who has never walked along a country road at night. Start your sentence with either of these word groups: *Walking along a country road* or *To walk along a country road.*
10. Use *however, nevertheless, on the other hand,* or *moreover* after the word *believed* in this sentence: We all believed that she was lying.

PRONOUNS

Students who make serious errors in pronoun usage are responding to what is a more complicated system than need be. Black English vernacular, in a probable move toward simplicity, will juxtapose pronoun and noun to show possession (*at they party*). The existence of some pronouns that do not change to indicate case, number, or gender suggests that other pronouns may similarly be used, context and word position alone determining case, number, and gender. Further, many pronoun forms are redundant: what's happening with *who–whom* indicates possibilities that other forms may lose ground.

None of this is to justify incorrect usage, but merely to suggest again that student error results from thinking, from using a pattern which often does not follow—for whatever reason—the conventions of the language.

Though undoubtedly students in different geographical areas will show different kinds and degrees of pronoun errors, two types of mistakes, because of their frequency in the papers of inexperienced writers, need attention.

One problem is with antecedents and all the ways pronouns are tied to them. Students often use *they* or *he* as pronouns that can refer to singular or plural antecedents of either gender. This tendency points up an omission in the system: though third person singular pronouns respect gender (*he, she*), the plural pronoun (*they*) does not. *They* becomes an easy alternative, the word itself carrying no strong sense of plurality. And this usage is gaining ground everywhere in spoken language. A further result of the writer's tendency to blur the service of pronouns is the frequent shift in person. Shaughnessy sees this as an unstable sense of the writer-audience relationship, the shift to *you* signifying a more direct sense of audience. One example of this uncertain sense appears in this sentence: "A lot of people have been told if *they* want a good job *you* have to stay in school."

Depending upon the student's level of misunderstanding, instruction should clarify first the uses of the different pronouns, with special attention provided—where necessary— to the third person singular and plural. Comparisons to pronoun systems in other languages are very helpful. Spend some time on the generalized singular pronouns used so frequently in academic discourse—*he, one, everyone*. But do not fuss over the "Everyone should hand in his paper"; rather, explain how this use is in flux among educated people, and how *everyone* despite its singular form conveys in speech a sense of plurality which is changing the "rule." Formal written English still adheres to *everyone–he*, but for the writer on this level do not expect mastery of this rule. You want further to indicate the changing nature of language by discussing claims of sexism in pronoun use.

Another problem related to incorrect antecedents involves

the inexperienced writer's assumption that the reader will understand and recognize the referent for each pronoun he sees. Thus you might read:

The child's ball rolled into the garden and it looked strange.

Colorful audio visual presentations with varied inks for pronoun and antecedent will make graphic the chain of grammatical interrelationships that a writer constructs as he moves across the page. And sometimes an antecedent logically occurs after its referring pronoun:

Observing them unguarded, Caroline snatched the racquets and ran away.

Another characteristic problem involves inappropriate use of subject and object pronouns. Dealing first with the subject pronoun, present the singular and plural forms and indicate what happens if the subject is incorrectly compounded. Thus, though we'd never see "Me run" or "Him runs," we might indeed see "Him and me run on the golf course every Sunday." Teach the skill of correct pronoun selection in a compound subject by giving this hint to students:

Test each subject *alone* before you decide which pronoun to use. For example, suppose you do not know whether to use *her* or *she* in the blank space in this sentence:

My mother and _____ rushed into the house.

First say:
My mother rushed into the house.

Then say:
Her rushed into the house.
That would never sound right.

Then say:
She rushed into the house.
That is correct. Now combine the two subjects from the first and third sentences:

My mother and she rushed into the house.

Practice should include oral and written activities in which students select the correct pronoun for a subject position and generate their own sentences with correct subject pronouns as parts of compounds.

In dealing with object pronouns, present the list to the class and show how each corresponds to a subject pronoun. Then treat the pronoun as it functions as verb completer and as object of preposition. Few students will ever select a subject pronoun for the object position except when the pronoun is a part of a compound. Offer lessons that follow the pattern of instruction for compound subjects.

Students need practice in the use of prepositions and prepositional phrases. Some students may be unfamiliar with these as grammatical units, though the relational words themselves will not be unfamiliar. You might want to offer a list of several of the most important prepositions:

about, by	except, at	within, since	by way of
beneath	under, onto	beside, as to	by means of
inside	across, on	toward, at	because of
outside,	over, into	beyond, up	along with
above, for	after, to	before, like	in spite of
among, of	with, along	below, upon	in front of
	between	through	

Even inexperienced writers know how to use these as lead words in word groups like *by the lake, among friends, over the small gray bridge,* so your intention here is not to teach prepositional phrases as grammatical entities that one must underline in sentences or paragraphs. You can illustrate how the prepositional phrase offers a writer options for alternate expression and for variety in sentence order. For example, compare with the class the differences achieved in these sentences:

1	2
The tall, blonde, smiling woman rushed away.	With a smile the tall blonde woman rushed away.
	The tall woman rushed away with a smile.
	The tall woman with a smile rushed away.

Point out the flexibility of the prepositional phrase in allowing the writer to exercise stylistic options though not always without changes in meaning; and point out how too many adjectives before the noun make the prose dense, and how the prepositional phrase allows for a looser structure.

In this chapter on language I have explored the several possible routes to correctness in writing. If the material seems extensive, let me say without cynicism that I've left out enough to fill books. Individual problems by individual writers demand individual instruction and the experienced teacher has at his fingertips the most resources possible.

4

Support Services

Despite its potential for achieving broad educational objectives with heterogenous audiences, the traditional classroom setting has its limitations. Especially for basic skills students, who may for years have suffered schoolrooms with failure and disappointment, the need is acute to develop alternate learning environments. Toward that end my call for collaborative activities is an attempt to shift the teaching-learning spotlight away from the familiar instructor's stage in front of the room. But that general technique and others like it aimed at modifying the classroom scene in any course are too much to treat here and must be the subject of another book.

In this chapter, if I may borrow from Francis Bacon's language, I want to deal with instruments and helps for the beginning writer both within and without the classroom. After some preaching that you may have already heard from me for the creative use of nonprint media, I will deal here with writing centers, the tutorial setting now offered by many institutions as classroom adjuncts for beginners; and with the important, private conference between writer and writing teacher. Supporting day-to-day instruction are audio visuals, learning centers, and the conference—valuable supplements to any beginner's program.

AUDIO VISUALS: MACHINES AND PROJECTS

As a means of providing alternate instructional strategies, audio visual machines available to the teacher of writing can breathe life into the classroom. Besides, they save time and money: a single exercise on the overhead projector can economically replace dittoed pages for fifty students; notes co-

pied tediously onto a chalkboard with your back to the class
can be written instead with felt tip pen on plastic, enlarged
behind you by a projector as you face your students. Commercially prepared transparencies in English language skills,
slides or film strips and accompanying sound tracks on cassettes, records, video cassettes, films—these, wisely used to
complement instruction, are magical elements for students
lost too easily in the barrage of words demanded by lecture
or class discussion. For experienced teachers of beginning
writers, photography, television, film, and multimedia presentations are no strangers.

And yet for too many institutions the Audio Visual Service
Center is the institution's graveyard of lights and motors
dead long before their prime. At a community college in up-
state New York I watched a media services director display a
dazzling supply of educational technology—which, he noted
wryly, few teachers ever used. Sparkling new, exteriors
shiny, after daily dustings the machines slept day and night
the sleep of the unfulfilled.

Of course this director might have arranged for frequent
demonstrations in the use of the machinery by visiting departments, by explaining technology simply, by inviting faculty questions and experimentation. Sadly, however, few institutions provide adequate orientation to technology, so the
burden for learning is essentially on the instructor. The
sooner you meet the person at your school in charge of
audio visual equipment, the sooner you can start trying
things out. If you're like most people I know passionately involved with words and language, you suspect classroom machines, sense a conspiracy among them against your ability
to take command, feel weak kneed and clumsy and just plain
stupid in flicking a switch and in having to interact with a
hunk of metal. Yet the only way to rid yourself of machine
angst is to be a pest about learning how to use whatever
technology your school owns. Refusing to learn will set you
apart from students warm to visual and auditory stimulation.
Help the media services director set up weekly or biweekly
sessions for you and your colleagues. Get your hands on

those machines! Get familiar with the roar of the opaque projector which, despite its abilities to enlarge original pages and illustrations, makes you shout above it, your room in darkness. Try out various writing implements, grease pencils or felt tip pens, for the versatile overhead projector. Learn how to thread an 8- or a 16-millimeter film projector, a video tape machine, a reel-to-reel tape recorder. Discover how to rescue from disaster a session that stubs its toe on a machine that fails. Return to the media center frequently for more instruction.

If you're bored or anxious or depressed about having to take time to do all this, think of the dividends you will collect on these hours throughout your teaching career. Lest I seem needlessly to stress skills any new teacher would seek by instinct to develop, I have to report after many years of observing classroom instructors that not many capitalize upon the machine's potential as time saver and teaching assistant. It's the rare (and often the wonderful) teacher who turns to anything other than a blizzard of handouts—dittos, xeroxes, mimeographed objects—as instructional aids.

No Pollyanna about instructional media, I do have cautions to add. Bringing network television and commercially prepared slides, movies, or filmstrips into the classroom will not replace the tedious, discouraging process of learning to write, despite the seductions of electronic media. Too often a teacher, relying upon them for instruction, expects class members to harvest their own rewards. Lights go out; for half an hour or so students sit transfixed by flickering images and seductive sound tracks; lights go on; and efforts at discussion limp along, stimulated weakly by questions like "What did you think?" Just as in a reading or a writing task, without defining precisely just what the effort should yield, teachers shift a responsibility that is theirs into students' hands. Guide questions, comments before viewing, statements of objectives so everyone knows the kinds of outcomes expected of the experience—only such efforts make audio visuals into true classroom assets.

Beyond the use of professional media productions,

teachers of beginning writers are wise to encourage them to compose in nonwritten media, as a prelude to a written exercise. By nonwritten media I mean such diverse and original efforts as simple photographs on topics of interest, collages, photo essays made from newspaper and magazine presentations or from the student's own still or slide photography, original cassette recordings, student-made slide and tape multimedia productions, and other compositions that in their final forms can be independent of written vocabulary and syntax. When writing disappoints or even frightens the beginning writer for one reason or another, you can provide an intermediate means for him to convey his sensory responses. Nonwritten, often nonverbal, compositions allow students to grapple with creative instincts in a visual or auditory medium even before writing begins.

I have explained in detail elsewhere (see the Bibliography) a way to challenge writers with an assignment that leads first to media compositions and then to written themes based upon the same assignment. In that essay I also pointed out how other nonwritten compositions could precede—not supplant—some traditional activities offered in writing programs. Let me repeat, without attempting a comprehensive listing, some interesting possibilities for individual or group presentations in the media, presentations stimulated by traditional exercises for building rhetorical skills. Of course, written assignments always follow the media projects.

Rhetorical Skill	*Media Composition before the Written Exercise*
Description of a place	1. Visit some place which conveys a sharp impression—*quiet, noisiness, activity*, etc. Convey that impression with a camera and a tape recorder. 2. Prepare a collage on a place you know well, one which you can convey vividly in visual terms.

Narration	Prepare a photo essay (with your camera or with newspaper or magazine cutouts) in which you relate a story about a robbery, a day in the country, a train ride, a walk in the city at night.
Comparison-Contrast	1. In a photo essay, dramatize wealth and poverty in your community. 2. The high school student and the college student: record on a cassette the impressions, opinions, interests offered by students on each of these levels.
Argumentation	1. Invent a commercial product. Prepare three advertisements in which you attempt to convince people to buy your product. 2. Take pictures in your community in order to illustrate your opinion on a key social issue: pollution, women's liberation, urban problems, traffic. Prepare a sound track with words and music on tape cassette to accompany your visual presentation.
Description of a person	1. Prepare a collage which will introduce someone you know—relative, friend—to the people of the class. 2. Ask a volunteer to stand before the class and speak for five minutes about himself. Take photographs which attempt to convey some dominant impression you have about the person. Arrange the pictures and present them to the class.

Similarly, with narrative sequence, style, tone, using several supporting examples to develop a paragraph idea, classification, writing introductions and conclusions, figurative language—with all of these the student and instructor may experiment in the media before the written assignment. Admittedly, time for demonstration and discussion of projects bites heavily into classroom hours. Many instructors report, however, that work with visuals early in the semester is often followed later on by a more sustained interest on the students' behalf for building writing skills.

To hold an inveterate suspicion toward the nonwritten medium as if it debases the word as the golden means of communication is a narrowness of vision that will not serve the interests of this special generation of students. It is an uncomfortable contradiction, too, that many among us cannot warm to what for our students is the very life's blood. But to use the media composition in order to bring students to a pitch of excitement about words and their power is certainly no abdication to the nonverbal. It is instead a little pragmatism that enriches the learning experience.

WRITING CENTERS

As with classroom instructors, those charged with tutoring beginners one-on-one or in small groups have found few opportunities other than on-job training to learn how to perform their work efficiently. Coming of age like Topsy (and, unfortunately, like the basic writing teachers they serve), tutors and their directors are just beginning to analyze strategies for novice writers seeking institutional help outside the classroom.

Though not really numerous enough to serve students' needs, writing centers now appear at many institutions that perceive the growth of skills in written English as a major educational priority. Typically understaffed and overworked, writing centers—or writing labs or writing workshops—are places where students in a writing course come for extra, individualized help with their prose. (There are some but not many writing centers where all instruction takes place in tutorials without accompanying classroom sessions.) Sometimes tutors are college graduates without much training in writing or literature; sometimes (ideally, at least), they are good students and good writers only a year or two ahead of their tutees; sometimes they are graduate assistants or future teachers eager for experience with students.

It's also not unlikely that a new instructor of beginning writers will draw as part of his or her program an assignment as writing center tutor. Serving as a tutor, though, is no job to take lightly or without thought and planning.

The strength of a writing center lies in the quality of its tutors. Often through temperament as well as through talent, it is the tutor who can give that extra push for students to go beyond what the classroom offers, to stretch over the finish line with the skills that certify competence. A tutor must have not only a keen sense of writing abilities and how they grow and advance, but also a personality that encourages growth and advancement. Working with one student alone in a private session demands tact and rigor, forcefulness and reserve, abundant patience. A tutor knows when to talk and when to be still. He knows when to probe, when to prod, when to push hard. He knows how to draw others out. He knows how to work along with the writer and his instructor to plan a program of growth that will assure success.

At PSU when I directed the writing center, tutors were teaching assistants. To help orient new staff, my assistant, George McWilliams, and I prepared a set of principles for tutors based upon our observations of the writer-tutor relationship. Although not unlike the principles any good teacher of writing should follow in any setting, they nonetheless focus on the demands of individual or small group instruction. Here are ten touchstones for tutoring apprentice writers:

1. *The relationship of tutor to writer is that of a trained, sympathetic, and faithful reader.* Your training and experience in careful theme grading will serve well in your role as a tutor, but the special relationship you can establish in the writing center puts a highly personal cast upon your evaluation of writing by students. You see them as individuals, hear their specific complaints and problems as writers. Since you are usually meeting them one at a time, students do not

compete for your attention at the moment with twenty-five others. And you feel no strain to tend to those others as you explain a point particularly vexing to one of your students. The tutorial format leans toward sympathy and faithfulness because you have time to draw out and to understand the motivations that led the writer to certain lines of thought, to certain manners of expression. And since you most often do not grade the students you tutor, you can get them to accept your comments on their work as from a thoughtful reader and not as from a judge.

2. *Tutors should begin by seeing the student's strengths as a writer.* Those who come to the writing center have had very bad experiences with writing, and students sit before you, for the most part, unaware of their own linguistic resources. Therefore, point out these resources to them early on. Many beginners need to be shown by a sympathetic tutor that they have good foundations to build upon, that they are not starting from scratch. Once they recognize their strengths, they will be more eager to eliminate their weaknesses.

3. *Tutors should avoid discussing with students the fairness of an instructor's grade.* Offering responsible evaluations in the Writing Center is fraught with complications because some instructor has in all likelihood already read, evaluated, and graded the theme now before you in your role as tutor. You do not want to undermine the teacher's position in the classroom. Further, you must repeatedly emphasize knowledge as the main goal, not grades. Listen to complaints about bad teachers, bad assignments, unfair grades for about a minute of your assigned session—then push, hard, to move from gripes into actions to improve writing.

4. *Tutors should expect writers to improve and should let them know it.* Students need encouragement. Let them know early that writing is a skill that, with patience and practice, can be learned. Often the skill takes longer to develop than anybody likes, but work yields results.

5. *Tutors should deal with writing as an entity of com-*

munication and should fragment the writing only after discussing it as a whole. This point seems all too obvious, yet many tutors treat the tools of expression as though they were the finished product. If you show little concern for the ideas students are trying to convey, you have no grounds for demanding that they improve their writing skills. Related to this is point 6.

6. *Resist giving the impression that grammatical correctness is an end in itself.* Their bookshelves and file cabinets groaning with innumerable exercises in subject-verb agreement, in pronoun recognition, in comma splices, many writing centers find it hard to assert their essential priority: working on writing. All too typically, after a student arrives for an appointment, the tutor seizes a worksheet from a metal drawer and sits distractedly as the student underlines or circles grammatical probabilities. After ten minutes the reluctant pair discusses the exercise and parts finally without much talk about getting the writer's words down clearly on paper. Certainly drills are important exercises, especially when they aim at one student's special needs; but without constant reference back to the writer's own prose, with a succession of exercises you are piling up pebbles to see if you can build a rock.

7. *Tutors should emphasize organization as a way to avoid confusion, not as an academic exercise.* Again, the purpose of having students write in various forms is not to make them masters of narration or exemplification, but rather to allow them to explore the potentials of organizational patterns. Good organization promotes lucidity; poor organization promotes obscurity. Don't let the student be intimidated by form: like grammatical correctness, organizational principles serve the purpose of communication.

8. *Tutors should establish a priority of skills—both generally and in regard to specific students.* Spending twenty minutes to explain colon usage is nonsensical if the student does not know how to use a thesis statement to control the essay or how to use specific, concrete details to support a

generalization. Obviously, since some problems demand more attention than others, you need a sense of priorities, which you can adjust to fit the needs of individual students. By doing so, you make tutoring sessions as efficient as possible.

9. *Tutors should reinforce major skills throughout the term.* Students must use newly acquired skills habitually in order to discontinue unsuccessful practices. Of course, you cannot eliminate in one or two brief sessions mistakes formed over a lifetime of speaking, reading, and writing. Therefore, you need to review periodically students' major weaknesses to prevent reversion to bad habits. Boring as reinforcement might seem, you should encourage students to welcome the opportunity either to relearn or to prove their mastery of a skill.

10. *Tutors should not allow students to become too dependent.* Some writers will use tutors as a security blanket, and this practice is natural, up to a point. However, you do students a disservice if you do not finally abandon them to their own resources. Remember, your goal is to make each student a self-reliant writer.

With these principles up front I want to describe briefly a typical tutoring session in which you might find yourself, one that revolves around a student's paper graded and returned by the instructor in the course.

Such a session involves work on several fronts. First to insure that the entire session is productive, have the student work on something as you read the paper. Perhaps he or she can revise a few sentences of an older essay, can do an exercise in sentence combining, can read a brief chapter on this week's rhetorical strategy from a textbook other than his own. The important point is that the student not sit idle as you read his theme.

After reading the essay, m᷅ ᷍e a note, mental or otherwise, of what the instructor has ᷍aid. Start the session with a comment related to the generᴀl area of strength and weakness that the teacher has pointed out.

Though tutors might silently question the approach to grading here—circled errors, no comment on the writer's strengths which are several and noticeable—they must accept the scored paper as *primum mobile* for the tutoring session. In "The Old Bus Building" the instructor does, after all, provide for the tutor some cues in the marginal and end

The Old Bus Building

As the State College bus terminal stands upon its *passive* old foundation, many interesting things are noticed within its surroundings. (Cars) roaring up and down *cars look on? (1)* Highway 322 (three-twenty two) look on as an old grey haired custodian sweeps the sidewalks trying to brighten the appearance of the old paint-chipped building. Across the street the construction workers are putting *Can you be more specific? Stone? Tall? Concrete?* up a (modern) building with the sound of their chain saws and metal clattering together. Sitting on the *Who is sitting? That's "dangling"* curb the bitter poison-like taste of carbon monoxide and oil residue covering the blacktop seems to mysteriously enter the lungs. (2) Walking to the top of the *cars are walking and looking?* old cement stairs looking out over the cold railing, cars are zipping by in the distance and an old metal pushcart is located directly beneath the railing for the convenience of the customers luggage. (Busting) *ww* through the swinging metal doors within the walls of the old building bus drivers assemble socially sipping their coffee and telling (various) stories of the *can you be more specific?* road. Proceeding over the warped tile floor, sitting *dangling* down on the old wooden furniture, schedules of oncoming arrivals and departures are displayed. Bus *num?* drivers and terminal workers (are) in and out of this

walk?
dash? old building constantly but seem quite content and *what does*

accustomed to its old appearance, (which) in turn *which*

refer to?

adds an extra effect of cheerfulness upon the little

old building.

① "*Look on*" *has a leisurely feeling — these cars are* "*roaring.*"
② *Are the two sentences in that compound sentence equal?*
or logically a pair?

You're hampered by your topic sentence. It doesn't contain
a real idea. "*Many interesting things*"

What's your overall impression?

Your danglers are a real problem — more about that
in class today.

comments. That the piece is not properly governed by a
topic sentence can open a focused discussion. "Many interesting things" does nothing to limit the topic and, in light of
the details that follow it, does not accurately represent the
writer's attitude. The student's final statement about the "effect of cheerfulness" seems totally out of line with his details. In the question "What is your overall impression?" the
instructor rightfully notes the student's failure to com-
municate an idea clearly and to support it successfully with
images.

Consequently, a tutor's first priority here would be to show
the student how to generate a topic sentence that successfully governs the paragraph's details. Perhaps, in this case,
you can use the student's statement about cheerfulness as a
focal point for developing a topic statement like this one: "In
spite of (or even *because of*) the age of the State College
bus terminal, I find the place cheerful." But whatever the
final shape of the opening sentence, it should do three
things: introduce the topic, limit it, and suggest the writer's
attitude toward it.

This student has the same trouble with individual words

that he has with the topic sentence; because of imprecision they don't convey an idea accurately. The instructor has noted most of these words and has suggested alternatives, so your job as tutor would be to oversee the process by which the student chooses the most effective word from those suggested in the comments or, better, from those triggered by your discussion and out of his own language resources. Which word says best what the writer wants to say? Beginners do not ask themselves such questions often enough: Fuzzy thinking or carelessness, as well as weak vocabulary, can cause diction problems, so you must insist that the student take care about language.

After you have spent time on the ideas communicated by the paragraph, you can begin to take it apart to work on mechanics. Emphasize writing conventions as aids to communication, not as data that one memorizes for their own sake. In "The Old Bus Building" you can use the dangling construction as a lead-in to other problem areas. Since the instructor has promised to discuss danglers you have an opportunity to reinforce what the student discovered in class. You should have him first discuss what he learned, and then have him put the theory into practice by revising his errors. After revision, you can call attention to the need to separate participial phrases from main clauses, whether they occur fore or aft, with commas. Then you can explain how in the first sentence the passive voice construction, by eliminating the observer at the outset of the paragraph, led the writer nefariously to dangling.

A discussion based upon a scored paper, then, can expand understanding of readers' responses to the writer's ideas. Certainly there are other things to do in tutorials—teaching about language, guiding the adaptation of process to individual student needs, overseeing and stimulating original composition. But it is from work directed by judged writing that the tutor wins the writer's respect and energy, the classroom teacher's cooperation (not suspicion or enmity), and the joys of watching skills advance.

Even if you never serve as a tutor, you should find the previous discussion helpful. Knowing the principles that guide good tutoring, you can better understand the special role the tutor plays in a writer's growth of skills. If your institution has a Writing Center, visit it right away to explore its facilities, and have a talk with the director and some of the tutors. How, you will want to know, can they help your students who need support beyond the classroom? When you send members of your class to the Center during the semester, make sure that you characterize even in just a sentence or two on a referral form or on the bottom of a graded paper the problems you would like the tutor to examine. Lend your support by encouraging students to keep appointments promptly, by commending students' attendance at tutoring sessions, and by responding to any questions tutors may raise. Comment directly to tutors about their work with your students. Share your course syllabus and a copy of your text with the Writing Center. Discuss with individual writers any progress reports you have received from tutors, and use those reports to help you frame comments on themes.

Look at your relationship with tutors as a partnership: your classroom efforts will undoubtedly reveal gaps in knowledge for which students need the kind of personalized instruction that your own time schedule and work load often prevent. Tutors can provide that instruction and, in addressing a beginner's sticking problems, can help writers achieve their goals.

STUDENT-TEACHER CONFERENCES

There is no doubt about the value of the private conference between the classroom teacher and his or her students, and Shaughnessy crystalizes its merits when she points out that it "remains the best way to discover how students have perceived their instructions and to create the bonds of concern and encouragement that energize both teacher and student."

But like the tutorial in which the tutor is probably not the student's classroom teacher this kind of conference is by no means a simple affair to manage, especially if you like your students and are open and honest with them. You have to keep the time you've set aside for conference reserved for talk about writing, and that means you'll have to resist turning conferences into therapy sessions, gripe sessions, or sessions for the lovelorn and the homesick. What counseling you do on free time, of course, is service on the side of the angels; but office hours set for consultations with students about their writing should go only for that. There's serious business to carry out in conference and you need a "let's get to work" atmosphere for the most productive results.

Conference sessions help you to expand from class eleventh-hour explanations that need more ammunition and to single out special problems in writing. Aside from discussing individual progress, you can use the session as a tutorial, as if you were helping students in the Writing Center. What you teach about fragments to an inexperienced writer in fifteen minutes in the office can often succeed better than a full class-session on such a topic. Examine the corrections the writer has made from your comments on papers. Explore the main areas of strength and weakness. Ask the student to keep a record of the topics covered during conference; assign sections from the text to allow practice of newly learned skills. A shelf of good reference books in the office is indispensable; by studying explanations in a number of texts, students can often easily understand their major problems. Lend out desk copies to encourage study and practice.

In dealing with methods complementing and supplementing formal classroom instruction, I mean to solidify a point I've made several times before, a point your own experience and an open mind will lead you to almost immediately. The more alternatives you offer for learning the skills you have to teach, the better your chances of reaching the widest number of students. As varied as their interests, talents, and problems should be your own approaches.

5

Testing: What Beginning Teachers Should Know

Regrettably, the title of this chapter is much more ambitious than its intent, for I do not propose here to treat comprehensively the testing of writers' skills. The works of Lee Odell, Charles Cooper, Paul Diederich, Fred Godshalk, Richard Lloyd-Jones, in more detail than I have space for, define the principles behind testing student writers and offer practical suggestions for implementing those principles. Though I shall no doubt be dipping into their proposals to summarize a tried position or to make a new point, anyone charged with building or oiling or reconstructing test machinery must study those sources to set gears efficiently in motion. Other excellent resources for concepts and practices in testing writers is a bibliographic survey in *Basic Writing* (Spring/Summer, 1978) and one in *College Composition and Communication* (December 1979).

AN OVERVIEW OF TYPES

My main purpose in this chapter is to provide an overview of testing for the beginning teacher. Although much of what I say can relate to testing efforts at any school involved in the assessment of writing skills, my framework for discussion here is the college writing program. With examples of specific procedures at hand, I want to deal with tests as they bear specifically on the basic writing course and how that course and a testing program relate to a student's ability as a writer, to the shape of a writing program and the sequence of courses in its territory, and to the identity of an institution and its population. If those goals, too, seem ambitious they deserve no apology, however, because they have not, so far as I have seen, received the kind of attention they deserve in the context of specific institutional needs. Often tests grow apart from courses and what a teacher teaches there. Though that is probably good for certain kinds of evaluations, precisely what the tests are testing must always be clear all the way around. Further, tests are frequently unconnected to what an institution can achieve or what it says it wants to achieve.

I suppose, given the doubts easily raised about a one-shot writing exam that attests to a student's skills, one could argue against mass testing in any case. Indeed, some departments holding to the privilege of academic freedom insist on each classroom teacher's right—even duty—to be the sole judge of a student's competency. They reject out of hand any institutional testing toward such an end. Other departments through inertia or despair or lack of stated goals have succeeded in avoiding the testing issue completely. Nevertheless, and especially in the back-to-basics excitement of recent years, many institutions insist on some kind of testing program as a measure of writing achievement and of consistency in teaching and learning. College administrations prodded by legislatures clamoring for accountability and cost efficiency make the fact of uniform writing tests *de rigeur,* an issue no longer influenced by discussions at faculty councils or at department meetings.

With no great love myself for the one-shot test, I have come to see enough strengths in it as a means to evaluate fairly at a certain point or at certain points the status of a writer's progress. However I shall not ignore grievances lodged against tests and testers. I want to help anticipate the issues bound to arise as any thoughtful instructor takes a place in the testing effort.

Needless to say, a test for writing is still received as a volatile, highly political instrument, especially when it claims to test proficiency and by its results can exclude students from further course work. Although careful procedures help objify and limit (within ranges) evaluators' responses, reading and judging a writer's work are still irreducably subjective in nature, no matter how scientific the trappings, no matter how sophisticated the scale designed to assist the reader. For these and other reasons, tests that make students write in order to measure their writing skills (as opposed to short-answer tests) will always play to mixed reviews.

The first kinds of tests the new teacher is apt to face are tests for course placement. Prepared by the educational institution itself or commercially prepared by a publisher or by a large-scale testing company like the Educational Testing Service (ETS) in Princeton, these often use objective, multiple-choice components. At Penn State an exam prepared at the University questioned only vocabulary and usage skills to determine placement in writing courses. From ETS the Test of Standard Written English asserts an ability to predict qualities of a student's skill as a writer based upon his responses to objective questions. (Fred I. Godshalk—see the Bibliography—offers data to support the value of objective tests as predictors of writing ability.) Administrators defend short-answer tests because they cost less to support than do faculty readings of student essays; and because for the kinds of gross distinctions needed for placement either in the skills course or in the regular freshman course, a writing sample, one can argue, is unnecessary. A diagnostic essay early in the term can provide the basis for more discrete judgments to indicate a writer's strengths and weaknesses. Correlations between scores on objective tests and scores on written essays run high, the testers insist.

I have my own biases against short-answer exams at any point. I do not like what they say to beginning writers who might ask, "If you can tell how I write from an exam that requires no writing, why do I have to write at all?" No one has convinced me that objective questions about writing test much other than reading skills. Further, a school with a three- or four-tiered program—two basic skills courses followed by a term or two of freshman English—could no doubt improve the system for placing students by using, instead of a multiple-choice exam, a written sample for an entire entering class.

Still, budgets have a way of overriding sound pedagogy. But, conscious of costs, an institution that insits upon machine scored tests can heighten their reliability. The first essay of the term can back up objective questions and can provide needed data. Examining correlations between numerical scores on objective tests and those for written placement essays helps validate the axis drawn between pass and fail. Otherwise, placement scores established from correct or incorrect short-answer tests are arbitrary and themselves subject to politics and pressures to keep classes full or underenrolled, depending upon the caprices of budgets. One suggestion I can make is that for whatever objective exam upon which the institution insists, at least once, one whole entering freshman class should write placement essays for reading by the English department. (Some experts like Mina Shaughnessey have argued privately that a reading test— even a mathematics test!—could serve adequately under those conditions.) Scored essays would then be compared to scored short-answer exams for each student in that entire class. Based on correlations discovered in such a process, cut off points stabilized for long-range placement can relate even in subsequent years to this one-time consensus among writing teachers. Data from this and any further experiments help resist pressure to raise or to lower the objective test score required for course placement.

If they give in to objective exams as expedient placement tools only, experienced teachers are right to defend unflinchingly the need for a written sample to measure a writer's competence. For objections similar to but more serious than those I've named above about objective tests for placement, one can oppose them even more forcefully for writing proficiency. You judge *writing* by looking at *writing,* not at someone's skills at editing someone else's prose, not at command over syntactical operations performed on language the writer has not generated, not at intimacy with grammatical terminology or with labeling. Fortunately, many institutions have accepted the need for an essay as evidence of achievement. Usually that evidence is drawn around a line somewhere between the basic skills course and freshman English, so that a student who writes an acceptable theme under proctored exam conditions is deemed ready for "regular" freshman writing.

If the distinction I've made between exams for placement and those for certifying some level of competence implies a universal clarity in the conception, administration, and application of results of these writing tests, unfortunately little exists in fact. Questions and contradictions muddy the well. To deal with them throughout this discussion I will draw upon the experiences of three major institutions attempting to test writers' skills. I will describe those experiences rather fully because they exemplify recurrent issues in testing.

Since an exam for placement says that student X is either competent enough to take freshman English or unskilled enough to require a more basic writing course, the same exam, some argue, should also be able to certify a level of competency *after* preparatory course work is completed. Edward M. White, Director of the Freshman English Equivalency Examination for the California State University and Colleges, explains the positions both of those who oppose and of those who favor such an approach. Opponents insist that tests of any kind have limited purposes. Placement examinations (especially good ones that include writing segments) sample a wide range of possibilities, ultimately selecting for attention only those deemed essential by test makers. Tests to measure the effects of course work, on the other hand, must grow out of curriculum in order to determine whether students have learned what has been taught—and not what test makers say is important. Supporters of a single test for placement and competence say that if a placement test is accurate, whatever the student learns in class *should* lead to the kind of improvement that test *can* measure; he should be able to take a retest, then, and to apply newly developed skills. (White told me, however, that on limited experiments with the same testing instrument used before and after course work, not much evidence appeared for improvement in English skills on the second try. The placement test, it seems, could not effectively measure short-term gains.)

White and many of his colleagues are more convinced by those demanding different exams, and so on the one hand the State of California provides multiple tests for gathering and applying data about writing, and on the other allows individual campuses to establish methods for determining successful completion of courses. Currently, therefore, in California there is at one end of the spectrum a high school proficiency exam in writing, which is roughly equivalent to a diploma in that a student must pass it for admission from high school to a community college; and at the other end there is the English Equivalency Examination, a multisection test that includes writing and is designed for advanced placement, a student who passes earning as much as two terms of English credit at the California State University and colleges. There is also in the middle another and newer exam, the English Placement Test (see Appendix) with multiple choice sections on reading comprehension, on sentence construction, on logic and organization, and a forty-five-minute essay that may be used for determining students' course programs in college. I say "may" pointedly: to move from "remedial" to "regular" composition, students follow rules and procedures set at each campus.

In New Jersey, for those colleges and universities *electing* participation in the state sponsored program, the New Jersey Basic Skills Placement Test serves to identify students whose English language skills are not strong enough to guarantee successful reading and writing required in college freshman classes. Scores report an ability to answer questions on reading comprehension, on logical relationships, and on sentence structure, and an ability to write a twenty-minute sample that gives the reader "some sense of whether or not the student can organize ideas, can develop a logical argument, can provide specific examples, can use complete sentences, can spell, can punctuate, can interest the reader, can maintain a consistent tone, can express ideas precisely, or can do a score of other things that go into writing a good essay." The Jersey test is strictly advisory, again used essentially for placement purposes (see Appendix).

The Freshman Skills Assessment Program (FSAP) of the City University of New York has perhaps the most ambitious goals of any testing program I've worked with and perhaps the most complicated problems as well. Responding to a mandate by the City Board of Higher Education, the CUNY Task Force on Writing Assessment (of which I am a member) developed as part of a larger testing program an essay exam which would establish minimum standards of writing competency for CUNY students. Given *after* a student is admitted to the university, the test serves to measure entry-level skills and to assist a college in placing students in the correct writing course. Ideally, a college would allow students to take freshman English only if they passed the test, designed to measure skills that should have been developed in high school. However, and this is the rub, the test also measures *minimum* proficiency in writing by students moving from a community college or from any other lower division program to the upper division of a four-year college. (The test is saying that competent high school writers are ready to attempt upper division writing tasks.) To get beyond sixty credits of college work, therefore, students must pass the writing skills assessment test. What passing means was laid out clearly by the Task Force on a six-part descriptive evaluation scale, categories on the scale painstakingly defined and illustrated (see Appendix). Aimed at determining "the lowest level of writing ability which students should have in order to take advantage of what they will be taught in college-level composition," the test tells those students who pass on entry that they have minimal skills or beyond, and those students who fail on entry that they have two years to reach minimum levels. The test is not simply advisory. Faculty generally praise its intentions and believe it serves the best interests of both the students and the university.

Although as I write this the FSAP has not been in effect long enough for me to report on its impact at the two-year juncture in any student's program, the test is bound to raise quite a fuss when, despite years of formal pronouncements on the test's purposes, it stops a student's career and deprives a college of candidates for junior and senior courses. Exam procedures, too, lie open to questions. With no money to supervise centralized staff grading for all papers written by students at all the campuses (I'll say more about grading methods later), each college—though with precise guidelines developed by the task force—runs its own show. Hence, legally, one can question binding uniform proficiency standards from college to college within the university because conditions are subject to too many variables. How could a student at LaGuardia Community College, for example, be certain that graders at his institution were as fair as graders at Brooklyn or at Queens College? Whatever meaningful research might ultimately support or deny, the validity of an exam administered in such a way is impossible to encourage because of budgetary constraints. Another problem with CUNY's exams is simple logistics: the uniform calendar for testing chases its tail endlessly throughout the year. Each of the two annual waves of new entrants requires placement tests; and several retests are required for those who must show proficiency in order to continue their studies. Add to that erratic yearly study calendars from college to college (semesters starting and ending at different dates, one trimester system, one quarterly system) and you have dizzying predicaments.

Yet another difficulty, as you might have guessed from an earlier discussion, is the connection between the test used as a gauge of writing proficiency and the course designed to teach the required skills to those students who fail the exam the first time around. Because the test focuses essentially on a writer's ability to argue—students must take a position on some topic and then defend that position—and because argument is quite far along in the sequence of skills beginners need, many instructors believe that no single basic writing course can prepare students adequately for the assessment test. (The kind of course recommended by *The Writing Room* ends *months* short of instruction in argumentation.) This last problem has its positive implications: discovering that a single "remedial" course cannot help students achieve adequately in freshman English, local campuses are evolving a series of courses that will develop required skills sequentially. In California, too, White reports, the impact of the test upon curriculum has been profound and substantial. With a clear sense of standards it is hard for any institution to maintain ancient notions that the basic skills course is the same as freshman English, only less; and that a student who fails to demonstrate proficiency at some accepted level just needs to keep taking the same course over and over again.

As I've tried to suggest, these writing tests, their philosophies, procedures, and political implications resist any clear consensus upon which a beginning teacher can pin an absolute commitment. To complicate matters further, approaches on how to score the papers students write during an exam are similarly varied and hotly contested. Both the kinds of scales and the way to use them most fairly continue to stimulate debate in the profession.

SCORING THE WRITING TEST

Though there are many instructors who insist upon the sanctity of personal grading, many others agree with Diederich about the value of "staff grading." Staff grading insists that an entire composition faculty *together* in one room scores, impersonally, unidentified student papers. Personal grading has problems: prejudices toward a highly intelligent student one knows, or against a slothful one (as Diederich points out) can carry over easily into a grade on an essay. Besides, scores on a single paper can be jarring in their divergence when different teachers grade it privately. But it's possible for a set of readers after discussion and analysis to agree pretty closely upon grades for written essays. A student who writes a final in-class paper that will determine his course status has an added advantage: his teacher does not have to give grades on all the other essays written prior to the final and can concentrate exclusively upon comments designed to improve writing. (Anyone with experience in student conferences knows how much time is wasted when students insist on justification for grades, time better used in exploring ways to improve writing.) In a uniform exam students get a fair shake when idiosyncratic grading disappears. Such a condition is arranged with frequent discussions of sample papers to keep readers close to similar standards. Instructors learn enormously from the staff grading session: they improve the quality of their instruction, and they shore up their own confidence as graders. Thus, for beginning instructors, mutual scoring sessions are, I believe, indispensable.

Though conditions seem to be changing, one can only wonder why shared grading has been ignored over the country for so long. It wasn't until after ten years as a teacher of writing that I ever participated in a kind of group effort at grading, and even then it was a bungling though well intentioned session I planned myself during my first year as a freshman director. Perhaps it's been general neglect of instruction in how to teach writing that has kept prospective primary and secondary school teachers from learning from each other about how to respond to students' papers. And, encouraged by their professors, would-be college teachers (until this decade, anyway) would have shunned like gamma rays any "methods" course that might deflect the study of literature. If you're lucky, you will have had a bit of training in joint grading sessions in some teaching preparatory course somewhere along the line. Otherwise, start pushing for such sessions as soon as you can on your first job, whether you're a teaching assistant or a beginning teacher in elementary, junior, or senior high or in a college or university. An enlightened department chair or freshman director builds into any staff development program frequent meetings devoted to staff grading, even if they're just practice sessions and no uniform exams demand that a whole department work together on students' final papers. Despite the fact that you and some of your new colleagues may need to get this one rolling, it will probably be one of the most valuable elements in your own growth to excellence as a teacher.

I won't go into detail here about all the labels and distinctions made to describe the various evaluation procedures. But I do want to note briefly some important elements in methods for joint evaluation of student writing.

One of the important approaches to evaluating written essays involves *holistic scoring.* Here a reader (trained through practice) makes a quick, impressionistic judgment about a piece of writing and, without making corrections or comments on the paper, usually grades it with some numerical score based upon an agreed upon scale. (Four- or six-point scales, because they allow a broad enough range of analysis, are most popular.) At least two different readers examine each paper in an effort to rate fairly; grades that diverge by more than one point require a third reading.

As an aid to holistic scoring, testing supervisors have developed a variety of techniques. *Analytic scales* enumerate and describe in categories major features of some particular kind of writing. For each category the scale carefully describes high, middle, and low achievements. According to the reader's judgment of how a paper stands in each category, he assigns a numerical evaluation. Thus, on one such scale, for example, a paper in the low range in the category "ideas" or "organization" would earn a 2; a paper in the mid or high ranges would earn higher scores in those categories.

A *dichotomous scale* offers statements or questions that can be answered *yes* or *no* about a piece of writing.

Primary trait scoring insists that accurate holistic evaluations depend upon the reader's ability to define exactly the type of discourse awaiting judgment. "The chief steps in using the Primary Trait Scoring System," reports Richard Lloyd Jones, "are to define the universe of discourse, to devise exercises which sample that universe precisely, to ensure cooperation of the writers, to devise workable scoring guides, and to use the guides." To describe accurately the formal characteristics of a piece of writing in this system, scoring guides are usually lengthy and comprehensive (according to some, unmanageable as well). However, many researchers see primary trait scoring as the most promising type of holistic evaluation because of its potential impact on classroom instruction. Knowing primary traits for particular rhetorical tasks, a teacher can teach to them. These holistic evaluations and others researchers reporting in Cooper and Odell's book (see the Bibliography) explain in depth, offering examples and commentary.

Reading papers intelligently in the holistic method demands practice. To train fair, efficient readers, ETS (who oversees, among many other tests in English, grading procedures for the New Jersey Basic Skills Placement Test and for the California State University and College's English Placement Test) guides trial sessions for readers, no matter how experienced, *each* time an exam must be scored. For practice, gathered around tables (with each supervised by a table leader), all readers evaluate the same sample papers until each group can agree pretty closely on scores for them. (This activity is known as "range finding.") For direction readers may use a scoring guide that describes sample papers previously selected from that particular exam by table leaders. But the guide does not prescribe; it is added support for the sample papers which themselves are scoring models. Once a group has standardized judgments by its members and members of other groups, each reader can swiftly examine different sets of papers and can score them, knowing his or her evaluations will be similar to those made by others around the table and in the room. This procedure, often called "general impression marking," requires no rigid adherence to a written evaluation scale. Each test is its own "universe"; students' papers are scored relative to each other; and readers arrive at common standards by consensus each time around. (A shortcoming in this kind of holistic scoring is that it cannot measure a student's progress with any accuracy: comparative judgments do not allow longitudinal measurement of skills.)

The CUNY Freshman Assessment Test follows procedures similar to those in California and New Jersey, except that readers base their judgments on a prescriptive scale that lists different possible scores and describes the kind of writing required to earn them (see Appendix). The value of an explicit scale, argue its supporters, is that in it lies the capability for replicating a reader's judgment at other times and in other places. Readings without such a scale confine evaluations to the unique "universe" of essays read on that occasion alone. Each new reading, therefore, evaluates papers without regard for those judged at other points. With an explicit scale, however, papers judged from year to year have a potential consistency beyond the essays written at a given moment to essays written each time the test occurs.

Opposed to holistic readings, *feature counting* demands that a reader, using a detailed analytic scale for writing effectiveness, determine a score by *counting* certain elements in order to make a judgment. Thus, errors in syntax, punctuation, usage, and diction may be added up: any total above eight, say, would mean that a paper fails. Or, points may be given for positive elements—good thesis sentence, strong transitions, adequate details—and these would be weighted numerically and added together, a student passing only if his or her grade matches or exceeds a cut-off score.

Critics have pointed to strengths and weaknesses in both holistic and feature counting methods of scoring student's essays. Among the arguments in favor of feature counting are its possibilities for high rates of agreement among readers, especially when the count focuses upon error (a fragment is a fragment). Scores are easy to explain when there are countable elements; and students perceive that error and tallies minimize a teacher's subjective responses to an essay. Teachers, too, feel immunity to subjective appeals from students for passing grades based upon emotional, personal, or psychological conditions: "You have eight errors. There's no way to reconsider the score." Opponents to error counts insist that such procedures tend to stress surface features of the language and that no matter how insistently an accompanying scale asserts the need for clear, coherent prose, readers check for eight errors and make judgments accordingly. Errors other than those in mechanics or sentence structure resist fair and sensible counting. And counting further detracts the reader from following with all his faculties the clear flow of ideas, the accuracy of supporting details, the interaction of content and syntax. Readers could read each paper twice of course; but to have to look at the same essay more than once increases the reader's workload and cuts his efficiency.

Those who favor holistic scoring say it allows quick, fair evaluations based upon the usual conditions under which most readers operate when they judge some piece of writing. Thus, in the local newspaper an essay we consider as good or bad writing rarely results from our weighing the number of comma faults, subordinate structures, or subtle transitions. In holistic readings evaluation grows from form and content as they cohere upon the page. Yet for many tastes holistic reading treads too firmly in subjective territory, no matter how explicit and humane the analytic scale. After many hours at a table readers wear thin, their judgments questionable at day's end. And readers accustomed to marking up a paper rarely shake a sense that holistic scores cheat students with an unintelligent, unlabored grade. Finally there is the fear that holistic grading will replace for all writing the careful, thorough responses demanded of teachers concerned about a student's progress as a writer. Though not a necessary consequence, this fear is a real one: I have heard respected speakers for the profession praise holistic scoring as the way of a future already dim with over-sized writing classes and with excessive course loads for writing teachers.

For the beginning instructor, group efforts at scoring are extraordinary situations for learning about how to respond to student writing and about how to adjust one's standards to the needs of students as the department and the institution perceive them. Hearing experienced and inexperienced teachers offer reasons for their impressions about an essay helps to sharpen a skill not honed finely enough for many writing teachers left alone at their library carrels. I have scored papers and have led grading sessions using holistic and feature counting methods, and although I favor the former because it seems to me the fairer plan for students, the efforts of a whole staff working together bring rewards no matter what kind of scoring your institution has selected for a uniform essay.

I've offered this discussion as a primer really to show about testing the range and variety of issues that face the basic writing instructor just starting out. Asked to under-score my major concern among all the provocative issues the testing of writers raises in general, I'd have to wave the red flag I unfurled before: the relationship between the basic writing course and some test designed by the department or the university to measure levels of proficiency. No doubt it's easy to be cynical about the degree to which a beginning teacher can affect policy. Indeed, *experienced* teachers without much hope of influencing change often squeak and groan their way through elaborate testing machines that are inefficient, outdated, and unreliable. For placement testing (an old-timer on the academic scene) and for general proficiency testing (a relative newcomer but quickly entrenching itself) perhaps there's not much an individual can do single-handedly, except to speak up at every opportunity about the need for periodic evaluations of the goals and procedures of the testing program. But because not much thought has gone to connecting curriculum and exam, to allying course design and testing instruments, the aims and structures of a basic writing program and the aims and structures of a testing program often run on different tracks. With a sense of what a basic writing course (or courses) should teach, beginning instructors are perhaps the strongest forces in bringing logic to instruction and examinations. Remember, basic writing as a formal course of dignity and importance is a relative infant in the academic household (we've come a long way, fortunately, from the days of Bonehead English), and those of you reading this book are among the pioneers in the effort to teach novices from scratch, and gladly, and without contempt for those not yet skilled.

What I'm trying to say is that the teacher of basic writing, who sees himself as a professional, no matter how inexperienced in the classroom at the moment, needs to help focus for the academy the values and limitations of tests that exist apart from courses. If a college describes a minimum level of proficiency it wishes all students to demonstrate and constructs an exam that draws out fairly that level of proficiency from students, a course of study must stand in place (or at least must be on the drawing boards) to develop proficient writers as the institution defines them. Perhaps the least logical approach to developing good writers is, even in an honest concern for standards and achievement, to gather together a blue-ribbon panel of faculty experts to design a test. To be sure, for large multicampus universities sometimes such a dramatic effort is the only way to gather the flock, so to speak, to bring all the units (which tend to stray, for better or for worse) into the fold of some coherent, articulated, set of standards for writing. This drawing together can ultimately affect curriculum, as I've pointed out in the cases of CUNY and New Jersey and the California State system. But changes here are slow and painful.

A much sounder, more defensible effort at testing starts
first in a realistic appraisal of the needs of students at a
given institution, needs suggested by the students themselves, by the college faculty and its vision of a liberal education, by the practical demands made upon students' writing
skills by careers and by heterogeneous life styles. When con-
sulting with college English departments about their writing
programs, I resist talking about tests as long as I can, though
someone usually tries to lay the issue on the table as the first
order of business. To my way of thinking, tests come last. At
the outset, teachers need to ask and to answer questions
like "How do we expect students to perform as writers before they begin formal college instruction in writing?" and
"How do we expect students to perform as writers when they
complete their formal college instruction in writing?"

Answers to the first question—they can be molded into
statements of carefully worded goals—establish criteria that
do critical service. First, they are a message to institutions
preparing students who will become freshmen at your institution. You are offering not a statement of vague demands
but a list of clear expectations. Such a list helps junior and
senior high schools plan a logical writing curriculum for students soon to sit in college classrooms. Equally important,
the expectations become end points toward which a basic
writing sequence moves for men and women who do not
meet entrance criteria for college English. Next, with clearly
stated goals supported by the academic community, curriculum may then be designed to prepare students for the freshman English program. After defining requirements for entry
to it, writing faculty then can design a test to gauge whether
a student satisfies those requirements. Depending upon how
high they are set (given the student population and the institution's mission), either one course or a sequence of
courses can serve to prepare the inexperienced writer to
meet the goals measured by the test.

Answers to the question "How do we expect students to
perform as writers when they complete their final college instruction in writing?" yield similar kinds of results: state-

ments of goals carefully directed to students' needs, course structures and sequential curriculum for the writing program, methods for measuring whether or not students achieve at desired levels of proficiency.

With an approach such as the one I'm recommending the infamous pedagogical bugaboo "teaching to the test" can lose much of its bad reputation. If students must master specific goals for the basic writing course, the test that examines their accomplishments is a logical outgrowth of sequential instruction. The test invites teaching to it. There are few mysteries for students and for teachers; and a mutual accountability—teacher-to-student,   student-to-teacher—centers on achievements everyone works toward. Few things undermine successful teaching more than a test for which a course seems impossible to prepare.

I might just add in passing that an in-class essay exam is not always the best measure of achievement for each writing course. For example, a freshman course that stresses command over the seven or eight classical rhetorical modes or that stresses research techniques for writers would err in using a single final essay as a student's mark of proficiency. Evidence of strong writing in each of the modes must assert success with them in the first case. A formal research project must serve in the second case. An objective test on preparing bibliography and footnotes might tell the student knew *about* research but could not tell if he knew how to carry it out successfully.

I promised not much in the way of answers in this chapter, more than anything else a sampler of problems about testing and some institutional responses to them. The Appendix provides a few of those responses, which are varied enough to suggest possibilities for an institution not yet firm in its testing program. However, the tests and scales I've offered do not stand as magical solutions. The only way to approach testing is from institution to institution. Each must keep in mind the basic enigmas facing anyone charged with the responsibility of large-scale evaluation of writing. Let me end, then, by quoting from Cooper and Odell who state the issues precisely and succinctly: "In devising ways to measure students' growth in writing, we continually struggle with two problems: making judgments that are reliable, that we can reasonably assume are not idosyncratic; and making judgments that are valid, that provide significant information about the writing we are dealing with." Those are the issues underlying any reasoned approach to testing and evaluation.

6

Beyond Basics: An Overview

I have asserted all along that the basic course is first in a sequence designed to produce competent writers. Although my purpose in this book is to offer guidance for teachers of that basic course, I want to point out where writing programs might go from it so that an instructor knows the path a beginning writer could follow as he continues to learn his craft. I want also to suggest some bridges, ways of moving from the areas of instruction I've suggested for beginners to areas of more advanced skill. Hence this chapter.

SETTING GOALS

About the course for beginning writers one cannot help being struck by a grim paradox. On the one hand, beginning writers need extensive instruction and demand a careful breaking down of skills and their frequent, concentrated practice. But on the other, a single course does not seem to take students far enough—or as far as one would like them to go in a three-month quarter or in a five-month semester. From the few state-wide tests I know in mimimum writing competency, I cannot predict safely how many beginning students would, after the course I've laid out, survive those exams.

Of course, even beginning writers show wide ranges of abilities; and to move ahead to more complicated tasks, one can compress or eliminate skills that, on the whole, the class seems to command. Still, my experience with beginners suggests that most of them need close attention to the language-building skills, to the use of supporting detail, and to the rhetorical strategies, rudimentary as instruction in all these may be. Nearly all need close attention to the varied features of correctness in syntax or in word use that a beginner's idiosyncratic prose requires. There's more than enough to teach here in one course, yet not enough for many writers to achieve a high enough level of competency. What is well taught will certainly not be well learned without the students' commitment of time beyond the classroom, time spent writing and studying and conferring and working in labs or in learning centers to supplement the course of instruction. Furthermore, even with the best of intentions and the best of instructors there's no way to *assure* movement in competency from *X* to *Y*, no matter how sensibly one sets those points. People learn at different rates and under different, often unpredictable conditions.

As a former administrator, I know and appreciate the financial pressures that prevent an institution from offering all the courses writers need. There's no sense in arguing—lucid as such an argument might be—that a whole string of sequential courses is the best and the only response to beginners. But I do think that an intelligent writing program should base its course offerings upon where students taking those courses begin, and where the institution expects those students to be when they finish. Each school must ask first, "What specific skills do we expect students to have before they start the freshman English course?" and then, "What specific skills do we expect students to have after they complete it?" (I have asked similar questions in my exploration of testing in the last chapter.) Answers to those questions should define the range and depth of courses in the required writing program. (If those seem obvious questions, I assure you that not many institutions have formulated them. Defining minimal competency in some haphazard way, programs often lump together "remedial" students and the "regular" or "normal" students; and simply completing a course—not having to meet any clearly stated goals—frequently determines success. Often that course is vague and rarely consistent from room to room on one campus; and often the beginning writer fails the course and must take it again and again.)

Because student populations vary so according to needs and skills, every institution must itself map out a program suggested by responses to the above questions. At one school with students showing weak skills, a three-term sequence that ends in a one-term freshman composition course might work best. At another with different kinds of students, one basic skills course might precede a full year of freshman English. At most state institutions, teaching research skills in a one- or two-term required English course will steal time from instruction in skills that writers need more. Similar problems with time and course content will exist where a single composition course asks students to read and to analyze great ideas in literature, philosophy, religion, social science, or politics. Yet at an institution where entering students are highly skilled, basic writing classes are not useful, and a freshman English course might indeed focus on writing about great books, advanced research techniques, or literary criticism. (I don't know many institutions like this, however.)

Establishing a universal English curriculum in American colleges rubs against the grain of a heritage of varied institutions planning singular courses of study. There's little reason to propose changing that. However, one cannot escape insisting that the program of study in writing at least be *planned,* its goals laid out carefully and explained to students fully and in language they can understand. So, looking beyond the *first* course in writing skills for beginners, where do teacher and student go next?

In regard to correctness, advancing writers will be taking new risks in their prose; and those risks may invite patterns of error not before apparent. Thus, an instructor who in the first writing course spends class time on sentence fragments or dangling modifiers must expect again and again to teach about such errors throughout the writing program, though perhaps in less detail. More occasions than before will arise to deal with the demands of new syntactical operations, which you introduce at higher and higher rungs in the writer's climb to advanced skills. Instruction in sentence combining and embedding must continue, perhaps through modeling, as more sophisticated sentences by accomplished stylists are offered for imitation. Individual needs rooted in emerging skills will insist upon instruction that is repeated, sometimes condensed and simplified, other times taken to high levels of technical skill. And though the knowledge of grammatical terminology can for some writers enhance new sentence operations, and though it is perfectly sound for an institution to require command over language systems, offering instruction in grammar within a crammed writing curriculum is highly questionable, as I've asserted before.

NARRATIVE SUMMARY: FROM SENSORY DATA
TO EXPERT TESTIMONY

Correctness and syntax aside, instruction must help students support an assertion with data other than personal experience. I'm talking about the areas of expert testimony from which writers offer supporting material from books and magazines, from the media, and from reliable teachers, friends, and acquaintances. The kinds of details built from experiences are different from those built from these other important sources of data. Here the writer offers statistics, the language of facts and figures; he offers cases based on real events and conditions; he offers exact quotations and paraphrases in order to drive a point home.

In a coherent program that explores with writers the nature and use of detail, the transition from sensory data to testimony from a source beyond first-hand experience requires careful instruction. This area, as I pointed out earlier, is not given its due priority in the learning program, so I'd like to spend some time here considering how to teach these new skills.

After lots of practice with concrete sensory language, for

more objective writing than students have been doing you have to present other kinds of details and their possible sources. However, before turning students loose with an expository topic for which they not only must seek out sources of data, but also must choose from those sources appropriate *kinds* of supporting materials (or combinations of them), offer practice in which you limit considerably the base of data that will supply the detail. Summary writing is one valuable means of achieving that goal. Asking for a summary of a *narrative* provides a logical bridge between the sensory, subjective, and experiential writing stressed before and the research-oriented compositions to come, those frequently demanded by objective writing for other courses.

The summary-writing skill is not easy to develop. It requires an ability to separate major from minor detail and a keen sense of proportion; it requires a clear understanding of the sequence of events portrayed; it requires an ability to distinguish among the terms of summary, such as synopsis, abstract, précis, paraphrase, and summary itself. And finally it often insists upon close attention to quotation marks, mystifying creatures for many students.

A wise instructor will choose a written or spoken (or sung) narrative to have students summarize, and will consider those cautions. The selection of the narrative used as the basis of the summary is critical. Shaughnessy points out the difficulties in summarizing when the intellectual structure of the work does not mirror the rhetorical structure. The main point of an essay is sometimes not stated until the end, where "the reader realizes only retrospectively how the parts contribute to the whole." In such an essay, the summary will often require a reordering of the contents of the selection. At this stage of the student's growth as a writer, it's essential to select for summary some clear narrative, one in which rhetorical and intellectual structure meet. Next, help students overcome the temptation to summarize as they read. Ask the writer first to state in his own words the main idea of the selection in one correct sentence. Then, following Shaughnessy's recommendations, make no attempt yet to teach or to require the use of quotes from the original. You should not expect the student to attribute ideas to the author. And you must point out that summary excludes the summary-writer's *interpretation* of the events he's summarizing. Only later on as part of much more advanced instruction should students learn those refinements I'm suggesting you eliminate here.

One way to lead into the assignment in summary is to use a visual element. Select a picture of some dramatic event, perhaps a photograph of an accident or of a person in action or of a crowd clearly bent on some activity. Try to select a photo that, despite a clear single intent, has nonetheless some extraneous detail. Ask the class to look carefully at the picture and to state in their own words in a *written* sentence the main idea of the photograph. Then ask that from the photo students state the details that support the main idea. Call one or two students to the chalkboard to record all the details named by their classmates, after everyone agrees that the detail does indeed support the main idea. Make no comment about the list. Instead ask why certain details were not included. In a photograph, as students should conclude, there are often extraneous details, which may or may not make some small contribution to the photographer's point but which have no major role in the picture. From that you can move to the concept of *major detail* and *minor detail,* gathering definitions of those ideas from students. Now look together at the list on the chalkboard and ask the class to suggest details that might be excluded because they are not as significant as others. After reducing the initial list considerably, use an overhead projector and write out a paragraph synopsis of the photograph from sentences the students construct out of details listed on the board. A student might write the summary at the projector. Or ask students to write independently from the chalkboard list.

The photo is a good place to begin for summary activity because, despite the liveliness of action represented in the picture, there is really no sequence of events distinguishable in the flash of time frozen by the camera. In effect, then, this practice is in the summary of the *description* of some scene represented on film. In naming details from a picture, we record them generally in a spatial way; and the language of space and position will now present few problems for students. Details of summary will develop as the author moves from left to right, right to left, top to bottom, and so on, even though summary of a narrative will demand more advanced skills. But you have taught with this exercise the notion of compressing detail and of distinguishing major from minor detail and have thus laid important foundations for the writing soon to come.

Your next work is to involve students in an activity that allows them to summarize some story with a clear sequence. Here, perhaps, play some musical selection (a current song or a folk song) that presents a clear narrative. Ask students to take notes as they listen; then ask someone to summarize the events as someone else writes. How does the summary compare with the original? How does it contrast? What elements does the summary exclude? There are bound to be problems in using sequence vocabulary, too. Here, the difficulty will be to avoid excessive use of sequence words and to use, when necessary, sequence words of sufficient variety.

Some instructors like to demonstrate the need to keep sequence clear by creating sentences with two time elements, the second of which occurs in time prior to the first. This is on a small scale what Shaughnessy means when she says that the intellectual and rhetorical structures do not always match in a given piece of writing. Examine this sentence:

He enjoyed the cold salami and cheese, several olives and small tomatoes, a banana and an apple—all spread out upon the white formica table—although shortly before arriving he had eaten an enormous breakfast at Steve's Diner, following that with a cup of coffee and a doughnut from a small truck on the corner of Maple and Allen.

To summarize the key information in that sentence the student must first puzzle out the sequence before he can begin to reject some details as being less significant than others. A way to present a sentence like this one is to write it out on four different cards, each card corresponding to a different sentence element. For example, put on the first card the words from *He* to *apple;* on another card write the words from *all* to *table;* on the next, *although* to *Diner;* on the last *following* to *Allen.* Ask students to help arrange the cards in the correct *chronological* order—the order in which the events occurred. How do the members of the class account for the wide difference between the writers presentation of the information and the actual chronology? Here again is a good place to discuss the options open to writers when they write: How could the sentence be rearranged with clear connecting words so that the syntax matches the chronology? What other arrangements might the writer have chosen?

Then reinforce the notion of major and minor detail. Ask students to discuss the main point of the sentence. Which details might the writer of a summary be able to exclude because of their minor nature? Which details would have to be included because of their importance? Any decisions about including or excluding detail in a summary must be related to the author's main idea. Students should come away from this activity with that understanding.

It should be clear that though these recommended activities seem extensive, they are taking the place of the main elements in *prewriting.* In the summary-writing exercise, the stage of invention is pretty much bypassed, materials for writing controlled by the segment for synopsis. Despite its complications, however, the summary does not plunge students into the same kinds of choices they must make when they write description, say, or narration. Certainly the writer needs to select the details he sees as important in preserving the sense of the narrative he is summarizing; and certainly he must create his own syntactic structures as he represents the story in his own language (although in a précis the writer will try to preserve the style and stresses of the original). Still, the writer of the summary is not inventing his own subject matter. It is all there in the piece he is summing up. So attention in this activity moves from the area of invention toward the special requirements of form and content imposed by the summary assignment. And any information the student presents within his summary he develops not from experiential reality into sensory detail, but from someone else's perceptions that need restating in the student's own language. Here then begins practice that leads to skill in the use of expert testimony; and beyond that grows into competence with citation and with the complex interweaving of original and quoted language that is the mark of a skillful research writer.

After warm-up activities that encourage practice in summary skills, students should write a narrative on their own.

What kinds of narratives stimulate clear summaries? Again, the imaginative instructor sees no limits to possibilities. Here are some options:

- Use the students' own previous narratives as the basis for the assignment. Arrange to have members of the class exchange papers. Using a classmate's narrative as the source, each student must first identify the main idea of the selection and then must make a list of key details that support that idea. This will be a simple task if the topic sentence is the first sentence in the paragraph. From their notes students then write a one-paragraph synopsis of the narrative.

- Use newspaper clippings of current, local stories. Ask each student to bring in an article that narrates some event (an accident, a ceremony, an itinerary of a diplomat, the events in the day of a famous star). From these stories students write their summaries either alone or in groups.

- Ask students to watch the same episode of a situation comedy show on television and to take notes with the purpose of summarizing the story. This will be a more difficult assignment because of the quantity of detail that must be excluded. Writers will need to be very cautious about stating the main idea of the show. A special caution here about interpretive comments is in order: *funny, cute, hilarious*—temptations to use such adjectives must be overcome. The summary has as its purpose only to relate the main events in their order of occurrence.

• Ask the class to read a narrative from the textbook you are using. Or, select some brief, simple narrative from a novel or collection of stories you know. Read it aloud twice, once so students can determine the main idea and next so that they can take notes on important details. Ask each member of the class to write a synopsis of the major events. Simple fairy tales from Grimm have been used successfully by some instructors for this assignment.

A check list for the summary might look like this:

• Read (or listen to) the selection carefully.

• Be sure you can state the main idea of the selection.

• Take notes so that you keep a record of the major details.

• Keep in mind the proportion of your writing to the selection you are summarizing. Your writing should be about a third of the length of the selection.

• Keep the sequence clear. Tell the events in the order in which they occurred.

• Repeat information accurately. Use your own words as you restate the author's ideas.

By adapting someone else's language by means of a summary, students now familiar with some options for selecting detail can face the demands of exposition more confidently. A topic like "women's liberation," for example, might develop through widely divergent presentations of detail. The writer could offer sharply drawn instances in which she has confronted prejudice because of sex; has worked with women in professions thought essentially for men; has been the child of a working mother and can call up through images feelings of loneliness or neglect; or has read or heard the latest from Betty Friedan or Simone de Beauvoir, has viewed on television a rally for women's rights, or has been inspired by the pages of *Sexual Politics.*

As the course of instruction progresses, therefore, the student develops a vision of the available areas to which to turn in order to support a topic in writing. Before they begin to write any theme, encourage students to ask themselves these important questions:

1. What have I experienced in my own life that I can recall vividly enough to help me support with details some aspect of the topic?
2. What have I read lately (or can read easily and quickly) that will help me support with details some aspect of the topic?
3. What have I seen or heard on television, in the movies, on the radio, or from my friends, relatives, or teachers that will help me support with details some aspect of the topic?

If the student has an answer to question 1, he knows that the substance of his paragraph should rely upon sensory detail for concreteness: he might even develop a narrative paragraph to advance his position on an abstract idea. If question 2 inspires thought, the student knows his concrete details should be paraphrase or quotation with some reference to source of information. Details selected in response to question 3 may be developed with an eye to both—or either—the sensory or the supportive material available through paraphrasing or quoting statements, examples, statistics, or cases.

When the student moves to more abstract regions of argument, then, he is armed with a variety of approaches to detail. With the nature of detail clearly in mind, beginning writers may meet more easily the problems of form. The theme below suggests the potential of instruction in detail, instruction that moves from concrete sensory language to data drawn from other sources. In a paragraph of illustration the writer holds the reader in no small part through the pertinence and specificity of detail:

The Dangers of the Automobile

Automobiles are dangerous because they pollute the air with harmful chemicals and because they are frequently unsafe to drive in. Polluting the air, the exhaust emissions of a car make people ill every day. Aside from its stress on heart ailments, carbon monoxide fumes cause nausea and dizziness. Writing in *Highway Homicide,* Paul W. Kearney reports that a faulty exhaust system that fed CO_2 into his car lulled him to sleep at the wheel, forcing him to drive clear across the four-lane divided Taconic State Parkway, and escape death by a miracle. Other hydrocarbons, nitrogen dioxide, and lead similarly make breathing hard to bear and may contribute to paralysis, blindness, insanity, and sterility. Poisonous car emissions also cause other fatal diseases. One is emphysema, a respiratory ailment; between 1950 and 1959, reports Gerald Leinwand in a study of air and water pollution, deaths from this disease rose from 1.5 in every 100,000 to 8 per 100,000. Bronchial asthma is another condition often aggravated by air pollution and after a person with asthma is disturbed for a long time by smog, he may die from lack of oxygen. Other diseases linked with air pollution are lung cancer and chronic bronchitis. But in addition to the danger of pollution, cars are often unsafe for the driver and his passengers because of bad design and construction. The Chevrolet Corvair was a perfect example of a car unsafe to the driver. Ralph Nader in *Unsafe at Any Speed* shows how one woman in 1961, Mrs. Rose Pierini, lost her left arm when her Corvair suddenly turned over on its top just beyond the San Marcos Overpass in Santa Barbara, California. Furthermore, the instrument panel can cause many dangers to the passenger. Nader says, "Dr. William Haddon of the New York Department of Health tells how one of his cases, a young girl, lost her eye by the instrument panel. When the car jerked forward, the girl's eye went into a protruding knob on the dash board." Announced in a Cornell study, the total injuries from the instrument panel range from simple fractures of the pelvis to crushed chests. There is no doubt that in the areas of pollution and safety, automobiles are very dangerous; but with an educated public, well aware of these problems, important changes can be brought about.

ADVANCED RHETORICAL STRUCTURES

I have indulged my concerns for instruction in detail and have allowed them to carry me somewhat afield of my intention in this section: to provide a general overview of the kinds of skills students need to develop after the first basic course in writing. Beyond detail, beginners need more than the three simple rhetorical structures—description, narration, illustration—I've defined as the heart of early instruction. Loosely in this sequence because of their increasing complexity and their dependence upon each of the proceding forms in the continuum, the rhetorical strategies of process analysis, of comparison and contrast, of definition, and of division and classification require investigation.* Methods of organizing data and the way those methods relate to thought processes are important new skills to teach, includ-

*During my year in State College an elaborate argument between some of the members of the PSU's Freshman English Committee and other teaching faculty focused on the value of separating these closely related strategies. Insisting that division—analysis, really—is a breaking down into particulars whereas classification is a building up into categories, the first group asserted that the two techniques *opposed* each other in intent. Louise Rorabecker in her text *Assignments in Exposition* speaks for the separatists.

The other group, citing presentations in major texts that almost always united the two and taught them as flip sides of one coin, insisted that division and classification work together, that one could rarely establish categories without first dividing some larger whole. *The Harbrace Handbook,* perhaps unwittingly, speaks for the joiners in this succinct sentence that starts its discussion on classification: "To *classify* is to *divide* into categories" (emphasis mine). Randolph Decker in *Patterns of Exposition* follows a similar route.

ing here causality and inductive and deductive reasoning. And the vast sea of argumentation and persuasion will require close instruction in logic, in the discovery of arguments, and in confirmation and refutation. Although I myself will usually ask students to practice each new rhetorical strategy in a single paragraph theme (in that way at early stages of instruction, the whimsies of essay form draw no attention), developing writers need ultimately to move into more open formats, first to the clearly delimited essay of four or five paragraphs, then to the expansive essay limited only by the demands of content and by the audience's needs. From a one-paragraph theme the topic sentence can expand into the introductory paragraph of an essay. Paragraph subtopic sentences can serve as openings for body paragraphs now more richly than before developing ideas through detail. Transitional elements—like a subordinating structure that refers back to the substance of a previous paragraph—provide fuller connections than a single paragraph usually allows. And a closing sentence can be expanded to teach the conclusion, where a writer may try to set his topic in a new perspective. At the heart of all these concerns with form, of course, lies the essence of content revealed through concrete detail.

I've used the word *overview* pointedly in the title of this chapter: though I can name many I've overlooked here, I have no intention of laying out *all* the elements every apprentice writer needs to learn in order to succeed. In the first place, I don't know them. Each writing task throws up its own barriers, uncovers its own problems. So, ultimately, only practice under a watchful eye can assure continuing advancement. (More often than not, that eye is the writer's own.) Second, and as I've explained, each institution must define its own concept of success in writing, taking into account many conditions—the mission of the school, its populations and their needs and talents, the life's work for which an education must prepare that population, the standards for excellence agreed upon by the faculty. I cannot insist enough upon how widely those conditions can vary from school to school (and, from year to year, decade to decade, even within the same school); and how easily an institution can ignore those conditions in its desperate search for students, in its sometimes hardened curriculum designed for another age, in its unexamined marriage of convenience to the status quo.

Finally, I don't want to try to lay out all the skills and techniques apprentice writers need because it will, I am sure, insist I answer a question I have successfully avoided for many years (though I am asked it with increasing frenzy each year): "How many courses must a successful writing program offer?" Only an English department guided by a strong writing program administrator and supported by an informed faculty in other disciplines can answer that one. It is an answer locked in the institution's own identity.

APPENDIX

A

Suggested Day Plans

If a book describing a course of instruction invites jabs from those with divergent philosophies and approaches, a daily calendar for basic writing teachers can draw a merciless left hook to the chin.

One inescapable conclusion about calendars without apology is that they mandate actions, suggesting to many (myself included) the kind of mindless behaviorism that sings the "If this is Tuesday it must be run-ons" blues. Creative teachers abhor day-by-day schedules prepared in advance by others. There are many obvious reasons to marshall against standard courses and daily plans. Undoubtedly the problems of different students in different classes on different campuses will vary. Some classes may not need two or three full sessions on sentence fragments. Other classes may demand sessions on agreement and on verb tense long before those skills appear on the calendar. Still others will require instruction not even touched upon in the course plan or will require frequent repetition of skills allotted only minutes on a single day. Surely, only the instructor's awareness of the students' capabilities can establish the true logic for each course.

And yet in keeping with the spirit of this book, the calendar is a logical extension of earlier pleas for sequence in writing skills instruction. In a way, the daily plan is merely a time map that places Chapters 1, 2, and 3 in the practical context of the classroom, where they belong (hence, the accompanying column of reference pages). The two calendars below*—one for the quarterly system and a slightly different

* I'd pick the semester any day as a superior term structure for beginning writers, the quarter to my way of thinking a cost efficient expediency without much pedagogical value, especially for students who learn more slowly than others. Since there are more days and more weekends over the semester, writers have more time to let their ideas congeal, more time to work through drafts, more time to write more often with reduced suffering.

one for the semester—simply offer a program for one course that works well enough to be a guide for beginning teachers. They, no doubt, will draw upon their own creativity, resourcefulness, and adaptability to build their own courses. The sequence represented in these calendars is also one that works: in rhetoric it moves from the simple to the more complex; in language skills it moves after critical work with sentence patterns from those serious errors for which readers have little tolerance to those less serious (though important) violations of convention. Other things, too, are worth noting. Aside from the brief, dictated "exam" on problems arising from theme one, students do not deal at all with error until the eighth class of the quarter or until the thirteenth class of the semester. Also, reworking rough drafts in groups under the teacher's benign supervision takes significant class time, as do frequent explorations of syntactical options. And always before students submit a finished theme, they receive their previous work, fully evaluated, so that they can learn from the strengths and weaknesses to which the reader calls their attention. At the end of each recommended plan I have allowed for final in-class essays, assuming that they grow out of course instruction and that they certify a writer's achievement of course objectives, command over skills taught during the term. Teachers faced with more formal testing programs (uniform exams administered during a finals' week for example) or with contracted or expanded terms need to adjust the calendar.

THIRTY-DAY PLAN (FOR THE TEN-WEEK QUARTERLY SYSTEM, CLASSES MEETING THREE TIMES A WEEK)

Class Topics	Refer especially to these resource book pages
1. Introduction. Twenty-minute diagnostic sample written in class. How writers work.	13–21, 28–33, 37–42, 110–14

Specific language (nouns, verbs, adjectives).

2. Assign paragraph 1, description of a room. Vocabulary. Concrete language and sensory detail. Return diagnostic. 21–25, 68–77, 110–14

3. Rough draft workshop. Suggested focuses: paragraph parts (topic sentence, closing sentence, appropriateness of detail, expansion of detail, titles). 33–37, 63–67, 110–14

4. Instruction in proofreading. Collect 1. The concept of a sentence: recognizing subjects and predicates; combining subjects and verbs; expanding kernel sentences and contracting long sentences. 37–42, 124–30

5. Assign paragraph 2, description of a person. Review of sensory details. Connotation and denotation. Vocabulary. 21–33, 68–70, 77–82, 110–14

6. Return 1. Correction workshop. Focus on major recurrent errors in a brief dictated "exam" made up of incorrect words and structures from students' papers. Individual spelling problems and how to deal with them. 33–37, 45–58 117–20

7. Rough draft workshop 2. Sentence embedding and combining. (Introduce relevant punctuation with each operation.) 68–70, 129–32, 181

8. Sentence boundaries: run on errors and comma faults. Collect 2. 135–41

9. Assign paragraph 3, narration. Vocabulary for narratives. Active voice. 21–33, 84–94

10. Return 2. Correction workshop. Dictated "exam" on major errors. Practice with embedding: appositives. 33–37, 45–58, 127–135

11. Rough draft workshop 3. Run-on review. Dictionary skills. 33–37, 114–17, 135–41

12. Sentence boundaries: fragments (no-subject, no-verb type). Collect 3. 141–49

13. Sentence boundaries: fragments (subordinate or relative clause type). Review of all fragments. Review of key principles of embedding. 127–32, 141–49, 149–53

THIRTY-DAY PLAN *(Continued)*

Class Topics	Refer especially to these resource book pages
14. Assign paragraph 4, narration, for in-class writing. Review of composing process for pressure-writing conditions. Vocabulary. Punctuation of direct and indirect quotes.	43–45, 94–95, 120–24
15. Return 3. Correction workshop. Focus on fragments from students' papers.	33–37, 45–58, 141–53
16. Write 4 in class. (Second exercise in narration.)	43–45
17. Subject-verb agreement (singular and plural nouns and verbs).	153–64
18. Review of subject-verb agreement. Practice embedding participial phrases (*-ing, -ed*) in various sentence positions. Use of comma for participial openers. Avoiding dangling modifiers.	133–35, 153–64 164–66
19. Assign paragraph 5, illustration (or summary of narrative). Vocabulary of transitions helpful in using illustration format (or vocabulary of summary).	96–106, 234–40
20. Return 4. Correction workshop: agreement and quotation errors from student papers.	33–37, 55–58, 120–24, 153–64
21. Dangling and misplaced modifiers (from paper 4). Students proofread 5 and check for dangling and misplaced modifiers. Collect 5.	27–40, 164–60
22. Assign 6. Illustration.	21–33, 96–106
23. Return 5. Correction workshop: review of major errors.	33–37, 45–48
24. Basic tense formations. Irregular verbs. Tense consistency. Collect 6.	166–71
25. Review tense. Capitals. Possessives.	166–71, 172–80
26. Return 6. Correction workshop: capitals, possessives, tense errors, comma uses.	33–37, 55–58, 166–71, 172–80, 181–83

27. Write 7 in class. (Practice for final achievement theme.)   43–45
28. Special usage problems. Pronouns as subjects and objects. Pronoun reference and agreement.   183–87
29. Return 7. Correction workshop: focus on major sticking errors.   33–37, 45–58
30. Final in-class achievement theme.   43–45, 209–27

FORTY-TWO-DAY PLAN (FOR THE FOURTEEN-WEEK SEMESTER SYSTEM, CLASSES MEETING THREE TIMES A WEEK).

Class Topics	Refer especially to these pages
1. Introduction. Twenty-minute diagnostic sample How writers work. Specific language (nouns, verbs, adjectives).	13–21, 28–33, 37–42, 110–14
2. Specific language. Concrete detail. Vocabulary of description.	68–72, 110–14
3. Return diagnostic. Assign paragraph 1, description of a room. Review sensory detail.	68–77, 110–14
4. Paragraph parts: topic sentence, closing sentence, titles.	63–67
5. Review of detail: appropriateness, expansion, precision, showing vs. telling.	110–14
6. Rough draft workshop: focus on review of paragraph parts.	33–37, 63–67
7. Instruction in proofreading. Collect 1. Connotation and denotation.	37–41, 41–42, 111
8. The concept of a sentence: recognizing subjects and predicates; combining subjects and verbs; expanding kernel sentences and contracting long sentences.	124–30
9. Assign paragraph 2, description of a person. Review sensory detail. Vocabulary of description.	68–70, 77–82, 110–14
10. Return 1. Correction workshop. Focus on major recurrent errors in a brief dictated	33–37, 45–58, 117–20

FORTY-TWO-DAY PLAN (*Continued*)

Class Topics	*Refer especially to these pages*
"exam" made up of incorrect words and structures on students' papers. Individual spelling problems and how to deal with them.	
11. Sentence embedding and combining. Introduce relevant punctuation with coordinate and subordinate operations.	127–32, 181
12. Rough draft workshop 2: focus on expanding, embedding, and combining sentences.	33–37, 68–70, 127–32
13. Sentence boundaries: run-on errors and comma faults. Collect 2.	135–41
14. Vocabulary for narratives. Dictionary skills.	84–85, 114–17
15. Assign paragraph 3, narration.	21–33, 84–94
16. Practice embedding appositives.	127–35
17. Return 2. Correction workshop. Brief dictated "exam" on major errors.	33–37, 45–48
18. Rough draft workshop 3. Run on review.	33–37, 135–41
19. Sentence boundaries: fragments (no-subject, no-verb type). Collect 3.	141–49
20. Sentence boundaries: fragments (subordinate and relative clause type).	149–53
21. Review of all fragments. Review of key principles of embedding.	127–32, 141–53
22. Assign paragraph 4, narration for in-class writing. Review narrative principles (eye on problems students had in paragraph 3). Review of composing process for pressure writing conditions.	43–45, 84–94, 94–95
23. Vocabulary of narrative. Punctuation of direct and indirect quotes.	120–24
24. Return 3. Correction workshop: focus on fragments from students' papers.	33–37, 45–58, 141–53

25. Write 4 in class (second exercise in narra-   43–45
    tion).
26. Subject verb agreement (singular and   153–64
    plural nouns and verbs).
27. Review and continuation of principles of   153–64
    subject verb agreement.
28. Review of principles of sentence expan-   133–35, 164–66
    sion, combining, and embedding. Prac-
    tice embedding participial phrases (-*ing*,
    -*ed*) in various sentence positions. Use of
    comma for participial openers. How to
    avoid danglers.
29. Assign paragraph 5, illustration (or sum-   96–106, 234–40
    mary of narrative). Vocabulary of transi-
    tions helpful in using illustration format
    (or vocabulary of summary).
30. Return 4. Correction workshop: focus on   33–37, 55–58,
    agreement and quotation errors from stu-   120–24, 153–64
    dents' papers.
31. Rough draft workshop (for 5). Focus: par-   33–37, 96–106,
    ticipial embedding.   133–35
32. Dangling and misplaced modifiers (from   37–41, 153–64,
    4). Students proofread 5 and check for   164–66
    agreement errors and dangling modifier
    errors. Collect 5.
33. Assign 6. Illustration.   21–33, 96–106
34. Return 5. Correction workshop: review of   33–37, 45–48
    major errors.
35. Basic tense formations. Irregular verbs.   166–71
    Collect 6.
36. More on tense. Tense consistency.   166–71
37. Capitals. Possessives.   166–71, 172–80
38. Return 6. Correction workshop: Capitals,   33–37, 55–58,
    possessives, tense errors, comma uses.   166–71, 172–80,
                                               181–83
39. Write 7 in class (practice for final achieve-   43–45
    ment theme).
40. Special usage problems. Pronouns as   183–87
    subjects and objects. Pronoun reference
    and agreement.

FORTY-TWO-DAY *(Continued)*

	Refer especially
Class Topics	*to these pages*
41. Return 7. Correction workshop: focus on major sticking errors.	33–37, 45–48
42. Final in-class achievement theme.	43–45, 209–27

B

Short Takes: Seventeen Informal Writing Exercises

The early chapters in this book and the day plans that map out possible programs include several formal writing assignments, large-scale exercises that move from prewriting through several drafts before submission as clean copy. But, as I've pointed out, beginning writers need to write a great deal, much more than carefully structured weekly assignments will require. Certainly sentence-level activities like combining or embedding extend the territory for practice when they demand syntactical operations in each student's original prose. But there are other kinds of exercises, done in class or away from it, that can provide beginners with the important experience of simply putting pen to paper and can help them in overcoming reticence they feel about themselves as writers. In some of these "short takes" you might stress a particular skill in language or syntax. Or, students may write just for practice, unrestricted by any special attention to one skill.

These activities need not present any special burden for the teacher who grades seriously the students' work: some papers can be checked for particular elements in class by students themselves working in groups, some papers only briefly and cursorily by the teacher, others perhaps not at all.

What follows are suggestions culled from my own experiences and from those of successful classroom teachers I've known, many at LaGuardia and at Penn State where I've taught. With no attempt at exhaustiveness I hope these will arouse other brief, informal exercises.

• **Journal Writing**

The journal is a fairly common method of getting students to write. Its value for teaching specific skills is, at best, questionable, but it can be effective in helping students over that initial "I have nothing to write" hurdle.

To be effective, journal writing should probably begin soon after classes begin, when students are at their most reticent. After explaining that many writers use journals to record spontaneous ideas and observations that may later be used in more disciplined writing exercises, point out that journals are like diaries in that the writer records whatever private thoughts he feels like recording at whatever moment he chooses to record them.

It is of course in that feature that the main contradiction lies for teachers who assign journal writing, which they then collect to read, reading even with great generosity of spirit and without making comments. A writer's journal, so far as I'm concerned, is for its creator's eyes alone. Using journals to loosen up students by telling them to write whatever they please and then insisting that they submit their words for a reading works against whatever relaxation about writing that journals allow. With someone looking over their shoulders journal writers always hold back.

But if you have no intention of reading what students write in their journals, you can use them to insist upon daily written records. Approach the journal as you would timed writing by setting a task and by supervising its execution. "Turn to the first page in the notebook you plan to use as a journal, write down today's date, and write for the next five minutes your impressions of today's class. Write whatever comes to mind. Don't stop, even if you can't think of anything more to say; just keep writing. Keep the pen going for five solid minutes. Don't look up; just write. What you write is for your eyes only. No one but you will read it."

One instructor suggests that a way to connect the value of journal writing with more formal exercises is on the very next day to ask the class to write, for collection, four or five sentences to answer the question "How was your English class yesterday?" Checking their journals, students can compose a measured response based upon spontaneous entries recorded at the previous class.

To encourage habitual entries, for the first couple of weeks you want to allow time at the start of each class for students to write in their journals. Expecting entries every day, you can spot check to show that you care by asking that students bring their journals to class and by asking occasionally to see the page for yesterday's entry. Promise not to read the words; just move between the chairs for a spot check.

• Epitaphs

Students write a few sentences for the tombstone of some familiar or famous person. These may be humorous or serious, contemporary or historical, poetic or straightforward.

• Advertising Copy

Ask students to invent a product and then to write four or five complete sentences that highlight its strengths and that convince readers of a magazine or newspaper to buy the product. Or ask the class to write copy for the basic writing course they're in now. Those musically inclined can write advertising jingles, but with only complete sentences allowed.

• Boasts

Students enjoy a four or five sentence exercise in which they tell what makes them exceptional. Say, "What do you know, or what have you done, or what can you do, or what is it about your looks or physique or personality that makes you the stand-out that you are? Let yourself go. Don't worry too much about the truth. Boast."

• Fables

This project provides practice in writing dialogue and in understanding such distinctions as concrete/abstract and general/particular. It's probably necessary to read a few simple fables to the class to set the mood.

First provide a situation or a choice of situations: for example, a conversation that might take place between a dog and a squirrel on the campus, between a bee and a fly, a bee and a squirrel, or between a mouse in the classroom and a bird on the windowsill outside. The fable consists of a dialogue followed by an aphorism or moral—a generalization realized from the particular conversation.

• News-story Openers

Ask the class to write the first sentence or two of a newspaper story about some important local event.

• Letter to the Editor

Focusing on some current issue, students can write brief letters to the editor of campus or local newspapers.

• Picture into Words

Ask the class to look at some action-filled snapshot from the local paper and to write two or three sentences to describe the main point of the picture. A cartoon without words (a caricature, for example) works nicely, a political cartoon with somewhat more difficulty.

• Sensory Riddles

Ask students to select some familiar object and to describe it in a few sentences—without mentioning its name—so that readers can identify it easily. There should be a number of concrete details that appeal to color, sound, action, smell, touch. Offer this example of an ice-cream truck:

White Rectangle

This smooth rectangle sputters up Polo Road every evening with the clink of bells and squealing children down the street. One youngster steps up to the rectangular object, holds out a silver coin, and a man in a white hat swings open a door with a thump. Smoke curls out, and the odor of chocolate and strawberry and coldness fills the air.

• A Person in a Sentence

As a volunteer stands before the class, ask students to write a single sentence describing the person, a sentence rich in sensory diction. Here's an example:

Staring through gold-framed glasses, Jean brushes a soft strand of brown hair off her forehead and then coughs nervously into a trembling hand.

• Job Description

Ask students to write a few sentences which characterize their ideal job.

• Want Ads

Have the class write want ads (in full sentences) for jobs they invent to deal with important issues of today.

• Career Goals

Students can write several sentences to describe what they want to be or to do when they leave college.

• Self-portrait

Ask people in the class to look into a mirror and to write a few sentences about what they see.

• Introductions

Students can write brief introductions of themselves to the
rest of the class. Or a student can interview the person sitting at the next desk and can introduce that person to the
rest of the class.

• TV Guide Program News

A good, short exercise asks students to write a few sentences of copy about a television show that will appear next
week, the copy designed for release in a television pro-
gramming magazine.

• Personifications

Pretending they are some inanimate objects, students can
write five sentences of "gripes" from the point of view of the
object.

APPENDIX

C

Sample Writing Tests

(Only the essay components of the various tests appear below; frequently, accompanying sections attempt to measure other skills such as reading, sentence structures, vocabulary, logic, or organization.)

THE NEW JERSEY COLLEGE BASIC SKILLS PLACEMENT TEST, 1979*

Sample Essay Question and Instructions

Time—20 minutes

You will have 20 minutes to plan and write an essay on the topic assigned. DO NOT WRITE ON A TOPIC OTHER THAN THE ONE ASSIGNED. AN ESSAY ON A TOPIC OF YOUR OWN CHOICE IS NOT ACCEPTABLE.

The essay is assigned to give you an opportunity to show how well you can write. You should, therefore, take care to express your thoughts on the topic clearly and effectively. Be specific. Remember that how well you write is much more important than how much you write.

Your essay must be written on the lines provided on your answer sheet. You will receive no other paper on which to write. You will find that you have enough space if you write on every line, avoid wide margins, and keep your handwriting to a reasonable size.

Read this topic carefully before you begin writing.

Throughout history, older people and younger people have tended to blame each other for what is wrong with the world. The truth of the matter probably is that each group does some things wrong and some things right.

*From *Scoring the Essays for the New Jersey College Basic Skills Placement Test.* Copyright © 1979 by Educational Testing Service. All rights reserved.

What are some things members of your own age group are doing right? Choose one or two things you admire most about people your own age. In a well-organized essay, describe the things you admire and tell why you admire them. Use specific examples.

Excerpts from Principles of Scoring

There are four points to the scale used in scoring; each reader can award a paper a 4, 3, 2, or 1, with 4 being the highest score. The total score for a paper is the sum of two readers' scores: 8, 7, 6, 5, 4, 3, or 2. Papers that are judged off-topic are given 0.

Readers are instructed to rank papers against each other, not against some ideal. This insistence on dealing with the papers at hand is designed to prevent readers from setting up a standard that even the very good student could not meet when writing an essay on a given topic in 20 minutes. In using the four-point scale, which deliberately has no middle point, readers must first judge whether the paper, in the light of other papers written on this same topic, is "upper half" (3–4) or "lower half" (2–1) and then whether the paper is far enough into the "upper half" category to receive a 4 or far enough into the "lower half" category to receive a 1. Because only four different scores can be awarded by any one reader, each score must necessarily represent a range of ability. Readers are accustomed to referring to a paper as a "low 2" or a "high 2," for example, even though the recorded score for that paper can be only a "2." Sometimes, papers are classified by readers as "splits"; these papers receive an almost equal number of different but adjacent scores on the four-point scale. That is, for example, a paper may receive a "3" from half the readers and a "2" from the other half. In the actual scoring, this paper is expected to receive a score of 5, a score of 3 from one reader and a score of 2 from the other, for it is probably a paper that falls exactly in the middle of the score range. Papers that receive scores of 4 and 1, 4 and 2, and 3 and 1, however, are read again to resolve a discrepancy in readers' scores that cannot be tolerated in a reliable reading.

To judge the essays fairly, readers must read the entire essay. Some writers make a poor beginning, but write better and better as they warm to the task. Some writers begin splendidly and then fall into problems of organization or development that mar the essay considerably. A long essay is not an automatic indication of a good essay; nor is a short essay indicative of a writer who has little control of sentence structure, organization, logic, or other aspects of writing. Some essays are not completed in the 20 minutes allowed. Such essays are judged on the quality of the writing found in what the student has accomplished; the writer is not penalized for failing to complete the task in the short period allowed for it.

• Selected Sample Essays in Different Score Categories and Commentary by the New Jersey Basic Skills Council

Total score: 7
(a score of 4 from one reader and 3 from the other)

Sample C

Several important things have been accomplished by the members of my own age group. All have been aimed at the establishment and betterment of social conditions. People in my age group today have set higher goals for themselves and are achieving more than previous generations. They are now well-educated and are more aware of the crisis surrounding them, if there happens to be one existing at the present time. They strive towards peace and equality in society. They have bought down many old ideas, social barriers, and have, for the most part eliminated racism. They are discouraged and dissapointed about the corruption they see in the higher echelons of our government, and plan to do something to change it for the better.

The younger people today are not divided, as the previous generations were, by race, color, sex, or creed. There is no caste system in this country, and the younger people today act in unison while striving to accomplish their goals. The world left behind by the older generation is one that has been wracked by war, genocide, poverty, and crime. With the betterment of our educational system, our younger generation can possibly learn from their forefathers mistakes and make this world a prosperous and harmonious place in which to live our lives.

Sample D

Teenages today may seem to have lack of respect for the moral code of their elders, but this is a false supposition. Young people today have spontaneity, and a great deal of courage. They also have the ability to both learn and love.

Courage for teenagers doesn't necessarily mean courage enough to defy your parents or your school, but it means courage to accept every challenge that comes along, and not give in unless there is defintely no answer that they are able to give. They don't bow down until they are absolutely sure that there is nothing left for them to do.

A great gift that teenagers have is spontaneity. They react quickly with their emotions, but not unwisely. Many people would say a better word to use than spontaneous would be adaptable. Teenagers adapt themselves well to any and every situation.

Lastly, teenagers have a great ability to learn and love. By learning, it doesn't necessarily mean schooling. They keep their senses alert and learn about life through them, and with them. They don't stand by and let life go on as they watch. The young people jump in with both feet to take part. As for their ability to love, it reaches every corner of the world. Teenagers aren't afraid to love someone of a different race or creed. They may not always show patience towards others who are not as good physically or mentally, but then teenagers still have a long way to go in the "growing up" process. Their love encompasses all, and especially themselves.

Youth today have many problems, but with a little time and encouragement from their peers and elders, they will get by. Who knows, someone sitting in this room right now might be another Thomas Edison, or Madame Curie, or any one of a dozen brilliant people. It may sound "old hat", but it just might be true.

Sample C is well written, but it does not exhibit the command of the language seen in the two samples that received a score of 8. There is a fairly successful attempt to present a logical, unified argument; this argument, however, is married by such statements as "They . . . are more aware of the crisis surrounding them, if there happens to be one existing at the present time" (where one part of the sentence weakens the other) and "With the betterment of our educational system, our younger generation can . . ." (where no concrete attempt has been made to tell us just how the betterment of the educational system affects the younger generation or will effect the changes alluded to).

Nevertheless, on the whole, the essay is "upper half" and far enough into the "upper half" in the judgment of readers to warrant a 7.

Sample D is the work of a fluent writer. It is basically well-done, with a consistent and clear argument presented. However, the writer does not follow exactly the organizational plan outlined in the first paragraph and ends the essay with a paragraph that does not relate at all to that plan. Moreover, there is a problem of pronoun reference in the second paragraph and a superfluity of commas in various compound structures throughout the essay. Nevertheless, readers who judged the essay as a whole and who rated it against other essays on the same topic saw enough merit in the essay to rank it as decidedly "upper half" or better. When presented to the entire group of readers, the paper received a score of 3 from some readers and a score of 4 from others.

Total score: 5

(a score of 3 from one reader and 2 from the other)

Sample G

In history, older people and younger people have tended to blame each other for what is wrong in the world. This is because the two groups have a hard time of understanding each other. The older people were brought up in an different environment. Many of these individuals did not change with the times, and live in the old days. Their inability to change, is the real generation gap. Examples of this could be rock music, dress, hair etc. which are important to today's youth. Parents especially have a hard time understanding these things which are important to their children. Older people especially senior citizens even fear today's young people with their long hair, jeans and loud music. It is true that some youth oftens abuses today's older citizen (robbings, vandalism etc) but that is only a small minority. Newspapers seem to blow everything up of proportion when it comes to todays youth. (example: There can be a thousand kids at a rock concert, and out of a thousand three light up a joint, and the next day the papers print that their was a wild concert with everyone smoking dope. Today's young people often resent their elders because they represent authority. Authority to them means doeing things against their will. I'm not saying don't listen to authority but to distinguish between what is right and what is wrong. today's young people are more rational than does of twenty years ago. They live in a more sophisticated world. Adults should not compare their childhood to that of today's. They were two completely different worlds. Today's young people live in a better society, scientifically, economically etc. Today's young people are more aware of what is happening in today's world.

Sample H

Many young people today are leaning towards correcting the problems that have come about through carelessness of the entire population. They are striving to clean-up the land that they live on, the air that they beath and the water that is near them.

It is the younger group of people who have pushed for many antipollution laws to be passed and many recycling programs. They are the one who have brought these problems to the older people who are really the people who work out the programs and write the laws.

Many younger people are more interested in the ecology of our country and the rest of the world. They are beginning to realize that these problems must be taken care of now, before its to late.

The younger group of people are those that work for these programs for waste recycling are the ones who will determine how long we, as human beings, can live at the pace we do today. Through their hard work and education we can develope better ways in which to conserve what we have, to clean up our world and try to make so that people will be living, like we are or maybe even better, on this earth for many years to come.

Both the writer of G and the writer of H exhibit control of sentence structure and both make an attempt to present a logical argument. However, in spite of the kind of syntactical structure and diction exhibited in each essay, each paper has major flaws. The writer of H, for example, not only fails to introduce the topic of the essay directly, but also ends up with an essay that is more like a list than an organized whole. The writer of G writes one long paragraph. Readers judging these essays as a whole were divided in their scoring of them. Some thought the essays written well enough to deserve an "upper half" rating; others saw qualities that made the papers "lower half" in their eyes. Note that the divided scoring places the papers exactly in the middle of the score range. These are, in essence, the "average" papers in the group.

Total score: 4
(a score of 2 from each of two readers)

Sample I

The first accomplishment I see that members of my own age group are doing right is excepting the special child in society. New organizations are developing and helping them to live in this world without being stared at or run away from like they have some kind of diesease. I have to admit that at first I myself felt sorry for these people but by just sitting down and talking to them I see they are as intelligent as anyone in this world.

People my own age seem to have a more interest in the athletic field. I think this is a very important factor since fitness as become such a big deal in are health care.

What I really admire most in are age group is that people are doing and saying what they think is right, speaking out there own mind so people can live better. We shouldn't be scared to say what we think or care what other people think of us if we know we are right.

Sample J

The younger people today are more open towards other people, in spite of the fact of their race ore religion. However, the older generation may still have a little prejudice within them.

In school, for example, youths are always socializing with people they don't even know, and will make each other feel comfortable by the things they say to each other.

The youths are also concerned about their career ahead of them. They are eager to better their lives in any way possible. Most youths are already getting jobs to be able to futher their education and/or to live their lives to the fulliest.

The basic problem with J is its tendency to force the reader to supply the logical connection between parts of the argument, an argument, incidentally, that is not illustrated in any convincing way. For example, the first sentence leads the reader to believe that the writer will discuss better relations between peoples of varied backgrounds. The specific example supplied does not deal with that topic at all. Note that the writer does, however, show command of sentence structure, punctuation, and spelling. It is the flawed logic of the paper and its lack of depth that put it in the "lower half."

Sample I reveals that the writer needs some help in using the conventions of the written language as well as in developing a logical, unified argument. The flaws in the paper, however, are not sufficient to put the paper in the lowest score category.

THE CALIFORNIA STATE UNIVERSITY & COLLEGES ENGLISH PLACEMENT TEST (CSUC-EPT), 1979–80, SAMPLE ESSAY TEST QUESTION*

Directions: You will have 45 minutes to plan and write the essay assigned below. Before you begin writing, consider the topic carefully and plan what you will say. Your essay should be as well organized and as carefully written as you can make it. Be sure to use specific examples to support your ideas. Write only on the topic assigned; an essay on another topic will receive no credit.

The sample topic printed below is similar to the topic that you will be assigned to write on in Section IV of the test. You may want to write an essay on this sample topic for practice.

No one's life runs perfectly smoothly. We all encounter problems, whether major or minor, whether in school, at work, at home, in our social lives, in our relationship to the world. Sometimes we are successful solving these problems and sometimes we are not.

Describe in detail one problem you have encountered fairly recently, discuss how you went about trying to solve it, and indicate to what extent your solution seemed to work.

THE PENNSYLVANIA STATE UNIVERSITY FINAL ACHIEVEMENT THEME FOR ASSESSING PROFICIENCY IN BASIC WRITING SKILLS, 1976.

(Students are placed in the basic skills course by means of The Pennsylvania State University English Test, a multiple-

*Reprinted by permission of Educational Testing Service, the copyright owner.

choice exam on vocabulary, punctuation, grammar, and diction. Passing the final achievement theme in the basic writing course, students then take English I. Topics for the in-class theme vary each year, but teachers at campuses throughout the state use the same pool of topics for their classes.)

Grading Standards for English 4 Achievement Theme

(*Themes are graded on* Pass *or* No-Pass
by two readers for each paper)

1. Meaning and ideas
   a. Is the topic clearly stated?
   b. Are there sufficient concrete supporting details?
   c. Is the length adequate (approximately 250 words as a minimum)?
2. Structure
   a. Is the selected structure appropriate to the development of the subject?
   b. Are transitions effective and efficient?
   c. Does the syntax display an ease and familiarity with a variety of sentence structures?
   d. Is the closing appropriate?
3. Mechanics
   a. Are sentences complete and separated in correct ways according to the conventions of edited American English?
   b. Are verb forms correct and consistent?
   c. Is the spelling correct?
   d. Are modifiers properly placed?
   e. Are punctuation and capitalization correct?
   f. Are pronouns correctly used?
   There should be no more than 3 errors in a and no more than 8 major errors of the kinds listed in a–f.
4. Language
   a. Is word choice appropriate to the purpose and idiom?
   b. Are the words chosen specific enough?

Sample Paper and Commentary by Graders

A
Eating Out

1   Knowing no Chinese and little Dutch, makes eating at a chinese
2   restaurant in Holland frustrating. Opening the large glass door of the
3   restaurant, I was confronted by the tranquilizing smell of oriental cooking.
4   My stomach began to secrete digestive juices in expectation of the coming
5   meal. Being greeted by a oriental looking man in a clean black and white
6   suite, caused me to expect quality oriental cuisine. He spoke, and not
7   understanding I just shook my head, with this he turned and nodded for me
8   to follow him through the mase of black tables and red chairs.
9   The gold walls trimmed with red borders, supported small framed
10   pictures of chinese cities. Large white painted lamps with varies images
11   of chinese dragons and people, nearly touched when heads came pasted.
12   Upon receiving a seat and menu I began the hapless task of ordering a meal.
13   After smelling the oder and seeing an appatising surroundings, my
14   stomach beg my mind to to this quickly. This was difficult since the
15   menu contained only two langues. Chiness and Dutch. I know no chinese
16   and the Dutch I had known did not appear on the longe list of black
17   letters. My only hope was the waiter standing patiencely near a waiting
18   my order, realizing my problem and in perfect English, he asked, "May I
19   help you". Together we worked out an appricating order but as he walked
20   away I sat staring at the black letters and realized how so frustrating
21   it is to be in a beautiful restaurant and country not even being able to
22   order a meal.

This writer has attempted to present a narrative over a brief span of time and has wisely limited his topic to a single meal. There are occasional uses of sensory detail—the waiter's clothing, the concrete images of the walls and furniture, the image of the long list of black letters on the menu. Though these show an awareness of the need for sensory detail, the student misses the notion of concreteness more often than not. The restaurant has no name; the place the writer tries to describe is never individualized enough (beyond the images of walls and furniture) for the reader to see it clearly; we see nothing of the waiter's face. Although there is a good attempt to limit the topic through some opinion, the writer does not let us experience the sense of frustration: the details do not support the idea that there were difficulties until the third paragraph. Knowing the need to include detail, the writer nonetheless has difficulties integrating the details with his purpose: it is for this reason that he creates a separate paragraph for those details, closing it suddenly with another reference to his stated topic. One paragraph rich in detail to support his topic would have sufficed. In regard to error this paper shows typical problems of inexperienced writers. (In the third paragraph we see a number of careless errors, indicating, no doubt, that the student could not use efficiently the time provided for writing.) Spelling errors are abundant; the writer's sense of sentence boundaries is vague and leads him to write a fragment, and two comma faults, errors serious enough alone to indicate that he has not yet reached the desired level of proficiency.

Line-by-line Critique

1 incorrect use of comma between subject and verb, writer obviously confusing gerund phrase—the subject of the sentence—with an introductory participial phrase
2
3 unexpected—and unnecessary—use of formalese is distracting ("confronted"); "tranquilizing smell" is poor writing
4
5 "an" required for "a"; "Oriental" requires capital; hyphen for "Oriental-looking" (a clumsy phrase)
6 "suit" misspelled; again, incorrect use of comma after participial phrase which serves as subject; capital for "Oriental"
7 comma after "understanding" for clarity; comma splice after "head"
8 "through" and "maze" misspelled
9 comma after "borders" is wrong
10 "Chinese" requires a capital; "various" misspelled
11 incorrect use of comma between subject and predicate; peculiar spelling of "Past," the writer probably confusing "past" with "passed" and coming up with "pasted";

APPENDIX C

the meaning of this sentence is unclear: what touched?
who came past?

12 comma after "menu" required; does the writer want
    "hopeless" or "hapless"?
13 dangling modifier; "odor" and "appetizing" misspelled
14 "begged" required for "beg"; "do" required for the sec-
    ond "to"; personification strained; referent for "this"
    not clear in either case
15 "languages" misspelled; sentence fragment; "Chinese"
    misspelled and then correctly spelled without a capital,
    however; comma required after "Chinese" (two in-
    dependent clauses joined by coordination)
16 "long" misspelled
17 sentence beginning "My only hope" tangled; "patiently"
    and "awaiting" misspelled; "near" should probably be
    "nearby"
18 comma splice after "order"; comma after "problem"
    necessary for clarity
19 punctuation after "you" should be a question mark and
    should be inside the quotation mark; "appricating" a
    misspelling for some word; which, even if correctly spel-
    led, is probably the wrong word anyway; comma after
    "order" required;
20 comma required after "away"; "so" out of place
21 the second half of this sentence is not parallel in struc-
    ture to the first half—the student uses the structure
    "being-able" instead of "to be able"; the coordinating
    conjunction is omitted after "country"

CITY UNIVERSITY OF NEW YORK (CUNY) WRITING SKILLS ASSESSMENT TEST, 1979.*

Essay Question

Directions: You will have fifty minutes to plan and write the essay
assigned below. You may wish to use your fifty minutes in the follow-

* By the Chancellor's Task Force on Writing, the City University of New York.

ing way: 10 minutes planning what you are going to write; 30 minutes writing; 10 minutes rereading and correcting what you have written.

You should express your thoughts clearly and should organize your ideas so that they will make sense to a reader. Correct grammar and sentence structure are important.

Write your essay on the lined pages of your booklet. You may use the inside of the front cover of the booklet for preliminary notes.

You must write your essay on *one* of the following assignments. Read each one carefully and then choose either A *or* B.

A.

It always strikes me as a terrible shame to see young people spending so much of their time staring at television. If we could unplug all the TV sets in America, our children would grow up to be healthier, better educated, and more independent human beings.

Do you agree or disagree? Explain and illustrate your answer from your own experience, your observations of others, or your reading.

B.

Older people bring to their work a lifetime of knowledge and experience. They should not be forced to retire, even if keeping them on the job cuts down on the opportunities for young people to find work.

Do you agree or disagree? Explain and illustrate your answer from your own experience, your observations of others, or your reading.

Evaluation Scale for Writing Assessment Test

6

The essay is competently organized and the ideas are expressed in appropriate language. A sense of pattern or development is present from beginning to end. The writer supports assertions with explanation or illustration.

Sentences reflect a command of syntax within the ordinary range of standard written English. Grammar, punctuation, and spelling are generally correct.

5-4

The writer introduces some point or idea and demonstrates an awareness that development or illustration is called for.

The essay presents a discernible pattern of organization, even if there are occasional digressions.

The essay demonstrates sufficient command of vocabulary to convey, without serious distortion or excessive simplification, the range of the writer's ideas.

Sentences reflect a sufficient command of syntax to ensure reasonable clarity of expression. The writer generally avoids both the monotony of rudimentary syntax and the incoherence created by tangled syntax.

The writer demonstrates through punctuation an understanding of the boundaries of the sentence.

The writer spells the common words of the language with a reasonable degree of accuracy. Exceptions can be made for the so-called spelling "demons" which frequently trouble even an advanced writer.

The writer shows the ability to use regularly, but not necessarily fautlessly, the common forms of agreement and of grammatical inflection in standard written English.

3-2

An idea or point is suggested, but it is undeveloped or presented in a purely repetitious way.

The pattern of the essay is somewhat random and relationships between sentences and paragraphs are rarely signaled.

The essay is restricted to a very narrow range of language, so that the vocabulary chosen frequently does not serve the needs of the writer.

The syntax of the essay is not sufficiently stable to ensure reasonable clarity of expression. The syntax often is rudimentary or tangled.

The writer frequently commits errors of punctuation which obscure sentence boundaries.

The writer spells the common words of the language with only intermittent accuracy.

The essay reveals recurrent grammatical problems; if there are only occasional problems, this may be due to the extremely narrow range of syntactical choices the writer has used.

1

The essay suffers from general incoherence and has no discernible pattern of organization. It displays a high frequency of error in the regular features of standard written English. Lapses in punctuation, spelling, and grammar often frustrate the reader. *OR,* the essay is so brief that any reasonably accurate judgment of the writer's competence is impossible.

Selected Sample Essays in Different Score Categories and Commentary by the CUNY Task Force on Writing.

Score of 6

(1) Television is a modern form of entertainment which has become so popular that almost every American family owns at least one T.V. (2) Many people enjoy watching movies and variety shows on television, in the comfort of their own homes. (3) If we didn't own televisions, we'd be going out more at night, spending money at theaters and seeing plays. (4) Although these are enjoyable forms of entertainment, it is usually more convenient and economical to stay at home. (5) Television also offers a variety of entertainment while a single theater does not.

(6) Since television has such a great popularity, educators are striving to offer shows which provide education and not just entertainment. (7) Young people, especially, are very attached to watching television, since they have grown up with it. (8) For this reason, it is important that the daily practice of television viewing be put to good uses.

(9) Unfortunately, television is often misused. (10) Young people are allowed to see and hear things which they don't understand, and this can be harmful. (11) This is why it is most important that parents supervise what their children watch. (12) The businessmen behind television, as with every form of entertainment, offer what the public wants to see. (13) This is how they make their money. (14) Therefore, parents and educators should encourage their chidlren to watch shows which provide some educational as well as entertaining value.

(15) Children often choose to watch cartoons which provide little or no educational value. (16) Instead, these shows are usually based on some sort of violence. (17) Since children are easily swayed, these shows can prove to be harmful on a child's

outlook on life and on his relationship with others. (18) Children should be encouraged instead to watch shows like Sesame Street, which offers educational entertainment. (19) This is an excellent program: viewers can learn how to build relationships, how different nationalities can live together in harmony, how to count and read on an elementary level. (20) All these things are taught by colorful puppets and happy people and funny cartoons. (21) From my personal experience in watching several children viewing Sesame Street, the show is one of the best children's shows available.

(22) Children use their creativity which evolves from what they see and hear around them. (23) Parents should put good television programs to use by helping children to relate to the programs. (24) Of course, other sources of entertainment and education, such as books and outdoor trips are also important.

(25) Like anything else in life, too much television may be harmful. (26) But treated in the right respect and with proper guidance, television can be the great invention that it was meant to be.

This essay is a 6 because it has a clear and sustained pattern of organization. The writer's use of connecting words and phrases holds the argument together. For example, she makes a general statement (sentence 18), a supporting point (sentences 19, 20), and then a personal observation (sentence 21), drawing clear relationships among these levels of generality. She also understands and mentions an argument other people might raise to challenge her point (sentences 24–26).

The writer's sentences are varied in length and structure. She subordinates ideas in different ways (sentences 3–6) and varies sentence length, using short sentences to good effect (sentence 13). In sentence 5, she accurately balances two parallel ideas through sentence structure.

The essay does, however, have limitations. There are occasional clichés (sentences 19, 26), the style is sometimes stilted or repetitious (sentences 8, 14, 23), and some sentences are unnecessarily wordy (sentence 11). Subject-verb agreement is occasionally weak (sentence 18). In addition, the logic of some sentences is unclear (sentence 12).

Score of 4

(1) Television has a harmful effect on young people. (2) If a child is watching television he cannot explore the outside world

for himself. (3) The violence on these shows could make him believe there is no good only bad and television takes away the child's ability to imágine, think or play.

(4) If a child is in the habit of watching television he cannot use his sense of curiosity to learn about things around him. (5) The television does this for him, he does not initiate this feeling on his own. (6) It might be good for a child to see a flower, for example, on t.v. but nothing can show how it really is, to take it in your own hands and describe it for yourself. (7) This is what t.v. is taking away from today's children. (8) Their sense to learn and to explore on their own. (9) These young people are depending on t.v. for something which they have already, but just do not use.

(10) Most of what is shown on television today is violence. (11) Since young people are watching so much t.v. violence could be the only thing that appeals to them and they could carry this destruction to their own every day lives. (12) Children watching violence so much could get used to it, not care about real murders or wouldn't think a second time about picking a gun and killing somebody because his hero "Kojak" constantly does it on t.v. and he wants to be just like him. (13) Young children might not know the difference between the good guy or bad ones and sometimes on t.v. today the bad guys are the heros the roles have changed considerably.

(14) Television takes away the child's ability to imagine, play and think for himself. (15) If a child is constantly watch t.v. he doesn't have time to imagine or play or think for himself. (16) Playing is good for a young child because he learns how to share and understand others by the use of toys. (17) By thinking a child can determine his values not use his favorite t.v. characters' values which might be invalid ones. (18) Imagining is taken away from the child because of t.v. advancement children can now go off to those far of lands that they used to imagine.

(19) Television has a distructive effect on a child. (20) He becomes addicted to it and does not go, outside to explore. (21) The child can take on invalid values seen on t.v. like violence. (22) T.V. can take away the ability for the child to use his own mind in everyday life.

This essay is a 4 and not a 3 because it has a clear pattern of organization. The writer follows a simple five-paragraph form. She states her position and gives three reasons to support it in the first paragraph. She develops each reason in the next three paragraphs. And she concludes by restating the introduction. Each paragraph holds together pretty well. Specific illustrations help develop the argument in the middle paragraphs. The meaning of most sentences is clear, and the sentences are varied enough in length and structure to keep the reader interested. The writer's vocabulary seems adequate to her needs.

Despite these strengths, however, this essay is not a 5 because the writer does not connect ideas from paragraph to paragraph. This lack of transition weakens the overall logic of the essay. In addition, sentence beginnings and endings are sometimes not clear (sentences 5, 6, 8, 19). The writer tries to put two or three ideas into the same sentence without sufficient skill in handling sentence structure to allow her to do something meaningfully (sentences 13, 14, 19). Occasionally the writer uses language imprecisely (sentence 21) and is repetitious (sentences 15, 16). She also misspells some common words.

Score of 3

(1) I disagree with the statement that television has a harmful effect on young people. (2) If we unplug all the TV set, it may result in an opposite way rather than it said in the passage. (3) This result maybe that children become ignorant and blind to the modern society. (4) Another words, they will not know what is going on in this world by means of news cast on television.

(5) However, it's undeniable to say television also has a harmful effect to the children because of some series shown on TV that deal with actions and violences. (6) But besides those series, there are programs that are shown to provide to the young people the necessary knowledge and education. (7) These programs are often seen on channel thirteen which is considered an educational broadcasting company. (8) Many programs shown on which are excellent and interesting, and providing real and scientific knowledges to the viewers, such as NOVA, VISA and many others. (9) I have been watching these programs many times, although not becoming omniscient, I now understand more, so do the other people, the gradual advancement and improvement of this world.

(10) It is not necessary to have this kind of programs only on this public TV company. (11) Good programs can also be seen on

those commercial TV broadcasting companies too. (12) There are certain hours that those channels will present some special series that are good to be watched. (13) For example, There are programs like "The Last of the Wild", "In Search of . . .", etc. shown on these channels.

(14) Again, it is not necessary to watch just these excellent series. (15) There are news broadcasting on most of the channels too, and which gives the viewers the events of the world. (16) A television is good for those who are illiterary but able to listen and for those who are lazy enough to pick up a copy of a newspaper.

(17) It is true that children in recent years have imitated the characters on the TV shows and done the things these characters did. (18) Sometimes crimes are resulted. (19) It is also true that children become lazier on their homework but spend their times on TV. (20) Besides these weakness that the TV provides, remember, there are good programs described above. (21) There is only one way to stop the belief of a harmful effect of television, which is to find a way to halt those violent shows on TV and concentrate on those more educational programs.

This essay is a 3 and not a 2 because the writer makes her point, sticks to it, and offers some specific details to support her views. She is able to introduce a number of different aspects of her subject and keep them in a reasonably clear relation to one another. The writer establishes useful paragraph divisions (with the exception of the misplaced sentence 5) and, in her final paragraph, she points out opposing points of view (sentences 17–19).

This essay is not a 4 because the details the writer introduces are unexpanded and therefore unexplained (sentences 8, 13, 15). As a result, although the writer has many potentially interesting ideas, they are not well-developed.

In addition, the writer's control of language and sentence structure is inconsistent. Her sentences are often tangled because of incorrect verb forms or lack of punctuation (sentences, 8, 9, 18). She confuses singular and plural forms (sentences 2, 3, 4, 8, 10, 20), and misuses or omits articles (sentences 3, 6, 16). Although the writer has a generally adequate vocabulary, she frequently puts words together incoherently and in that way confuses the reader. For example, "it may result in an opposite way" (sentence 2), and "there are news broadcasting" (sentence 15).

THE COLLEGE OF GREAT FALLS (GREAT FALLS, MONTANA) EXIT EXAMINATION FROM THE BASIC SKILLS COURSE, ENGLISH III, SPRING, 1979.

Sample Exam

We are all made up of many selves. Describe some of your various selves—for example, food checker at a supermarket, big brother to a foster child, sole wage-earner in a large family, CB radio fan, member of an athletic team, etc. How different are those selves? What do they have in common?

Grading Criteria for Papers

Students take two exams, the second graded only if the score on the first falls below a departmentally established cutoff point. To fail the course students need to do poorly on both tests.

In judging papers (which require a method of paragraph development calling for *illustration,* a method taught during the course), readers analyze organization, quality and appropriateness of specific detail, and sentence maturity.

Organization: 1. A paper should have a good topic sentence that names the topic and makes a focused point about the topic with an attitude or opinion word.

2. The topic should be supported with two or three appropriate examples.

3. The examples should be introduced with subtopic sentences.

4. The paper should have an appropriate concluding sentence.

Specific Detail: The specific detail should be appropriate, lively, and colorful. Writers should be especially rewarded for using appropriate dialogue and details appealing to sound, touch, and smell, as well as to sight.

Sentence Maturity:	1. Readers should look first for sentence completeness (absence of run-ons, comma splices, and fragments).

2. Other grammatical problems should be noted (verb forms, capitals and apostrophes, pronoun forms), but these should not be weighted as heavily as sentence-completeness errors.

3. Writers should be rewarded for attempting a variety of sentence patterns.

After reading each paper, each reader will independently assign one of the following scores.

6 Reserve these grades for papers which meet most of the
5 above criteria.
   A six paper should meet all the criteria; a five paper can vary from the criteria somewhat (i.e., fail to have a summary sentence, have less colorful details than a six paper, have several of the less important grammatical errors). No paper with errors in sentence completeness can receive a 6 or 5.

4 Reserve these grades for papers that show progress to-
3 ward meeting the criteria but that are marred by larger errors. Papers in this range should be successful in at least one of the major categories of criteria. Examples of papers in this range would include: A well-organized paper with dull or insufficient detail; a poorly focused or organized paper (i.e., with a poor topic sentence, no subtopic sentences) but with good details showing strength with concrete language. Papers in this range can make one or two sentence completeness errors but should generally show an understanding of sentence structure.

2 Reserve these grades for papers which show little if any
1 progress toward meeting the criteria.
   Papers with a distracting number (3 or more) of sentence-completeness errors should be assigned a 2 or 1 even if the paper has other strengths. If a paper makes

few sentence-level errors, it should be assigned a 2 or 1 only if it is hopelessly disorganized or undeveloped. Seriously undeveloped papers (i.e., 150 words or fewer) should be given a 2 or a 1 depending on the quality of the sentences.

Spelling: For the initial grading, discount all spelling errors. Rather, mark an "S" after the grade for writers who have serious spelling difficulties. Thus a 4 paper with a lot of misspellings should be marked 4S.

Procedure: After "norming" on the first ten papers, readers will mark each paper independently. A student's final score will be determined by adding each of the reader's scores. When the reader's scores differ by more than one point, the paper will be referred to a third reader.

After all papers are marked, the readers will compile a distribution table and decide upon the pass/fail cut-off score.

• Selected Sample Essays in Two Score Categories

RATING: 2

We, the people of the United States are our selves. We act and speak as we feel appropriate, to our own tastes and ideas, as opposed to acting how we think we should, in the eyes of other people. We are not completly ourselves if we are dependent upon other people in any way. For Example: A small business man running a sporting goods store. The business man is completely dependent apon trucking operations to supply the Inventory for his store. The business man is also dependent upon demand for these products. If people don't come in to buy these products, he will go out of business

The United States is strong because of all the states united together. The people living here could then be called Unitied Individuals.

RATING: 5

I met myself last Thursday, while I was filling in for a secretary at IBM. I sat behind Carol's desk, half bored and half contemplative when I saw myself walking past the glass doors on the way home from the supermarket.

I ached when I saw her, eighty years old, the cheap nylon scarf tied under her chin in a large untidy knot. Her shoes were grey with tiny holes pierced through them, and her dun-colored hose hung in folds at her ankles. She walked as though it were an act of perpetual motion, an unconscious ritual that had continued for years or decades.

I am that old lady, walking though life, knowing I have done it before, and feeling I will do it again. I carry with me the same worn vinyl purse and brown grocery bag. As I sat there, at this secretary's desk, playing the role of efficiency, and understanding it only intellectually, I was cognizant, only for a moment, of being that old lady; all her aches were my aches, and all her fears laid crouching on the other side of the metal desk and plastic name plate. I knew, in the kind of knowing that comes only through experience, that I was myself; tall, brunette, student, lover, Jew, and secretary, that I was also more than myself, and more than I would ever be allowed to understand.

Once in a very great while I will meet myself in the way I met the old lady. I see me in a magazine, on the news, playing in a sand box, or on the Paris metro. And I see, at these moments, in colors brighter than earth-colors, and sounds more sweet than earth-sounds that I am many different selves, an infinite number of identities in a cosmic dance of love, hatred, death, birth, wekness and strength.

P.S. I sincerely believe I have answered fully the required essay question. If, however, you doubt that in any way, I will be glad to defend it.

Annotated
Bibliography

prepared by
Theodore F. Sheckels

Journal abbreviations used in this bibliography are:

CE College English
CCC College Composition and Communication
EJ English Journal
RTE Research in the Teaching of English

THE BASIC WRITING STUDENTS: UNDERSTANDING THEM

Bruner, Jerome S. *Toward a Theory of Instruction*. Cambridge, Mass.: Harvard University Press, 1966.
It is possible to prepare a student for college work after he arrives there, but it will take some remedial students far longer to acquire the necessary knowledge and skills than others.

Carroll, John. "A Model of School Learning." *Teachers College Record*, 64 (1963), 723–33.
It is possible to prepare a student for college work once he is there, but the time it will take an unprepared student to grasp the necessary material will vary tremendously from case to case.

Cosin, B., et al. *School and Society: A Sociological Reader*. Cambridge, Mass.: MIT Press, 1972.
Language differences among students and between students and teachers affect education.

Cross, Patricia. *Beyond the Open Door: New Students to Higher Education*. San Francisco: Jossey-Bass, 1971.

To be exhaustive (or even nearly so), an annotated bibliography of studies pertinent to the teaching of basic writing would have to be book length. When selecting studies to include, I leaned heavily toward work that is recent, readily available, significant, and directly relevant to the teaching of basic writing. To make the bibliography as full as possible, I kept the annotations brief. When the title of the study described it fully, I did not offer an annotation.

The kinds of students who in the 1970s entered American colleges under "Open Admissions" policies.

Daly, John A., and Michael D. Miller. "Further Studies on Writing Apprehension: SAT Scores, Success Expectations, Willingness to Take Advanced Courses, and Sex Differences." *RTE,* 9 (1975), 250–56.
Connections between high writing apprehension and low success expectations; writing apprehension more frequent among males.

Ginsburg, Herbert, and Sylvia Opper. *Piaget's Theory of Intellectual Development: An Introduction.* Englewood Cliffs, N.J.: Prentice-Hall, 1969.

Harris, Muriel. "Individualized Diagnosis: Searching for Causes, Not Symptoms of Writing Deficiencies." *CE,* 40 (1978–79), 318–23.
Describes a procedure to ascertain a student's previous experience as a writer and attitudes toward writing.

Kressy, Michael. "The Community College Student," *CE,* 32 (1970–71), 772–77.
The commuting, community-tied student is, except in being an underachiever, "advantaged" compared to the typical senior college freshman.

Lederman, Marie Jean. "A Comparison of Student Projections: Magic and the Teaching of Writing." *CE,* 34 (1972–73), 674–89.
Beginning-writing students seem to have a considerably lower view of themselves than students admitted to "regular" composition courses.

Linn, Bill. "Psychological Variants of Success: Four In-Depth Case Studies of Freshmen in a Composition Course." *CE,* 39 (1977–78), 903–17.

Musgrave, Marian E. "Failing Minority Students: Class, Caste, and Racial Bias in American Colleges." *CCC,* 22 (1971), 24–29.

Nordstrom, Carl, Edward Friendenberg, and Hilary A. Gold. *Society's Children: A Study of Resentment in the Secondary Schools.* New York: Random House, 1967.
Secondary schools teach "culturally rich" students a depersonalized language foreign to their own voices, and they resent being deprived of their language.

Ornstein, Robert. "Teaching the Disadvantaged." *CE,* 32 (1970–71), 760–71.

Disadvantaged students prefer to write poetry. Their writing problems are largely attitudinal.

Piaget, Jean. *The Language and Thought of the Child.* 3rd ed. New York: Humanities Press, 1959.
How children and adolescents learn to write.

Rich, Adrienne. "Teaching Language in Open Admissions: A Look at the Context." *Harvard English Studies,* 4 (1971), 257–73.
Remedial writing students' backgrounds; their responses to literature.

Rubenstein, Bonnie. "Say Something in English." *Junior College Journal,* 38 (October 1967), 7–12.
Students' responses in writing to the word "English" suggest how they were taught—and how they learned—to write.

Selman, Robert. Review of Hans Furth and Harry Wach's *Thinking Goes to School. Harvard Educational Review,* 45 (1975), 127–34.
Some of the problems that arise when Piaget's theory is applied.

Sennett, Richard, and Jonathan Cobb. *The Hidden Injuries of Class.* New York: Random House, 1972.
Class-based prejudices cause working-class students to be reluctant to commit their thoughts to paper.

Sharpe, Johnnie M. "The Disadvantaged Student Trapped Behind the Verb 'To Teach.' " *CCC,* 23 (1972), 271–76.
Teachers of beginning writing must understand the nature of both language-interference and culture-interference.

Sternglass, Marilyn S. "Dialect Features in the Compositions of Black and White College Students: The Same or Different?" *CCC,* 25 (1974), 259–63.
Virtually no qualitative difference between groups of essays.

THE WRITING PROCESS

General Descriptions or Discussions

Burgess, Tony, ed. *Understanding Children Writing,* Harmondsworth, England: Penguin, 1972.
The writing process described as children go through it writing both formal and expressive compositions.

Cooper, Charles, and Lee Odell, eds. *Research on Composing: Points of Departure.* Urbana, Ill.: National Council of Teachers of English, 1978.

Includes Loren S. Barritt and Barry M. Kroll's "Some Implications of Cognitive Developmental Psychology for Research in Composing"; Gabriel M. Della Piana's "Research Strategies for the Study of Revision Processes in Writing Poetry"; Janet Emig's "Hand, Eye, Brain: Some 'Basics' in the Writing Process"; Donald M. Murray's "Internal Revision: A Process of Discovery."

Denman, Mary Edel. "The Measure of Success in Writing." *CCC,* 29 (1978), 42–46.
Noncognitive processes can improve attitudes toward writing and, thereby, writing performance.

Emig, Janet. *The Composing Processes of Twelfth Graders.* Urbana, Ill.: National Council of Teachers of English, 1971.
Students do not compose as we think they do. We set up—or, more often, fail to set-up—the environment which compels them to write.

Gebhardt, Richard. "Imagination and Discipline in the Writing Class." *EJ,* 66 (December 1977), 26–32.
Strategies for teaching all parts of the writing process.

Graves, Donald H. "An Examination of the Writing Process of Seven-Year-Old Children." *RTE,* 9 (1975), 227–41.

Kinneavy, James L. "Theories of Composition and Actual Writing." *Kansas English,* 59 (December 1973), 3–17.
There are eight steps in the composing process; current approaches emphasize some but ignore others.

Koch, Carol, and James M. Brazil. *Strategies for Teaching the Composition Process.* Urbana, Ill.: National Council of Teachers of English, 1978.
Strategies for teaching all parts of the writing process. Emphasis on self-discovery through writing.

Lawrence, Mary S. *Writing as a Thinking Process.* Ann Arbor: University of Michigan Press, 1974.
The nature of academic writing.

Mischel, Terry. "A Case Study of a Twelfth-Grade Writer." *RTE,* 8 (1974), 303–14.

Rothman, Donald. "What Students Don't Realize." *CCC,* 29 (1978), 196–97.
Students do not understand how writers work.

Somers, Nancy I. "The Need for Theory in Composition Research." *CCC,* 30 (1979), 46–49.

The writing process is too often assumed to be linear. We lack an adequate vocabulary to talk about revision.

Stalker, James. "A Linguist's View of the Composing Process." *CEA Critic*, 40 (May 1978), 15–23.
Examines a sample composition from three linguistic perspectives; searches for sources of problems in the writing process.

Stallard, C. K. "An Analysis of the Writing Behavior of Good Student Writers." *RTE*, 8 (1974), 206–18.

Stallard, Charles. "The Process of Composing: A Learning Activity Packet." *North Carolina English Teacher*, 35 (Fall 1977), 13–17.
Exercises to help students overcome common difficulties encountered during the writing process.

Tuttle, Frederick B., Jr., "We Can Teach Students to Write." *Connecticut English Journal*, 9 (1977), 135–41.
Outlines writing process.

Invention

Baden, Robert. "Pre-writing: The Relation Between Thinking and Feeling." *CCC*, 26 (1975), 368–70.
Methods designed to provoke feelings as the first step toward successful writing.

Baldwin, Dean R. "Introducing Rhetoric in Remedial Writing Courses." *CCC*, 29 (1978), 392–94.
Describes "prewriting sheets" designed to help beginning writers understand their rhetorical situation.

Denman, Mary Edel. "I Got This Here Hang-Up: Non-Cognitive Processes for Facilitating Writing." *CCC*, 26 (1975), 305–9.
Exercises designed to free students of their hang-ups about writing.

Flower, Linda S., and John R. Hayes. "Problem-Solving Strategies and the Writing Process." *College English*, 39 (1977–78), 449–61.
Strategies for discovering ideas, analyzing one's audience, and gauging if one's communication is sufficiently clear for that audience.

Harrington, David V., et al. "A Critical Survey of Resources for Teaching Rhetorical Invention." *CE*, 40 (1978–79), 641–61.

Herrick, Michael J. "Discovering the Journal." *Teaching English in the Two-Year College*, 2 (1976–77), 89–94.

The possible content of student journals; ways of commenting on journals.

Hillocks, George. *Observing and Writing.* Urbana, Ill.: National Council of Teachers of English, 1975.
Theoretical connections between observing and writing; fifteen games that can be "played" in the classroom to teach observation.

Jurkiewicz, Kenneth. "How to Begin to Win Friends and Influence People: The Role of the Audience in the Pre-Writing Process." *CCC,* 26 (1975), 173–76.

Kennedy, Marilyn Moats. "A Journalistic Approach to Composition." *CCC,* 21 (1970), 386–90.
Numerous techniques developed in journalism courses to help a student find something to write in detail about.

Kytle, Roy. "Prewriting by Analysis." *CCC,* 21 (1970), 380–85.
A strategy involving analysis, limitation, more analysis, and formulation to move the student from topic to thesis.

Larson, Richard L. "Invention: Discovering One's World." *Kansas English,* 59 (December 1973), 18–24.
Specific exercises.

Larson, Richard L. "Invention Once More: A Role for Rhetorical Analysis," *CE,* 32 (1970–71), 665–72.
How to move from illustration to meaning in an orderly fashion.

Long, Littleton, ed. *Writing Exercises From Exercise Exchange.* Urbana, Ill.: National Council of Teachers of English, 1976.
Strategies to help students with prewriting, diction, paragraphing, prose style, etc.

Macrorie, Ken. *Uptaught.* Rochelle Park, N.J.: Hayden, 1970.
Describes the prewriting process.

Murray, Donald M. "Write Before Writing." *CCC,* 29 (1978), 375–81.
Pinpoints forces that block and compel forward during prewriting; discusses prewriting exercises.

Odell, Lee. "Measuring the Effect of Instruction in Pre-Writing." *RTE,* 8 (1974), 228–40.
What students learn specifically about the writing process if prewriting techniques are explicitly taught.

Odell, Lee. "Responding to Student Writing." *CCC,* 24 (1973), 394–400.

Students' habits of thinking about and responding to experiences; strategies teachers can use to help them develop new approaches.

Paull, Michael. "Invention: Understanding the Relationship Between Sensation, Perception, and Concept Formation." *CCC*, 25 (1974), 205–09.
Exercises to move a student from perception to conceptualization.

Paull, Michael, and Jack Kligerman. "Invention, Composition, and the Urban College." *CE*, 33 (1971–72), 651–59.
A number of exercises.

Radcliffe, T. "Talk-Write Composition: A Theoretical Model Proposing the Use of Speech to Improve Writing." *RTE*, 6 (1972), 187–99.
Writing seems to be enhanced when the writer first talks through his ideas.

Snipes, Wilson C. "Oral Composing as An Approach to Writing." *CCC*, 24 (1973), 200–205.

Southwell, Michael G. "Free Writing in Composition Classes." *CE*, 38 (1976–77), 676–81.
The advantages of free writing as a heuristic and an anxiety-reducing exercise.

Stallard, Charles. "Composing: A Cognitive Process Theory." *CCC*, 27 (1976), 181–84.
Verbalizing exercises to help students explore their changing cognitive structures prior to writing, while writing, and while revising.

Vygotsky, Lev. *Thought and Language.* Cambridge, Mass.: MIT Press, 1962.
Academic writing is itself a dialect with not only a unique syntax and vocabulary but also a unique cognitive style.

Waldschmidt, Elmer C. "Peers Paired for Talk-Writing." *Illinois English Bulletin,* 62 (May 1975), 2–8.
Based on Zoellner's theories, a strategy to facilitate writing in which paired students act as writer and audience.

Washington, Eugene. "Wh-Questions in Teaching Composition." *CCC*, 28 (1977), 54–56.
Questions can generate a mixture of general and specific details; questions can help students see the need for organizational signals.

Wiener, Harvey S. "Media Compositions: Preludes to Writing." *CE,* 35 (1973–34), 566–74.
Collages, photography, and tapes to bring beginning students to the brink of useful writing.

Writing, Revising, Proofreading

Arbur, Rosemarie. "The Student-Teacher Conference." *CCC,* 28 (1977–78), 338–42.
How to plan and conduct conferences.

Beach, Richard. "Self-Evaluation Strategies of Extensive Revisers and Non-Revisers." *CCC,* 27 (1976), 160–64.
Compares those students who revise extensively to those who do not and uncovers a number of telling differences about the way students perceive writing and the way teachers evaluate it.

Dworsky, Nancy. "The Disaster Workshop." *CE,* 35 (1973–74), 194–95.
Never deal with finished student writing but rather with writing that the student feels is a "disaster."

Elsasser, Nan, and Vera P. John-Steiner. "An Interactionist Approach to Advancing Literacy." *Harvard Educational Review,* 47 (1977), 355–70.
Exercises to make students aware of audience needs.

Goodman, Kenneth. *Miscue Analysis.* Urbana, Ill.: National Council of Teachers of English, 1973.
Techniques for diagnosing reading problems. Insights into student proofreading difficulties.

Jacobs, Suzanne E., and Adela B. Karliner. "Helping Students to Think: The Effect of Speech Roles in Individual Conferences on the Quality of Thought in Student Writing." *CE,* 38 (1977–78), 489–505.

Klammer, Enno. "Cassettes in the Classroom." *CE,* 35 (1973–74), 179–89.
Record a student's essay onto a cassette with commentary added as you read; then have the student revise the composition using the cassette.

McDonald, W. U., Jr. "The Revising Process and the Marking of Student Papers." *CCC,* 29 (1978), 167–70.
Argues for multiple drafts; suggests how to comment on drafts.

McNamara, John. "Teaching the Process of Writing." *CE,* 34 (1972–73), 661–65.
Strategies for collaborative writing.

Murray, Donald M. *A Writer Teaches Writing: A Practical Method of Teaching Composition.* Boston: Houghton Mifflin, 1968.
Focuses on the composing process; numerous examples, showing what rewriting and revising should consist of.

Murray, Donald M. "Teaching the Motivating Force of Revision." *EJ,* 67 (October 1978), 56–60.

Odell, Lee, and Joanne Cohick. "You Mean, Write It Over in Ink." *EJ,* 64 (December 1975), 48–53.
Useful techniques for revision.

Popovich, Helen Houser. "From Tape to Type: An Approach to Composition." *CCC,* 27 (1976), 283–85.
The advantages of using cassette recordings of students' writing in helping them learn how and what to revise.

Primeau, Ronald. "Film-Editing and the Revision Process: Student as Self-Editor." *CCC,* 25 (1974), 405–10.
Editing an essay and editing a film are analogous; students should be taught to proceed as a film editor does.

Pumphrey, Jean. "Teaching English Composition as a Creative Art." *CE,* 34 (1972–73), 666–73.
A collaborative writing procedure which focuses class discussion on the problems encountered while writing.

Thompson, George J. "Revision: Nine Ways to Achieve a Disinterested Perspective." *CCC,* 29 (1978), 200–202.

Weigl, Bruce. "Revision as a Creative Process." *EJ,* 65 (September 1976), 67–68.
The fallacies handbooks often present about revising; guidelines.

Evaluating

Allen, Walter P. "Using Word Groups in Correcting Compositions." *CCC,* 26 (1975), 379–83.
We should analyze faulty student sentences phrase-by-phrase as we correct to see where the sentences went wrong.

Blake, Robert W. "How to Talk to a Writer, or Forward to Fundamentals in Teaching Writing." *EJ,* 65 (November 1976), 49–55.
What is essential in high school writing instruction, from the

composing process itself to the types of writing taught and the stylistic skills stressed; how a student's paper should be responded to.

Bolker, Joan L. "Reflections on Reading Student Writing." *CE,* 40 (1978–79), 181–85.
Ways to write comments which engage students in a meaningful dialogue concerning their writing.

Cooper, Charles, and Lee Odell, eds. *Evaluating Writing.* Urbana, Ill.: NCTE, 1977.
Includes Mary H. Beaven's "Individualized Goal-Setting, Self-Evaluation, and Peer Evaluation" and Kellogg W. Hunt's "Early Blooming and Late Blooming Structures." The latter helps define the "syntactic maturity" we hope beginning writers will reach.

Crew, Louie. "The New Alchemy." *CE,* 38 (1976–77), 707–11.
A reflective essay on teachers' capricious, unfair ways of grading students who write in a nonstandard dialect.

Dieterich, D. J. "Composition Evaluation: Options and Advice." *EJ,* 61 (1972), 1264–71.
Reviews research.

Diederich, Paul B. *Measuring Growth in English.* Urbana, Ill.: NCTE, 1974.
A guide rich in scholarship to evaluating student writing.

Dudenhefer, John Paul. "An experiment in Grading Papers," *CCC,* 27 (1976), 406–7.
Slightly better to assign grades only after all revisions have been made than to assign them immediately.

Foley, Joseph J. "Evaluation of Learning in Writing." In *Handbook on Formative and Summative Evaluations of Student Learning.* Ed. Benjamin S. Bloom et al. New York: McGraw-Hill, 1971. Pp. 769–813.
A detailed anatomy of the act of writing, suggesting modes of evaluation appropriate at each stage.

Foliman, J C., et al. "Effects of Time and Typface on Level and Reliability of Theme Grades." *RTE,* 4 (1970), 51–58.
Typeface has no effect on grades; themes graded later are graded more leniently than those graded earlier.

Gee, T. C. "Students' Responses to Teacher Comments." *RTE,* 6 (1972), 212–21.
The value of positive reinforcement.

Hiatt, Mary P. "Students at Bay: The Myth of the Conference." *CCC,* 26 (1975), 38–41.
With certain kinds of students (basic writing students dominant among them), conferences, unless very carefully handled, can be detrimental.

Hickman, Walter R. "Second Aid for Freshman English, or What the Doctor Can Do Now That He's Here." *CE,* 35 (1973–74), 481–82. See *CE,* 35 (1973–74), 482–84, for commentaries.
Especially in remedial work, problems grading student writing can be solved by changing roles from teacher to professional critic.

Jerabek, R., and D. Dieterich. "Composition Evaluation: The State of the Art." *CCC,* 26 (1975), 183–86.

Judine, Sister M., I.H.M., ed. *A Guide For Evaluating Student Composition.* Urbana, Ill.: NCTE, 1965.
Essays by junior and senior high school teachers discussing aspects of evaluation.

Judy, Stephen N. "Writing for the Here and Now: An Approach to Assessing Student Writing." *EJ,* 62 (1973), 69–79.
Use publishability (i.e. the presence of an authentic voice and a sense of audience) as the primary criterion.

Kehl, D. G. "The Art of Writing Evaluative Comments on Student Themes." *EJ,* 59 (1970), 972–80.

Kline, Charles R., Jr. "I Know You Think You Know What I Said." *CE,* 37 (1975–76), 661–62.
Contradictions between the instructional emphases and the evaluative criteria used by teachers of freshman writing.

Knapp, John, V. "Contract/Conference Evaluations of Freshman Composition." *CE,* 37 (1975–76), 647–53.

Lamberg, Walter J. "Feedback on Writing: Much More Than Teacher Corrections." *Statement: The Journal of the Colorado Language Arts Society,* 12 (May 1977), 33–38.
Reviews theories and research.

Lemke, Alan K. "Writing as Action in Living." *CCC,* 25 (1974), 269–73.
Content and expression should not be separated when evaluating student writing.

Lewis, Paul. "A Generation of Prophets: The Writing Teacher and the Freshman Mystic." *CCC,* 26 (1975), 289–92.

Profitable ways of dealing with student papers about "profound" experiences.

Lynch, Catherine, and Patricia Klemans. "Evaluating Our Evaluations." *CE,* 40 (1978–79), 166–70, 175–80.
How students respond to different types of teacher comments.

Memering, W. Dean. "Talking to Students: Group Conferences." *CCC,* 24 (1973), 306–7.
Except for the real "problem students" (academically or emotionally), group conferences can be successful and time-saving.

Olsen, T. "Grading Alternatives." *EJ,* 64 (March 1975), 106–8.
Reviews research on and opinions about options to traditional grading.

Platt, Michael. "Correcting Papers in Public and in Private." *CE,* 37 (1975–76), 22–27.
A procedure for correcting essays publicly.

Robinson, Bruce. "Is Literacy All We Want Out of Universal Higher Education?" *CE,* 31 (1969–70), 643–65.
Analyzes A, B, C, D, and F papers, indicating in each case strategies for improving the perceptual and expressive abilities of the students.

Tate, Gary, and Edward P. J. Corbett, ed. *Teaching High School Composition.* New York: Oxford University Press, 1970.
Fundamental, generally reflective essays on topics ranging from evaluation to prose style to the teaching of standard English as a second dialect.

Warnock, John. "The Relation of Critical Perspectives to Teaching Methods in Composition." *CE,* 34, (1972–73), 690–700.
Critical perspectives imprison the student and teacher of literature (who is also a student and teacher of writing) in inadequate ways of responding to student prose.

THE RHETORICAL "CONTENT" OF BASIC WRITING COURSES

Paragraphing

Bond, Charles A. "A New Approach to Freshman Composition: A Trial of the Christensen Method." *CE,* 33 (1971–72), 623–27.
Significantly superior to traditional methods.

Braddock, Richard. "The Frequency and Placement of Topic Sentences in Expository Prose." *RTE,* 8 (1974), 287–302.
The claims of most handbooks are patently false.

Christensen, Francis. "A Generative Rhetoric of the Paragraph." *CCC,* 16 (1965), 144–56.
Model paragraph organizations.

Cohan, Carol. "Writing Effective Paragraphs." *CCC,* 27 (1976), 363–65.
A strategy to help students with the sentences that follow a topic sentence by converting the topic sentence into a topic sentence question.

D'Angelo, Frank. *A Conceptual Theory of Rhetoric.* Cambridge, Mass: Winthrop, 1975.
Conceptual patterns characteristic of sentences and extended pieces of discourse match typical patterns of rhetorical invention.

Grady, Michael. "A Conceptual Rhetoric of the Composition." *CCC,* 22 (1971), 348–54.
Based on Christensen's methodology, paragraphs as a sequence of ideas, some introductory, some coordinate, some subordinate, etc.

Graves, Richard L. "Highlighting Techniques for Teaching Composition." *CCC,* 27 (1976), 165–70.
Techniques using overhead projectors and multi-color overlays to teach paragraph coherence.

Hagen, Lyman B. "An Analysis of Transitional Devices in Student Writing." *RTE,* 5 (1971–72), 190–201.
Most college freshmen have already internalized transitional devices for descriptive writing.

Halliday, M. A. K., and Ruqaiya Hasan. *Cohesion in English.* London: Longman, 1976.
Identifies three sources of coherence: situation, structure, and semantics; analyzes types of semantic cohesion.

Meade, R. A., and W. G. Ellis. "The Use in Writing of Textbook Methods of Paragraph Development." *Journal of Educational Research,* 65 (1971), 74–76.
Paragraphs are most frequently developed by examples, reasons, and additional comments, *not* by the methods stressed in textbooks.

Padkard, Dennis J. "From Logic to Composition and Reading." *CCC,* 27 (1976), 366–72.

A method for teaching coherence using formal logic; an exhaustive list of transitional markers.

Stalter, William. "A Sense of Structure." *CCC,* 29 (1978), 341–45.
Describes four basic and three combined relationships between sentences in a piece of discourse.

Stern, Arthur A. "When Is a Paragraph?" *CCC,* 27 (1976), 253–57.
The paragraph is not a logical unit of development; we should stop misleading our students by teaching it "by rule and formula."

Walshe, R.D. "Report on a Pilot Course on the Christensen Rhetoric Program." *CE,* 32 (1970–71), 783–89.
Positive and negative feelings.

Warner, Richard. "Teaching the Paragraph as a Structural Unit." *CCC,* 30 (1979), 152–55.
Generative models for paragraphs based on Christensen.

Winterowd, W. Ross. "The Grammar of Coherence." *CE,* 31 (1969–70), 828–35.
Outlines a grammar of coherence with "operations" such as "coordination" and "obsersativity" for building paragraphs.

Young, Richard E., and Alton L. Becker. "Toward a Modern Theory of Rhetoric: A Tagmemic Contribution." *Harvard Educational Review,* 35 (1965), 450–68.
Outlines rhetorical patterns for paragraphs.

Description, Narration, Summation, and Illustration—In Theory and Practice

Beach, Richard. *Writing about Ourselves and Others.* Urbana, Ill.: NCTE, 1977.
Outlines a writing program which leads the student through autobiography, memoir, and portrait, from self-discovery to discoveries concerning others.

Branscomb H. Eric. "Turning the Corner: Story to Meaning in Freshman Composition Classes." *CE,* 37 (1975–76), 663–67.
How to get students from typical freshman narratives to meaningful, significant ones.

Cohen, Ralph. "Reading and Writing Movie Reviews in Freshman English." *Freshman English News,* 4 (1975), 3–4, 11.

Comprone, Joseph. "Using Painting, Photography and Film to Teach Narrative." *CE*, 35 (1973–74), 174–78.

Corey, Chet. "The Obituary as an Exercise in Living." *CCC*, 23 (1972), 198–99.

D'Angelo, Frank J. "Advertising and the Modes of Discourse." *CCC*, 29 (1978), 356–61.
Analyzes advertising into descriptive, narrative, and "reason-why" copy.

Haich, George D. "If the Reader Never Saw One, How Would You Describe It?" *CCC*, 26 (1975), 298–300.

Harp, Richard L. "Using Elemental Literary Forms in the Composition Class." *CCC*, 29 (1978), 158–61.
Suggests the use of fables, proverbs, and other basic literature to generate narrative and other types of writing.

Kinneavy, James L. *A Theory of Discourse.* Englewood Cliffs, N.J.: Prentice-Hall, 1971.
Four "modes" of discourse (referential, literary, persuasive, and expressive) and four aims or ways of thinking about reality (describing, narrating, classifying, and evaluating).

Kraft, Robert G. "The Death of Argument." *CE*, 36 (1974–75), 548–51.
Description and narration are increasingly important as modes of argumentation.

Linn, Michael D. "Black Rhetorical Patterns and the Teaching of Composition," *CCC*, 26 (1975), 149–53. See *CCC*, 26 (1975), 399–400, for response.
Group composition and personal narratives can draw upon Black oral rhetorical habits at a writing course's beginning.

Moffett, James. *A Student-Centered Language Arts Curriculum: Grades K–13.* New York: Houghton-Mifflin, 1968.
Suggests sequences of assignments and exercises tied to student's development.

Moffett, James. *Teaching the Universe of Discourse.* Boston: Houghton Mifflin, 1968.
How a beginning writer should naturally progress from one kind of discourse to another.

Rayne, Ann. "Précis Writing: An Approach to Basic Composition." *CCC*, 27 (1976), 403–6.

Schuman, R. Baird. "Between the Lines in Student Writing." *English Education,* 6 (1975–76), 74–76.
Based on an analysis of ghetto students' papers, assignments to avoid and some to use.

Schultz, John. "The Story Workshop Method: Writing from Start to Finish." *CE,* 39 (1977–78), 411–36.
Outlines instructions given to oral storyteller. If teller follows these, the transition to writing will be eased.

Shiflett, Betty. "Story Workshop as a Method of Teaching Writing." *CE,* 35 (1973–74), 141–60.
A method which helps students develop their own writing voices.

Stoehr, Taylor, et al. "Writing About Experience: A Report on Freshman English." *CE,* 32 (1970–71), 9–44.
Eighteen innovative methods to teach writing using student experience as a springboard.

Stoll, Patricia. "You Must Begin at Zero: Story Workshop." *CE,* 35 (1973–74), 256–66.
A prewriting strategy which emphasizes the student's personal growth.

Thomson, George H. "The Four Story Forms: Drama, Film, Comic Strip, Narrative." *CE,* 37 (1975–76), 265–80.

Wiener, Harvey S. "The Single Narrative Paragraph and College Remediation." *CE,* 33 (1971–72), 660–69.
The single narrative paragraph is the ideal place to begin in a course for beginners.

Wolfe, Don M. "Realistic Writing Program for Culturally Diverse Youth." In *Education of the Disadvantaged.* Ed. A. Harry Passow. New York: Holt, Rinehart and Winston, 1967. Pp. 415–23.
Autobiographical writing is a natural place to begin with beginning writers.

Details and Vivid Language

Blinderman, Abraham. "What's the Good Word?" *CCC,* 21 (1970), 198–99.
A procedure to enrich students' diction using professional writing with the "enriched" words deleted.

Gach, Vicki, "Graffiti." *CE,* 35 (1973–74), 285–87.

Kligerman, Jack. "Photography, Perception, and Composition." *CCC,* 28 (1977), 174–78.
The study of photographs will enhance descriptive abilities.

Labov, William. *Language in the Inner City.* Philadelphia: University of Pennsylvania Press, 1972.
The city dweller's vernacular can be used to enrich both the structure and the language of narrative writing.

Nilsen, Don L. F. "Cliches, Trite Sayings, Dead Metaphors, and Stale Figures of Speech in Composition Instruction." *CCC,* 27 (1976), 278–82.
Rather than criticize stale expressions, explore them with students in order to reveal the richness inherent in such sayings, metaphors, etc.

Petty, Walter, et al. *Vocabulary: The State of Knowledge About the Teaching of Vocabulary.* Urbana, Ill.: NCTE, 1968.

Rankin, David L. "Teaching Metaphor." *CCC,* 21 (1970), 273–75.
The difference between a "good' metaphor and a "bad" metaphor; classroom procedures to show students this difference.

Simpson, Mary Scott. "Teaching Writing: Beginning with the Word." *CE,* 39 (1977–78), 934–39.
Strategies to acquaint students with the evocative power of language and the importance of word choice.

Sossaman, Stephen. "Detroit Designers: A Game To Teach Metaphors." *Exercise Exchange,* 21 (Fall 1976), 2–3.
Teaching the richness of metaphorical language by playing with automobile names.

Speidel, Judith Douglas. "Using Art to Teach Writing." *Connecticut English Journal,* 9 (Fall), 66–70.
Slides of major works of art as the major component of exercises to increase student descriptive abilities.

Ullman, Stephen. *Semantics: An Introduction to the Science of Meaning.* Oxford: Basil Blackwell, 1970.
Distinction between transparent and opaque words (see chapter four) illuminates many of the vocabulary deficiencies and difficulties of basic writing students.

Western, Richard. "Teaching Whately's Fire; or, An Essay on Vagueness." *CE,* 32 (1970–71), 652–64.
The nature of vagueness and how teachers of composition have traditionally misunderstood and overemphasized it.

THE BASIC WRITING STUDENTS' ERRORS: UNDERSTANDING AND DEALING WITH THEM

Dialect-Related Problems

Aarons, Alfred C., et al., eds. "Linguistic-Cultural Differences and American Education." *The Florida FL Reporter,* 7 (Spring/Summer 1969).
Forty-three pertinent essays such as Roger D. Abrahms' "Black Talk and Black Education," Stephen S. Baratz and Joan C. Baratz' "Negro Ghetto Children and Urban Education," William Labov's "The Logic of Non-Standard English," William A. Stewart's "Urban Negro Speech," and Kenneth R. Johnson's "Pedagogical Problems of Using Second Language Techniques for Teaching Standard English."

Alatis, James E., ed. *Linguistics and the Teaching of Standard English to Speakers of Other Languages or Dialects.* Report of the Twentieth Annual Round Table Meeting on Linguistics and Language Studies. Washington, D.C.: Georgetown University Press, 1970.
A compendium of essays on the implications of theoretical linguistics for the teaching of standard English as a second dialect and the implications of applied linguistics and sociolinguistics. Among the essays are William Labov's "The Logic of Nonstandard English," Virginia French Allen's "A Second Dialect is Not a Foreign Language," William A. Stewart's "Sociopolitical Issues in the Linguistic Treatment of Negro Dialect," and Ralph W. Fasold's "Distinctive Linguistic Characteristics of Black English."

Burns, Shannon, and Lois Burns. "Ethnic and Regional Literature: Making Connections to Composition." *EJ,* 66 (March 1977), 34–36.
Such literature fosters dialect awareness and toleration.

Catford, J. C. "The Teaching of English as a Foreign Language." In *The Teaching of English.* Ed. Randolph Quirk and A. H. Smith. London: Oxford, 1964. Pp. 137–59.
Description of English-as-a-Second-Language techniques.

Cazden, C. B., et al., eds. *Functions of Language in the Classroom.* New York: Teachers College Press, 1972.
Essays to make teachers aware of disadvantaged dialects and how they are so often misunderstood or suppressed in the classroom.

Davis, A. L., ed. *Culture, Class, and Language Variety: A Resource Book for Teachers.* Urbana, Ill.: NCTE, 1972.
Essays exploring the differences between standard English and nonstandard dialects, problems nonstandard users have with standard grammar, the phonological and morphological features of nonstandard English, and systems of nonverbal communication of nonstandard dialect users.

Davis, L. M. *A Study of Appalachian Speech in a Northern Urban Setting.* Chicago: Center for American English, Illinois Institute of Technology, 1971.
Describes a regional, nonstandard dialect.

Dillard, J. L. *Black English.* New York: Random House, 1972.
A history of Black English, glancing at its structure and comparing and contrasting it with pidgin English and southern dialect.

Douglas, Wallace W. "On the Crisis in Composition." *ADE Bulletin,* no. 40 (March 1974), 3–11.
A review of recent work on dialectology noting what is now known and what remains unknown.

Fasold, Ralph W., and Walter A. Wolfram. "Some Linguistic Features of Negro Dialect." In *Contemporary English.* Ed. David Shores. Philadelphia: Lippincott, 1972. Pp. 53–85.

Fisher, John C. "Generating Standard Sentence Patterns and Beyond." *CCC,* 21 (1970), 264–68.
Exercises, modelled after those used in foreign language teaching, to teach nonstandard dialect speakers the features their dialects lack.

Fox, Robert P., ed. *Essays on Teaching English As a Second Language and As a Second Dialect.* Urbana, Ill.: NCTE, 1973.
Essays on the history, techniques, and problems of teaching English as a second language or dialect.

Garcia, Richard L. "A Linguistic Frame of Reference for Critiquing Chicano Composition," *CE,* 37 (1975–76), 184–88.
The nature of the linguistic interference experienced by Spanish speakers trying to write in English is phonological and morphological not syntactic.

George, H. V. *Common Errors in Language Learning.* Rowley, Mass.: Newbury House, 1972.
The errors common to second-language learners.

Geuder, Patricia A. "A Writing Seminar For Speakers of Black English." *CCC,* 23, (1972), 417–19.

Examples of where Black English interferes with the learning of standard English.

Gray, Barbara Quint. "Dialect Interference in Writing: A Tripartite Analysis. *Basic Writing Journal,* 1 (Spring 1975), 14–22.
Three patterns of dialectic interference; specific strategies for dealing with each.

Hess, K. M. *Basic Report for Targetted Communications: Teaching a Standard English to Speakers of Other Dialects.* St. Louis, Mo.: Central Midwestern Regional Education Laboratory, 1972.
A synthesis and interpretation of research up to 1971 on nonstandard dialects of American English.

Hoover, Mary Rhodes. "Community Attitudes toward Black English." *Language in Society,* 7 (1978), 65–87.
Correlates levels of dialect use to the writer's social and cultural situation.

Kirshner, Samuel A., and Howard G. Poteet. "Non-Standard English Usage in the Writing of Black, White, and Hispanic Remedial English Students in an Urban Community College." *RTE,* 7 (Winter 1973), 351–55.
Basic writing students, regardless of cultural background, exhibit the same writing problems.

Labov, William. "The Study of Language in Its Social Context." *Studium Generale,* 23 (1970), 30–87.
Introduces sociolingistics and illustrates the field's usefulness by studying in detail Black English and "hypercorrect" Lower Middle Class English.

Labov, William. *The Study of Nonstandard English.* Urbana, Ill.: NCTE, 1970.
Surveys the work done up to 1970 on nonstandard dialects.

Labov, William, et al. *Study of the Non-Standard English of Negro and Puerto Rican Speakers in New York City.* 2 vol. New York: Columbia University Press, 1968.
The difference between nonstandard Black and Puerto Rican English and standard English.

Lay, Nancy. "Chinese Language Interference in Written English." *Basic Writing Journal,* 1 (Spring 1975), 50–61.

Lin, San-Su C. "An Experiment in Changing Dialect Patterns." *CE,* 24 (1962–63), 644–47.
English-as-a-Second Language techniques applied to dialect-related writing problems.

Loflin, Martin D. "A Teaching Problem in Non-standard Negro English." *EJ*, 56 (1967), 1312–14.
Nonstandard Black English is not at all like the dialect spoken by southern whites. English-as-a-Second-Language techniques should be used to teach standard English to speakers and writers of Black English.

Nattinger, James R. "Second Dialect and Second Language in the Composition Class." *TESOL Quarterly*, 12 (March 1978), 77–84.
English-as-a-Second-Language students and students learning Standard English as a second dialect should not be in the same class.

Nauer, Barbara. "Soundscript: A Way to Help Black Students to Write Standard English." *CE*, 36 (1974–75), 586–88. See *CE*, 37 (1975–76), 419–24 for debate which ensued.
Recommends teacher-made tape recordings of disadvantaged students' prose which they use to rewrite their essays.

Nist, John. *Handicapped English: The Language of the Socially Disadvantaged.* Springfield, Ill.: Charles C Thomas, 1974.
Describes a wide group of Americans who, due to many reasons (dialect interference primary among them), are at a disadvantage.

Pearlman, Daniel. "The Cognate Trap in Writing by Hispanic Students." *CE*, 39 (1977–78), 844–46.
Examines A Hispanic student's unintelligible passage, made so because of the student's vocabulary problems.

Rizzo, Betty, and Santiago Villafane. "Spanish Influence on Written English." *Basic Writing Journal*, 1 (Spring 1975), 62–71.

Shuy, Roger W., and Ralph W. Fasold, eds. *Teaching Standard English in the Inner City.* Washington, D.C.: Center for Applied Linguistics, 1970.
Practical essays including Irwing Feigenbaum's "The Use of Nonstandard English in Teaching Standard" and Fasold and W. A. Wolfram's "Some Linguistics Features of Negro Dialect."

Simons, Herbert D. and Kenneth R. Johnson, "Black English Syntax and Reading Interference." *RTE*, 8 (1974), 339–58.

Smith, H. "Black English: Considerations and Approaches." *EJ*, 62, (1973), 311–18.
Reviews research up to 1972 on the teaching of standard English to speakers and writers of other dialects.

Sternglass, Marilyn S. "Dialect Literature: Positive Reinforcer for Writing 'In' and 'Out' of Dialect." *CCC*, 26 (1975), 210–4.

Stevens, Peter. "Second Language Learning." *Daedalus,* (Summer 1973), 149–60.
Possible strategies for teaching writing to students proficient in nonstandard dialects.

Williams, Frederick, ed. *Language and Poverty: Perspectives on a Theme.* Chicago: Markham Publishing Company, 1970.
Essays including William Labov's "Logic of Nonstandard English," Siegfried Engelmann's "How To Construct Effective Language Programs for the Poverty Child," and William A. Stewart's "Toward a History of American Negro Dialect."

Wolfram, Walter A. *Sociolinguistic Description of Detroit Negro Speech.* Washington, D.C.: Center for Applied Linguistics, 1969.
Dialect differences within Detroit Black community.

Wolfram, Walter, and Ralph W. Fasold. *The Study of Social Dialects in American English.* Englewood Cliffs, N.J.: Prentice-Hall, 1974.
The assumptions, methods, and conclusions of sociolinguistics.

Mechanical Problems

Blair, T. R. "Spelling, Word Attack Skills." *The Reading Teacher,* 28 (1975), 604–7.
Reviews current research on spelling.

Brengelman, Frederick H. "Dialect and the Teaching of Spelling." *RTE.* 4 (1970), 129–38.
Strategies (primarily for elementary school but to some extent adaptable) to teach spelling to students who are proficient in different dialects.

Brown, H.D. "Categories of Spelling Difficulty in Speakers of English as a First and Second Language." *Journal of Verbal Learning and Verbal Behavior,* 9 (1970), 232–36.
Both those learning English as a first language and those learning it as a second language exhibit remarkably similar difficulties with low frequency, high regularity words.

Buck, Jean L. "A New Look at Teaching Spelling." *CE,* 38 (1976–77), 703–6.
A complete course designed to teach basic writing students to spell and to overcome attitudinal difficulties.

Farrell, Thomas J. "Differentiating Writing from Talking." *CCC,* 29 (1978), 346–50.

Outlines differences; describes a program of instruction for basic writing students, especially those learning standard English as a second dialect, based on a recognition of these differences.

Geedy, P. S. "What Research Tells Us About Spelling." *Elementary English,* 52 (1975), 233–36.
Reviews research on spelling.

Golladay, W. M. "The Teaching of Spelling to Low Ability Classes." *Elementary English,* 48 (1971), 366–70.
Low ability adolescents should be drilled in word pronunciation and syllabification.

Hanna, Paul R., et al. *Phoneme-Grapheme Correspondences as Cues to Spelling Improvement.* Washington, D.C.: United States Department of Health, Education and Welfare, 1966.
Ways to classify student spelling errors.

Hanna, Paul R., et al. *Spelling: Structure and Strategies.* Boston: Houghton Mifflin, 1971.
Strategies for conquering spelling problems of elementary students. Adaptable.

Horn, Thomas D., ed. *Research on Handwriting and Spelling.* Urbana, Ill.: NCTE, 1966.
A collection of research reports, most giving some insights into handwriting and spelling deficiencies.

Laurence, Patricia. "Error's Endless Train: Why Don't Students Perceive Errors." *Basic Writing Journal,* 1 (Spring 1975), 23–42.
Outlines the errors basic-writing students make, suggests strategies for dealing with them, and ties many of them to perceptual and cognitive confusion.

Valmont, W. J. "Active Pupil Involvement in Learning to Spell." *Education,* 93 (1972), 189–91.
Reviews studies of spelling up to 1971 and seriously questions most current practices.

Grammatical and Stylistic Problems

Allen, Robert L. *English Grammars and English Grammar.* New York: Charles Scribner's Sons, 1974.
Introduces "sector analysis," a grammatical system used by many ESL teachers.

Brooks, Phyllis. "Mimesis: Grammar and the Echoing Voice." *CE,* 35 (1973–73), 161–68.
Paraphrasing exercises to develop style.

Carkeet, David. "Understanding Syntactic Errors in Remedial Writing." *CE,* 38 (1976–77), 682–95.
Describes two general kinds of syntactic errors—retention errors and blends—and outlines ways of analyzing them so that basic-writing students will see their mistakes.

Chaika, Elaine. "Who Can Be Taught?" *CE,* 35 (1973–74), 575–83.
Grammar exercises to teach students how to build sentences.

Chaika, Elaine. "Grammars and Teaching." *CE,* 39 (1977–78), 770–83.
Transformational grammar offers students insights into why given syntactic structures are more appropriate or more correct than others.

Christensen, Francis. *Notes Toward a New Rhetoric: Six Essays for Teachers.* New York: Harper and Row, 1967.
Outlines a method for analyzing and constructing sentences and paragraphs.

Clapp, Ouida, ed. *Classroom Practices in Teaching English, 1977–78.* Urbana, Ill.: NCTE, 1977.
Collected essays on précis writing, outlining, proofreading, sentence errors, and spelling difficulties.

Cooper, Charles R. "An Outline for Writing Sentence-Combining Problems." *EJ,* 62 (January 1973), 96–108.

Daiker, Donald A. "Sentence-Combining and Syntactic Maturity in Freshman English." *CE,* 29 (1978), 36–41.
Sentence-combining exercises increase syntactic maturity and improve writing.

D'Angelo, Frank J. "Imitation and Style." *CCC,* 24 (1973), 283–90.
A procedure of sentence pattern imitation which should lead to a greater stylistic repertoire.

Elgin, Suzette Haden. "Don't No Revolutions Hardly *Ever* Come by Here." *CE,* 39 (1977–78), 784–89.
Exercises to prompt students to derive transformational grammatical rules.

Emig, Janet A., et al. *Language and Learning.* New York: Harcourt, Brace and World, 1966.
The implications of linguistic research for the teaching of writing.

Gebhardt, Richard C., and Barbara Genelle Smith. " 'Liberation' Is Not 'License': The Case for Self-awareness through Writing." *CCC,* 26 (1976), 21-24.
Advocates a free approach to writing, one that does not ignore issues of corrections but puts them in their proper place.

Gliserman, Martin. "An Act of Theft: Teaching Grammar." *CE,* 39 (1977–78), 791–99.
Problem-solving, worksheets, and grammatical poetry to teach grammar.

Griffin, Jacqueline. "Remedial Composition at an Open Door College." *CCC,* 20 (1957), 360–63.
Describes an eclectic approach to the teaching of grammar (an approach combining the "best of" Allen, Christensen, and Chomsky) designed specifically for beginning writers in colleges.

Fagan, William T., et al. "Measures: Writing." In *Measures for Research and Evaluation in the English Language Arts.* Urbana, Ill.: NCTE, 1975. Pp. 185–206.
Fourteen measures, one useful for syntactical maturity.

Faigly, Lester L. "Generative Rhetoric as a Way of Increasing Syntactic Fluency." *CCC,* 30 (1979), 176–81.

Halsted, Isabella. "Putting Error in Its Place." *Basic Writing Journal,* 1 (Spring 1975), 72–86.
Errors should be put in such a "place" that they do not inhibit the basic-writing student from understanding writing as communication.

Harris, Muriel. "Contradictory Perceptions of Rules for Writing." *CCC,* 30 (1979), 218–20.
Examines students' comments on the rules they learned in high school.

Hunt, Kellogg W. *Grammatical Structures Written at Three Grade Levels.* Urbana, Ill.: NCTE, 1965.
Guidelines for measuring syntactic growth.

Kline, Charles R., Jr., and W. Dean Memering. "Formal Fragments: The English Minor Sentence." *RTE,* 11 (1977–78), 97–110.
Analyzes the kinds of intended fragments; distinguishes them from "broken sentences."

Krishna, Valerie. "The Syntax of Error." *Basic Writing Journal,* 1 (Spring 1975), 43–49.
We should teach students to place main ideas in subject and verb

positions to minimize many of the syntactical problems in papers by beginning writers.

Kroll, Barry M., and John C. Schafer. "Error-Analysis and the Teaching of Composition." *CCC*, 29 (1978), 242–48.
Making errors is a part of learning. Teachers should search for the causes of error and design exercises to help students confront the sources of their mistakes.

Long, Ralph B. "English Grammar in the 1970's." *CE*, 31 (1969–70), 763–73.
Surveys twentieth-century developments in grammatical theory.

Lunsford, Andrea A. "What We Know—and Don't Know—About Remedial Writing." *CCC*, 29 (1978), 47–52.
Describes the basic-writing student's difficulties in reading, with errors, and with writing processes; offers advice for instructors and program designers based on these observations.

Maimon, Elaine P., and Barbara F. Nodine. "Measuring Syntactic Growth: Errors and Expectations in Sentence-Combining Practice with College Freshmen." *RTE*, 12 (1978–79), 233–44.
Sentence-combining exercises help students become syntactically more mature. The rate of increase varies with subject matter; the number of errors increases as T-unit length increases.

Marzana, Robert J. "The Sentence-Combining Myth." *EJ*, 65 (February 1976), 57–59.
Sentence-combining only improves writing performance slightly; sentence-composing (after Christensen) is significantly better.

Meade, Richard A. and Elizabeth A. Haynes, "The Extent of Learning of Transformational Grammar in One School System." *RTE,* 9 (1975), 184–91.
Transformational grammar was learned only by high-IQ students.

Mellon, John C. *Transformational Sentence-Combining.* Urbana, Ill.: NCTE, 1966.
Describes a method of teaching syntax.

Mellon, John C. *Transformational Sentence-Combining: A Method for Enhancing the Development of Syntactic Fluency in English Composition.* Urbana, Ill.: NCTE, 1969.
Outlines a useful method for teaching nominal and relative embedding and other syntactic options.

Morenberg, Max, et al. "Sentence-Combining at the College Level: An Experimental Study." *RTE*, 12 (1978–79), 245–56.

Sentence-combining exercises help students become syntactically more mature and lead to better writing.

Ney, James W. "Lessons from the Language Teacher: Cognition, Conditioning, and Controlled Composition." *CCC*, 24 (1973), 182–87.
Cognitive and behavioral psychology point to a method for teaching composition, a method largely recognized by the recent theorists Mellon, O'Hare, and Christensen.

Ney, James W. "The Hazards of the Course: Sentence-Combining in Freshman English." *The English Record*, 27 (Summer/Autumn, 1976) 70–77.
Reservations about sentence-combining's efficacy.

Nugent, Harold E., and Darryl LeDuc. "Creating Sentence Combining Activities." *Connecticut English Journal*, 9 (1977), 106–16.
Students should work their own sentences, sentences they want to improve.

O'Hare, Frank. *Sentence-Combining: Improving Student Writing without Formal Grammar Instruction.* Urabana, Ill.: NCTE, 1973.
Describes the historical development of sentence combining techniques; describes an experiment in which students given no grammatical training per se but sentence-combining exercises improved the syntactical maturity of their prose considerably.

Pixton, William H. "The Dangling Gerund: A Working Definition." *CCC*, 24 (1973), 193–99.

Pixton, William H. "To Be *For All Seasons:* The Faulty Complement." CCC, 27 (1976), 383–86.
Three basic kinds of faulty complements.

Ross, Janet. "A Transformational Approach to Teaching Composition." *CCC*, 22 (1971), 179–84.
Some success in teaching stylistic techniques.

The Sentence and the Paragraph. Urbana, Ill.: NCTE, n.d.
Reviews studies on the sentence and the paragraph during the 1960s; reprints seminal artcles.

Shaughnessy, Mina P. *Errors and Expectations: A Guide for the Teacher of Basic Writing.* New York: Oxford University Press, 1977.
Shaughnessy anatomizes basic-writing students' errors and weaknesses in handwriting and punctuation, in syntax, in the fundamentals of grammar, in spelling, in vocabulary, and in para-

graphing, suggesting numerous explanations for the problems and many ways of combating them in and out of the classroom.

Sherman, H. Stephen. *Four Problems in Teaching English: A Critique of Research.* Scranton, Pa.: International Textbook, 1969.
Summarizes studies that indicate that transformational grammar instruction does not improve writing ability.

Sloan, Gary. "The Subversive Effects of an Oral Culture on Student Writing." *CCC* 30 (1979), 156–60.
Classifies the kinds of mechanical and grammatical errors caused by our contemporary oral culture.

Slotnick, Henry B., and W. Todd Rogers. "Writing Errors: Implications about Student Writers." *RTE,* 7 (1973), 387–98.
What kinds of students commit what kinds of errors?

Sternglass, Marilyn S. "Composition Teacher as Reading Teacher." *CCC,* 27 (1976), 378–82.
A strategy for approaching the basic writing student's problems with the sentence, a strategy combining reading and writing instruction.

Stewart, Murray F. "Syntactic Maturity from High School to University: A First Look." *RTE,* 12 (1978), 37–46.
College freshmen and sophomores do not mature syntactically far beyond the level reached by high school juniors and seniors; college upperclassmen do move forward.

Stewart, Murray F. "Freshman Sentence-Combining: A Canadian Project." *RTE,* 12 (1978–79), 257–68.
Sentence-combining and exercises based on Christensen led to increases in syntactic maturity.

Sotsky, Sandra L. "Sentence-Combining as a Curricular Activity: Its Effect on Written Language Development and Reading Comprehension." *RTE,* 9 (1975), 30–71.
A lengthy review article (with bibliography). Sentence-combining exercises can improve a student's syntactic sophistication.

Strong, William. "Back to Basics and Beyond." *EJ,* 65 (February 1976), 56, 60–64.
Sentence-Combining is absolutely basic. Strategies for the classroom.

Svindland, Arne S. "An Alternative Theory of Coordination." *Lingua,* 46 (1978), 29–48.
Analyzes types of coordination; discusses the frequency of each.

Taylor, Mary Valana. "The Folklore of Usage." *CE,* 35 (1973–74), 756–68.
Many of the "myths" we teach under the heading "correct usage" need to be exposed.

Walker, Robert L. "The Common Writer: A Case for Parallel Structure." *CCC,* 21 (1970), 373–79.
We should teach all kinds of sentences, especially complex sentences; we should stress parallelism.

CLASSROOM TECHNIQUES

Abercrombie, M. L. J. *Aims and Techniques of Group Teaching.* 3rd ed. London: Society for Research into Higher Education, 1974.

Baden, Robert. "College Freshman Can't (?) Write." *CCC,* 25 (1974), 430–33.
Students who experienced directive instruction wrote in more genres and styles and were more satisfied with their work.

Brosnahan, Leger. "Getting Freshman Composition All Together." *CE,* 37 (1975–76), 657–60.
A course devoted exclusively to the reading together of all the students' essays.

Bruffee, Kenneth A. "Collaborative Learning: Some Practical Models." *CE,* 34 (1972–73), 634–43.
For the teaching of literature, but easily adaptable.

Bruffee, Kenneth A. "The Way Out: A Critical Survey of Innovations in College Teaching, with Special Reference to the December, 1971, Issue of *College English.*" *CE,* 33 (1971–72), 457–70.
Surveys the innovations in collaborative learning; argues that collaborative learning is superior to traditional methods.

Bruner, Jerome. "The Uses of Immaturity." *Intellectual Digest,* 3 (February 1973), 48—50.
Collaborative approaches in teaching are better for disadvantaged students, for teacher-centered methods are laden with bad associations for these students.

Cassill, R. V. "Approaches to Semiotic Composition." *CE,* 37 (1975—76), 1–12.
A course in which students compose using not only words but pictures, shapes, symbols, and signs as well.

Clapp, Ouida, ed. *On Righting Writing.* Thirteenth Annual Report of

the Committee on Classroom Practices. Urbana, Ill.: NCTE, 1975.
Classroom techniques to motivate students to want to learn to
write.

Donelson, Ken, ed. "Rhetoric and Composition in the English
Classroom." *Arizona English Bulletin,* February 1974.
A far-ranging collection—from strategies for teaching description
to discussions of the applicability of formal rhetoric. Includes
Roland H. Dow's "The Writer's Laboratory—One Approach to
Composition," Russ Larson's "Teaching Writing to the New Stu-
dents of the '70s and '80s," Del Wait's "Descriptive Writing: An
Aid From Film and Story," Charles Davis' "Handwriting," and
Harrison J. Means' "Notions About Skills and a Sequence of
Skills in Written Composition."

Elbow, Peter. *Writing Without Teachers.* New York: Oxford University Press, 1973.
An extensive approach to the teaching of writing which frees the
student from the pressures and the blocks usually present in the
traditional classroom.

Evans, William H. "Another Hard Look at Written Composition." *Illinois Journal of Education,* 59 (December 1968), 43–50.
Thirty-one experimental approaches to the teaching of composition, none of which consistently works well.

Fisher, Lester A., and Donald Murray. "Perhaps the Professor
Should Cut Class." *CE,* 35 (1973–74), 169–73.
A conference-teaching program.

Flood, Ralph. "Reports on the Death of Student-Centered Teaching
Have Been Grossly Exaggerated."*CE,* 35 (1973–74), 475–78.
Attempts to expose numerous fallacious assumptions in the argu-
ments of those who oppose student-centered teaching.

Geuder, Patricia A., et al., eds. *They Really Taught Us How to Write.*
Ill.: NCTE, 1974.
The teachers of students who won high school writing awards
describe prewriting procedures, short writing assignments,
teaching techniques, long-term assignments, entire courses, and
grading methods.

Hardaway, Francine. "What Students Can Do To Take the Burden
Off You." *CE,* 36 (1974–75), 577–80.
Peer evaluation, conference teaching, and in-class prewriting and
editing improve writing instruction by making it less prescriptive.

Haring, Lee, and Ellen Foreman. "Folklore in the Freshman Writing Course," *CE*, 37 (1975–76), 13–21.
"Folklore"—in its broadest sense including games, proverbs, and song lyrics—can make basic writing more relevant to the students' reality and bridge the gap they perceive between speaking and writing.

Hawkins, Thom. "Group Inquiry Techniques for Teaching Writing." *CE*, 37 (1975–76), 637–46.
Special attention to the evasive techniques students may adopt, peer criticism, and the difficulties of task-making.

Hawkins, Thom. *Group-Inquiry Techniques for Teaching Writing.* Urbana, Ill." NCTE, 1976.
The problems the teacher is likely to encounter; what tasks the teacher can assign the groups to facilitate the acquiring of composition skills.

Hess, Karen M. "The Role of Objectives and the Teaching of Composition." *CCC*, 26 (1975), 272–78.
The kinds of behavioral objectives that might be useful, their proper use, and benefits to be derived from using them.

Hoover, Regina M. "Experiments in Peer Teaching." *CCC*, 23 (1972), 421–25.
In advanced composition course, but adaptable.

Judy, Stephen, ed. *Lecture Alternatives in Teaching English.* Urbana, Ill.: NCTE, 1971.
Essays outlining classroom-tested practices which transform a teacher-centered classroom to a student-centered one.

Karrfalt, David H. "Writing Teams: From Generating Composition to Generating Communication." *CCC*, 22 (1971), 377–78.
Group writing emphasizes the social nature of communication.

Kelly, Lou. "Toward Competence and Creativity in an Open Class." *CE*, 34 (1972–73), 644–60.
"Open class" techniques alter the student's negative view of the English teacher and convince the student that writing has a great deal to do with his life.

Laque, Carol Feiser, and Phyllis A. Sherwood. *A Laboratory Approach to Writing.* Urbana, Ill.: NCTE, 1977.
Rationale and full description.

Lindsay, Barbara. "The Class That Does Not Meet." *CCC*, 17 (1966), 258–60.

A writing course consisting solely of private conferences and group workshops.

Norell, Kathleen. "A 'Total-Effect' Workshop: Resources and Results." *CE,* 35 (1973–74), 190–93.
What the experience of being in a traditional classroom is like for the student; methods of getting around the problems a traditional classroom poses for the learner.

Ohmann, Richard M., and W. E. Coley, eds. *Ideas for English 101: Teaching Writing in College.* Urbana, Ill.: NCTE, 1975.
Twenty-three articles from *College English* (1967–75) discussing different conceptions of freshman composition, different methods for teaching it, and different tactics for classroom use.

Putz, Joan M. "Permission + Protection = Potency: A.T.A. Approach to English 101." *CE,* 36 (1974–75), 571–76.
A curriculum designed to take the student from writing for self (featuring "free writing") to writing for an audience of peers to writing for a public audience.

Rizzo, Betty. "Peer Teaching in English I." *CCC,* 26 (1975), 394–96.
Students, working in groups, can teach basic skills to each other.

Samuels, Marilyn S. "Choice for a First-Essay Topic." *CCC,* 27 (1976), 395–96.
"How to Write an F Paper" as a diagnostic writing assignment in basic writing.

Shugrue, Michael F. "New Materials for the Teaching of English: The English Program of the USOE." *PMLA,* 81 (September 1966), 3–38.
A number of innovative approaches to the teaching of composition.

Snipes, William Currin. "An Inquiry: Peer Group Teaching in Freshman Writing." *CC,* 22 (1971), 169–74.
Mixed results after experimenting with peer teaching. Structure should be provided by the teacher to prevent disintegration.

Steiner, Karen. "A Selected Bibliography of Individualized Approaches to College Composition." *CCC,* 28 (1977), 232–34.

Szilak, Dennis. "Tricks." *CE,* 36 (1974–75), 517–39.
The blocks "rules" and "facts" can be between the student and writing competence; some "situations" to put students into to circumvent these problems.

Tate, Gary, and Edward P. J. Corbett. *Teaching Freshman Composition.* New York: Oxford University Press, 1967.
A number of innovative approaches.

Wallace, Mary Lewick. "A Bibliography of Programmed Texts on English Composition." *CCC,* 30 (1979), 58–61.

Wilcox, Thomas W. "Varieties of Freshman English." *CE,* (1971–72), 686–701.
Surveys freshman English programs.

Zoellner, Robert. "A Behavioral Pedagogy for Composition." *CE,* 30 (1968–69), 267–320. See *CE, 34 (1972–73),* 603–8 for ensuing debate.

Index